TEXTS

SUNY Series in Philosophy
George R. Lucas, Jr., Editor

process of working through it will have produced a better understanding of the issues the theory seeks to solve. To guard against the dangers one must keep in mind the nondogmatic and heuristic aim of theories. The view presented here is meant as a conceptual framework whose function is to make sense of our experience, not to be superimposed on it.

The positions I defend in this book are intended to stand by themselves, but they become fully intelligible only when the logical grounds on which they rest are taken into account. Here is a summary of the pertinent grounds.[1]

I. The Logic of Texts

The conception of texts I adopt is expressed by the definition of texts as groups of entities, used as signs, that are selected, arranged, and intended by an author in a certain context to convey some specific meaning to an audience. This definition makes clear that texts are complex entities and therefore composed of other entities. It also makes clear that texts include such things as expressions, sentences, paragraphs, and books. *Don Quixote* is a text, but so are '2 + 2 = 4' and 'Fire!'.

Texts are composed of signs. The sentence, 'The cat is on the mat,' for example, is composed of the signs 'The,' 'cat,' 'is,' and so on. But signs are themselves constituted by entities that are used to convey meaning. Because these entities constitute signs and signs compose texts, these entities can also be said to constitute texts. Thus, the sentence, 'The cat is on the mat,' is composed of the signs 'The,' 'cat,' and so on and constituted by the marks on the page that also constitute the signs of which the sentence is composed.

It is important to distinguish the entities that constitute texts (ECTs), the signs that compose texts, and the texts themselves as well as the relation between texts and signs, on the one hand, and the entities that constitute them, on the other. Texts are composed of signs but texts and signs are constituted by entities that are used as signs to convey meaning. Thus the distinction between texts and signs, on the one hand, and the entities that constitute them, on the other, is that the latter, considered merely as the entities they are, have no meaning, whereas the former are related to a meaning an author or user intends to convey through them. The distinction between texts and signs rests on the fact that a text is always composed of more than one sign and the meaning of a text is at least in part the result of the meaning of the signs of which it is composed. Signs by contrast may be composed of other signs but their meaning is not the result even in part of the meaning of the signs of which they are composed.[2]

The entities that constitute texts have meaning only if they are used as signs which in turn compose texts; they have no meaning when considered in themselves, but they acquire meaning when they are used or taken as signs. Signs are those entities insofar as they are endowed with meaning. The marks on the page that constitute the sentence, 'The cat is on the mat,' have meaning only if they are used as or taken to be signs.

Textual meaning itself is conceived as what is understood when a text is understood and thus as related both to texts and to the act of understanding. This somewhat neutral conception of meaning allows the meaning of texts to vary; it can accommodate the three most popular views of meaning while avoiding their difficulties. These views are the referential, ideational, and functional. It accomodates the first because textual meaning can be conceived as the things or states of affairs that we understand when we understand a text; the second because textual meaning can be conceived as the ideas expressed by a text; and the third because textual meaning can be taken as that in virtue of which a text carries out certain functions.

That the primary function of texts is to convey meaning does not entail it is their only function. Texts may and often do other things than produce understanding, but to do those other things they must also produce understanding. The production of understanding is a necessary condition for any other function a text may have, even if that other function is primary in the intention of the author or user.

The definition of texts makes clear another important point about texts; namely, that texts always presuppose an intention. The use of a text makes no sense unless this principle is accepted. But intention should not be confused with full awareness of what is intended or with full awareness of the intention. One may not have full awareness of the meaning of a text and yet have the intention to communicate it. And one may not have full awareness of the intention to convey meaning and yet intend to do so.

An important corollary of the definition of texts is that texts are conventional entities. Their conventionality refers to the relation of their meaning to the entities that constitute them, for there is no natural semantic connection between the meaning of the signs that compose a text and those entities or between the meaning of a text and those entities. The connection is the result of a convention established by those who use the entities that constitute texts as signs and components of texts. Signs are never natural in the sense of having a natural connection to a meaning. This conventional character applies also to the semantic significance of the arrangement of those signs and the role of context.

Context is anything that, not being part of a text, can affect the meaning of the text. Some contexts may depend to a great extent on the type of text in question, whereas others do not. The importance of context can be gathered from the fact that texts are intended by authors for certain audiences, and thus presuppose a language and so on. It is also clear from the fact that most texts are elliptical and, therefore, meant to be completed by additions that are not part of them and can be supplied only by an audience in a determinate context. The dependence of texts on context does not entail that they are equally dependent

TEXTS

ONTOLOGICAL STATUS, IDENTITY, AUTHOR, AUDIENCE

JORGE J. E. GRACIA

STATE UNIVERSITY OF NEW YORK PRESS

Published by
State University of New York Press, Albany

Printed in the United States of America

For information, address State University of New York Press,
State University Plaza, Albany, N.Y. 12246

Production by M. R. Mulholland
Marketing by Nancy Farrell

Library of Congress Cataloging-in-Publication Data

Gracia, Jorge J.E.
     Texts: ontological status, identity, author, audience / Jorge
J.E. Gracia
        p.   cm. — (SUNY series in philosophy)
     Includes bibliographical references and indexes.
     ISBN 0-7914-2901-6 (alk. paper). — ISBN 0-7914-2902-4 (pbk. : alk. paper)
     1. Criticism (Philosophy)   2. Meaning (Philosophy)
 3. Hermeneutics.   4. Theory (Philosophy)   I. Title.   II. Series.
 B809.3.G73 1996
 121′ .68—dc20   95-9554
                                                          CIP

10 9 8 7 6 5 4 3 2 1

To Leonila

———

He who writes thereby exposes himself to criticism by everyone,
and appears before the tribunal of the whole world and every age.

John of Salisbury, *Metalogicon*

———

CONTENTS

PREFACE

Texts and textuality have become the source of considerable interest in recent years, not only in literary circles but also among philosophers. Texts have always been a focus of philosophical attention to some extent, because philosophers are concerned with philosophical views and these views are expressed in texts. Recently, however, philosophers have become interested in texts not only for the views they express but also for what they are. Apart from the more traditional epistemological issues involved in the understanding and interpretation of texts, questions have been raised concerning their ontological status and identity, and their relations to authors and audiences. The literature on these topics is already large and continues to grow at a steady pace, but so far no attempt has been made to explore some of these questions in the context of a theory that aims to provide a coherent and comprehensive approach to them. As a result, one frequently finds statements in the literature that appear shocking because they contradict long-held beliefs and much common sense. My aim in this book is to take some steps to remedy this situation by considering the questions of textuality together, as part of an interrelated set of issues, rather than in isolation from one another.

The questions I examine are closely related to, but do not overlap with, the ones raised in *A Theory of Textuality* (1995). The discussion is divided into four chapters, which are preceded by an introduction; a short conclusion is added at the end. The introduction aims to give a sample of the issues discussed in the book and summarize some of the conclusions reached in the logical part of the theory, presented in the earlier volume, that are pertinent for the understanding of the issues discussed here. The first chapter provides an ontological characterization of texts consistent with the conception of texts defended in the aforementioned study. The second chapter turns to the question of identity; it explores the issues involved in the identity of various texts and closes with a discussion of the epistemic topics of identification and reidentification. The third and fourth chapters take up matters that have to do with the author and the audience, their identities, functions, and relations to texts. Apart from the brief conclusion, a select bibliography and indexes of authors and subjects close the study. The bibliography records the sources cited as well as other materials consulted. Pertinent background sources have not generally been noted, but I refer the reader to the bibliography of *A Theory of Textuality*, which contains a more complete list of them.

In the preparation of this book I have used the following previously published materials: "Texts and Their Interpretation," *Review of Metaphysics* 43 (1990): 495–542; "Texts and Their Interpretation," in *Philosophy and Its History: Issues in Philosophical Historiography* (Albany: State University of New York Press, 1992), pp. 177–222; "Can There Be Texts Without Historical Authors?" *American Philosophical Quarterly* 31, no. 3 (1994): 245–53; "Can There Be Texts Without Audiences? The Identity and Function of Audiences," *Review of Metaphysics* 47 (1994): 711–34; "Author and Repression," *Contemporary Philosophy* 16, no. 4 (1995): 23–29; and "Textual Identity," *Sorites* 2 (1995): 57–75. I am grateful to the editors of the journals mentioned, Jude Dougherty, Nicholas Rescher, Peter Redpath, and Lorenzo Peña and to the director of the State University of New York Press, William Eastman, for their permission to use the materials in question. None of the materials borrowed appear without substantial modifications and elaboration.

I should also like to acknowledge my gratitude to those who read the whole manuscript or parts of it and gave me the benefit of their criticisms and suggestions. Among these I would like to mention in particular David Greetham, Edward Pols, Ignazio Angelelli, George Lucas, James Bunn, and Bruce Reichenbach, as well as Michael Gorman, Jeremy Fantl, William Irwin, Kenneth Shockley, Yishaiya Abosch, and Daniel Barwick. As my research assistants at various times during the preparation of this book, the last six helped me with research, proofreading, and the critical analysis of the ideas presented. I am also grateful to Kenneth Schmitz, Paul Eisenberg, and Rega Wood. The first two were my critics at a session devoted to my book, *Philosophy and Its History*, at the 1994 Eastern Division meetings of the American Philosophical Association, and raised questions that made me take a second look at some of the views I present in this book. The last was present at the session and raised interesting questions concerning my conception of the pseudo-historical author. To all I owe a debt that cannot be easily repaid.

INTRODUCTION

Are texts individual, universal, or both? It is not difficult to conclude that my cat Chichi or the pen with which I am writing these words is individual. And there is no difficulty in concluding that cat and pen, by contrast, are universal. But what do we make of texts? Unlike the examples of individuals and universals cited, texts appear to share some of the characteristics associated with individuals and some of the characteristics associated with universals. On the one hand, texts are historical entities, produced at a certain time by an author within a determinate set of circumstances and thus would appear to be, like all other historical entities, individual. Yet, on the other hand, they seem to be capable not only of instantiation but also of multiple instantiation; indeed, often there appear to be many instances of the same text. Consider the text of *Don Quixote*. On the one hand, the text of *Don Quixote* is a historical entity, published in the early seventeenth century by Cervantes, within a determinate set of circumstances, and thus it would appear to be, like all similar historical entities, individual. On the other hand, the text of *Don Quixote* seems to be capable not only of instantiation but also of multiple instantiation as the several copies of it in the library and the one I have in my office indicate.

The example of *Don Quixote* leads us into another issue, the question of identity. Several volumes in the library of the University at Buffalo bear the title *Don Quixote* whose author is identified as Cervantes. These volumes have important differences among them: They occupy different spatio-temporal locations; they are printed in different typescripts, on papers of different consistencies, with varying numbers of words per page, and so on. But, in spite of these differences, we regard these volumes as copies of the same text, and indeed, users of the library have no trouble identifying them as such. So we may ask: What makes them the same? Indeed, we may pose the more general question: What makes texts the same?

One possible answer points in the direction of the author. But this answer raises problems of its own, for it is not clear that all texts require intention and consciousness. Could not the proverbial monkey type a copy of Hamlet? This example seems farfetched, but it would not be as odd or unlikely for a monkey at random to press keys in a typewriter and produce an expression like "Fire!" or "Excuse me!" And yet, our intuition tells us that texts require intention and consciousness of their meaning on the part of those who produce them. A text is intended to say something. The monkey has no such intention, however, when it presses the keys of the typewriter, even if one were to concede it has some kind of intention. And the same could be said about the purported texts produced by computers or the expressions uttered by parrots. But if this is so, then texts do not require authors.

A similar question arises with respect to audiences. Some recent philosophers and literary critics have challenged the long-held view that texts without audiences are not texts. The claim that texts do not require audiences is based on various grounds, but perhaps the most impressive are the statements of certain authors themselves who say they do not have audiences in mind when they compose texts. Practitioners of the *nouveau roman*, for example, believe that for a writer the aim is to write, and whether the author is read or not is actually unimportant. From this point of view an audience is neither necessary nor important for the author, and if this is so, then its consideration could be neither necessary nor important for the existence or understanding of a text. Still it seems to be something in the nature of texts to have audiences because they are intended to be understood by someone. How can this intuition be reconciled with the view of those authors who reject the idea that they have anyone in mind when they produce a text?

These four questions should suffice to illustrate the problems that will be discussed in this book. These problems arise because we think about texts in what appear to be contradictory ways. We think of them as universal but also as individual, as one but also as many, and as having and not having authors and audiences. Philosophers have little tolerance, at least in theory, for inconsistency; it has always been their task to bring order into the conceptual frameworks we use, to understand the why and how, and to eliminate contradictions whenever possible. Hence the challenge texts pose for them. But there is more, for texts are the very stuff out of which philosophy is made. Some may want to think of texts as instruments of philosophy and others as essential to philosophy, but regardless of the view one adopts it is clear that philosophy as we know it cannot proceed independent of texts. If this is so, it would appear wise, and perhaps even necessary, for philosophers to address the philosophical questions we have raised in connection with texts.

This is what I have tried to do both in *A Theory of Textuality* and in this volume. In the former I have taken up primarily logical and epistemological questions, and here I turn to ontology, identity, authors, and audiences. Instead of the piecemeal approach characteristic of much contemporary philosophy, I proceed by presenting an overall view of textuality, for it is my belief that one cannot hope to solve the variegated problems that arise concerning texts unless one looks at the larger picture. This approach is unpopular today but I do not see how any other can yield the kind of understanding of textuality philosophers seek. Of course, there are dangers in such a procedure, but they are worth taking, for even if the theory presented here turns out to be inadequate, the on context or that they depend on context in exactly the same way. Different texts will depend on context in different ways and in different degrees.

One of the most significant results of the definition of texts I propose is that it narrows down the category of textuality considerably, ruling out all sorts of things that have been proposed as texts by recent hermeneuticists, literary critics, and philosophers of language. Texts constitute a narrow category of entities that have a very particular use, to convey meaning, and that are subject to strict conditions related to authorship, audiences, and contexts. At the same time, the conception of texts I propose allows complete freedom with respect to the choice of entities used as signs to make up texts. Indeed, the confusion between the two—namely, between texts and the entities that constitute them—is at least in part responsible for mistakenly extending the category of texts to entities that in fact are not texts.

The definition also makes possible the distinction between the category of texts and other categories sometimes confused with it, such as the categories of language, artifact, art object, and work. Most texts are composed of signs that belong to natural languages and those signs are arranged according to the rules of the natural languages to which they belong, but texts are not languages. Texts are not composed of rules, whereas languages are in part composed of rules. Texts have a concrete structure, whereas languages do not. Texts are historically determined, whereas living languages are constantly changing. Texts logically presuppose languages, whereas languages do not logically presuppose texts. Texts have particular purposes, whereas languages, except for artificial ones, do not. Most texts have identifiable authors, whereas that is not so with natural languages. Finally, texts have audiences, whereas languages do not.

The confusion of texts with languages may lead to the conclusion that texts, like most languages, are flexible, have no very strict identity conditions, and are independent of authors and audiences. The fact is, however, that texts are less flexible than languages, having concrete structures and generally identifiable authors and audiences. It is a mistake to conclude, then, that texts lack definition and determination. This is one of the reasons why it is important to understand the distinction between texts and language. Note, of course, that the distinction between texts and language does not imply that texts are not semantically flexible and are not dependent on their authors and audiences in various ways; it implies only that, if they are so, it is not because they are languages or like languages.

Texts should not be confused with artifacts either. The confusion of texts and artifacts is also understandable, for texts are always artifactual and therefore share with artifacts some fundamental features. Artifacts are entities that either are the product of intentional activity and design or, not being the product of intentional activity and design, have undergone some change or their context has undergone some change. This change, in either case, has to be the result of intentional activity and design and the artifactual entity must be considered in the context where the change has occurred rather than apart from it.

Something similar occurs with the category of art object. Although some art objects may be texts, not all art objects are texts and not all texts are art objects. For something to be an art object it must be an artifact and it must be capable of producing an artistic experience. The first condition ties art objects and texts for, like art objects, all texts are artifacts. But not all texts are capable of producing an artistic experience. The conditions for objects to be capable of producing an artistic experience are two: They must be regarded as artifacts and as capable of producing an aesthetic experience. Thus the conditions of being an art object include being an artifact, being regarded as an artifact, and being regarded as capable of producing an aesthetic experience. Art objects are not required to be composed of signs, and even if their aim were to convey meaning, their primary function has to do with the production of an artistic experience. Texts, by contrast, need not necessarily be regarded as capable of producing an artistic experience even if they share the conditions of artifactuality with art objects. Nor does it make a difference that they also share having authors and audiences.

Finally, texts should not be confused with works. Works are the meanings of certain texts. Not all texts have meanings that qualify as works; works are the meanings of those texts that a culture regards as works because they fulfill certain criteria developed by the culture. This entails that no general rules apply to what constitutes a work for all times and places. It is not length, the degree of effort that it takes to produce a text, or the fact that it may be open to many and conflicting interpretations that determines which texts have corresponding works. The notion of work is culturally conditioned and determined by the functions particular cultures attach to certain texts.

The introduction of the notion of cultural function leads naturally to the consideration of various types of texts depending on the functions they have. The notion of function plays an important role not only in the determination of whether a text's meaning constitutes a work, but also in the context of textual understanding and interpretation.

Function may be understood in various ways, two of which are pertinent here. The first is the notion of linguistic function. Texts are linguistic in character and therefore derive some of their functions from this fact. Like language, they can be used to inform, direct, express, evaluate, and perform. Less fundamental, but no less important, however, are the cultural functions a text may have that do not derive from its linguistic nature. They depend on various cultural phenomena and how they affect the uses to which texts are put. Thus texts may be classified as legal, literary, philosophical, scientific, religious, political, historical, pedagogical, confesional, entertaining, inspirational, mnemonic, and so on. None of the various functions identified is to be regarded as exclusionary. Texts may fulfill various functions at different times and at the same time, depending on a wide variety of factors. Nor are these functions jointly exhaustive, because they depend on many factors that may change according to the diversity of circumstances.

Texts may also be classified modally into actual, intended, or ideal. The actual text is the text that exists outside the mind of an interpreter. It is either the historical text, the contemporary text, or the intermediary text. The historical text is the text the historical author actually produced, whether we have it or not. The contemporary text is the text available to us in the original language in which it was produced; sometimes, when the historical text has survived intact, the contemporary text is the same as the historical text. The intermediary text is a text we do not actually have and is not the historical text but nonetheless existed at some time and functioned at that time as a contemporary text of an audience. The intended text is supposed to be the text the author of the text intended to produce but did not produce, althouth I have argued that this understanding of an intended text makes no sense. The intended text can be no more than a vague set of ideas and intentions concerning a text and its meaning. Finally, the ideal text is the text an interpreter thinks the historical author should have produced.

II. Outline

To facilitate the discussion of the issues I raise concerning texts in this book I have divided them into four different clusters, dealing respectively with ontological status, identity, author, and audience. Each cluster is discussed within a separate chapter.

Ontology seeks to develop a map of the world according to some fundamental categories. A substance-accident ontology, for example, will tell us that the world is composed of substances and accidents and will seek to explain the relations between the two. But an ontology that rejects substance will try to describe reality in other terms. Also, ontology will try to account for and explain the relations among the most fundamental attributes of being, such as unity, identity, similarity, and so on.

If ontology is a general investigation of the stated sort, an ontological characterization involves locating what is under investigation in a general categorial map. One might ask, for example, whether the thing in question is a substance or a feature. In turn, one might ask what a substance is and what its relation is to features. To define a human being as a featherless biped is not part of ontology, but it is part of ontology to determine whether human beings are substances or bundles of features.

Texts pose most of the fundamental questions that one may raise in ontological investigations. One may ask, for example, whether they are substances or features and what is the basis of their identity, among other things. I have, however, decided to focus the ontological investigation of texts around the following categories: universality, individuality, physicality, aggregate character, substantiality, existence, and location. I also discuss the historicity of texts.

A different issue has to do with identity. I have framed this issue in terms of sameness and difference. Simply put, the question has to do with the determination of the necessary and sufficient conditions of the sameness and difference of texts. Because I argue that texts can be universal and individual, and because sameness and difference are conditioned by temporality, the question is divided accordingly. Hence, I discuss the conditions of the achronic (apart from time), synchronic (in time), and diachronic (through time) sameness of both universal and individual texts. The conclusions reached in the analysis are then briefly applied, mutatis mutandis, to difference.

Two other issues are raised in the chapter on identity. They are epistemic issues and have to do with the identification and reidentification of texts. Identification means the process whereby a knower is able to pick out something in such a way that the knower can distinguish it from other things. Reidentification has to do with identification at two or more times.

A different set of questions involves the author and audience of a text. With respect to the author I explore questions of identity, function, need, repressive character, and subjectivity. Four types of authors are discussed: historical, pseudo-historical, composite, and interpretative.

Consideration of the audience raises several issues of philosophical interest. I begin with the question of identity and follow with discussions of function, need, subversive and repressive character, and subjectivity. As with the author, the audience may be classified in various ways. I discuss five of these ways explicitly: author as audience, intended audience, contemporaneous audience, intermediary audience, and contemporary audience.

With the general direction indicated by these preliminaries in mind, we can now turn to the more substantive and detailed part of the book. I begin with ontological status.

1

ONTOLOGICAL STATUS

Ontology is the branch of philosophy that studies being and seeks to establish its most general categories. The application of these categories to something is the determination of its ontological status. Philosophers have sought to identify many of these categories. Aristotle, for example, identified ten of them, and other philosophers have been adding to or subtracting categories from those ten ever since.[1] For our purposes, however, I believe it will be most profitable if we examine four pairs of categories: individual-universal, physical-nonphysical, substance-feature, and aggregate-nonaggregate. I have chosen these because they are very often used in philosophy and because at least some of them have been applied to texts.[2] The determination of the ontological status of texts, as will be undertaken here, will involve an inquiry into the suitability of applying these categories to them. Note that by using these categories I do not mean to endorse them. There are strong disagreements among philosophers about the viability of these categories, and therefore, I cannot settle these matters in the course of an investigation devoted to something else.

The most general ontological categories of the ones mentioned are individuality and universality, and for this reason, ontological status is usually taken in the recent literature to refer to these categories. Here, however, we will go beyond questions of individuality and universality and discuss also questions of physicality, substantiality, and aggregate character. In addition, because ontology is concerned with being, we will raise questions of existence, location, and historicity.

A text is a group of entities, used as signs, that are selected, arranged, and intended by an author to convey a specific meaning to an audience in a certain context. This entails that texts are artifacts, products of a conventionally established relation between certain entities and meaning in a context. Texts amount to the entities of which they are constituted (ECTs) considered as having a meaning that an author intends to convey through them. The main implication of this conclusion for the ontology of texts is that texts are the entities of which they are constituted considered as they stand in relation to the meaning and, therefore, their status is the same as the status of those entities with an added relation to meaning.[3] Texts are neither the ECTs considered

apart from meaning, meaning considered apart from ECTs, the relation between ECTs and meaning, or the context in which the relation between ECTs
and meaning is established.

There is nothing odd in this view, as is clear from the following example.
Consider a stone that is used as a paperweight. It is obvious that ontologically
the stone and the paperweight differ only in their use, which is established by
a relation of the stone to the user. Both have a certain weight and color, and so
on. The difference between them arises because the stone may be considered as
it is in itself apart from the relations it may have to a user who puts it down to
hold paper, whereas the paperweight is the stone considered as used by someone to weigh down paper. In the same way, a text is ontologically the entities
of which it is constituted (ECTs) except that, considered as a text, the ECTs
have a relation to meaning missing when they are considered merely as the entities they are apart from that meaning. The marks on a page that constitute a
text considered by themselves, apart from meaning, are not a text but merely
marks on a page.

One could argue that the fundamental question involved in the determination of the ontological status of texts concerns the determination of the status of the entities that constitute them. But this is not quite right, for meanings
are intrinsically related to texts. Hence, we must investigate the ontological status of meaning and the sort of relation ECTs have to it if we are to claim to have
provided a satisfactory ontological characterization of texts.

I.   Are Texts Individual or Universal?

For our discussion of texts, two pertinent questions can be raised concerning their individuality and universality. The first has to do with whether
texts are individual or universal. The second needs to be asked only if, in the
answer to the first, we conclude that there are individual texts; it seeks to identify the necessary and sufficient conditions of the individuality of texts.

Something is individual if and only if it is a noninstantiable instance of
an instantiable, whereas universals are capable of being instantiated, that is,
they are instantiables.[4] "Peter," for example, is individual because he is an
instance of human being but not itself instantiable. "Peter" is a noninstantiable
instance. By contrast, "human being" is universal because it can be instantiated, indeed it is instantiated in Peter, Mary, and so on. The same could be said
about "this white color" (a noninstantiable instance) and "the color white" (an
instantiable).

The first question that we have to address concerning the individuality
and universality of texts, then, is whether they are noninstantiable instances or
are capable of instantiation. If the first, then they are to be regarded as individual; if the second, then they are universal.

The distinction between individual and universal texts is equivalent to Peirce's distinction between a token and a type.[5] Terms and expressions function as *types* if they can be placed both before and after the copula in a true identity sentence such as 'A is A.' In this case 'A' stands for the type, and the sentence means that the universal A is the same as itself. Terms and expressions function as *tokens* in turn when they fail to meet that condition. In the example provided, it would be false that A is the same as A because the individual A at the beginning of the sentence is not the same individual at the end. The notions of token and type are subcategories of the notions of individual and universal. A token is an individual sign or text; a type is a universal sign or text. A text is a type because it is the sort of text of which token texts are instances, and a text is a token because it is a noninstantiable instance of a type of text. Tokens occur only once, but several tokens may belong to the same type. The notions of token and type do not apply, then, to objects except in cases where those objects are semantically significant. By contrast, the categories of individual and universal apply to all sorts of objects. To speak of token or individual texts and of type or universal texts amounts to the same thing.

Individuals should not be exclusively identified with substances, nor universals with features, even though these categories are frequently exchanged in philosophical discourse.[6] They are confused because substances are the most obvious examples of individuals found in our experience. Features, however, can be and often have been considered to be individual in the history of philosophy.[7]

Using a standard Aristotelian distinction, a substance is what can neither be predicable of nor present in something else.[8] "Predicability of" and "being able to be present in something else" are, then, the criteria that distinguish between a substance and its features. By contrast, the distinction between individual and universal has to do with noninstantiability and instantiability, and both of these categories may be applied to substances: an example of individual substance is the cat Chichi, an example of universal substance is cat. Likewise, although the black color of Chichi's coat is a feature, one could speak of instances of that black color (the individual black color of Chichi's coat) as well as the instantiable black color (the universal black color of Chichi's coat) of which the individual black color of Chichi's coat is an instance.

The issue of the individuality or universality of texts needs to be raised because on the surface it is not clear whether texts are individual or universal. Unlike the examples of universals and individuals given earlier, texts seem to have some of the features associated with individuals and some of the features characteristic of universals.[9] On the one hand, texts are historical, the results of the actions of an individual author working within a determinate set of circumstances at a certain time and thus would seem to be, like other historical entities, individual. On the other hand, texts appear to be capable not only of instantiation but of multiple instantiation. Consider the example of the text of *Don Quixote*. This text is a historical entity, published between 1605 and 1615 by Cervantes, and thus it would seem to be, like other historical entities, individual. However, the text of *Don Quixote* appears also to be capable not only of instantiation but of multiple instantiation, because there are several copies of it in the library and elsewhere.

In the sense that they appear on the surface to be both individual and universal, texts are very much like art objects.[10] For art objects seem to be individual and at the same time subject not just to instantiation but even to multiple instantiation. The original of Picasso's *Guernica*, for example, is in a museum in Spain, but there are reproductions of it in various places, including one in my office where I keep a postcard sent by one of my daughters from Spain. Insofar as some of these reproductions may be indistinguishable from the original, could we not say that they are instances of that original and, therefore, that Picasso's *Guernica* is instantiable and therefore universal? And yet the original of *Guernica* is a historical artifact that exists only in one place at a time and has all the marks normally associated with individuals.

The case with texts is even more puzzling, because the original printing of a text and subsequent printings of it appear, for all intents and purposes, to be indistinguishable as far as the text itself is concerned.[11] That is, although one may want to say that this or that printing is different, the text of the printings is regarded as the same. So, are texts universal or individual?

My response to this question is that the controversy concerning whether texts are individual or universal is the result of a confusion. Different persons answer the question of the individuality or universality of texts differently, depending on what they consider the text to be. Texts are complex and are composed of entities (ECTs) that are used to convey meaning. However, as shall become clear in Chapter 2, not everyone thinks of texts in this way. Some identify texts with their ECTs whereas others identify them with their meaning. This gives rise to different views concerning whether texts are individual or universal, because it is not obviously true that both ECTs and meaning can be individual and universal or, if so, whether they are always both individual or universal. My claim is that, once it is clear what a text is, the difficulties concerning the individuality and universality of texts can be settled.[12] I need to begin with the individuality and universality of ECTs.

A.   Individuality and Universality of ECTs

ECTs can be universal or individual. Anything whatever can function as an entity that, together with other entities, is used as a sign to convey meaning. I assume, moreover, that the categories of individuality and universality are jointly exhaustive and mutually exclusive, so that every single thing is either individual or universal, but not both. ECTs can be of various sorts. For example, there can be physical and mental ECTs. But this should not confuse us about the individuality or universality of the entities in question. Nor should the meaning of a text be confused with the universals of its ECTs. The universal physical ECTs are those of which there can be physical (e.g., written or spoken) noninstantiable instances; and the universal mental ECTs are those of which there can be mental (e.g., imagined) noninstantiable instances. The universal ECTs, however, are not the meaning that the individual ECTs are supposed to convey when used as texts but rather a type of the physical or mental individuals in question. This can be illustrated with the following texts:

1. $2 + 2 = 4$
2. $2 + 2 = 4$
3. Two and two make four.
4. Two plus two equals four.
5. Dos y dos son cuatro.

In texts 1–5 we have five sets of individual ECTs to which correspond only four sets of universal ECTs (since 1 and 2 are the same in type).[13] The ECTs of texts 1–5 instantiate four different universals: one consisting of mathematical symbols (1 and 2), two of English words (3 and 4), and one of Spanish words (5). And the same could be said for the corresponding oral or mental ECTs of the corresponding oral or mental texts. The oral ECTs would consist of the sounds we utter when we say the texts, and the mental ECTs would be the images we have in our minds when we imagine the texts. There is, therefore, no single universal set of the physical or mental ECTs considered as such, even when they may have the same meaning.

It should be obvious from what has been said that the classification of ECTs into universal and individual has nothing to do with the standard logical classification of propositions into universal and singular. Consider the following propositions:

6. All S is P.
7. All S is P.
8. Some S is P.
9. Some S is P.

According to the standard logical classification, 6 and 7 are universal and 8 and 9 are singular. But according to our classification, the ECTs of 6–9 are all individual. However, texts 6 and 7 are instances of the same instantiable, the universal "All S is P," and the same can be said about 8 and 9, which are instances of the universal "Some S is P." Thus, in 6–9 we have four individual sets of ECTs that are instances of only two universal sets of ECTs.

In short, the ECTs that constitute texts can be individual or universal, but what of meanings? We must examine the individuality and universality of meanings before we can settle the issue of the individuality or universality of texts.

B.   Individuality and Universality of Meanings

Meaning is a necessary condition of textuality but texts are not to be identified with their meaning. The meaning of a text is what we understand when we understand the text. Thus, for example, the meaning of '2 + 2 = 4' is that two and two make four. This, however, does not tell us whether meanings are individual or universal.

The ontological status of meaning is one of the most disputed issues in philosophy and thus it would be presumptuous to try to settle it in the short space I can give it in a book on texts. Nonetheless, something must be said about it so that the theory of textuality I am expounding may not be left incomplete, but what I say should be taken only as a tentative proposal.

One way to make some headway in answering the question of whether textual meanings are individual or universal is to look at some examples. Of course, meaning is not restricted to texts. Words, for example, have meanings and, according to the understanding of meaning I have proposed, the meaning of 'white,' is white. But here I am concerned only with textual meaning. Let us begin by considering the following texts:

10.   Cats are mammals.
11.   The cat Chichi is a mammal.
12.   Archangels are immaterial.
13.   The archangel Gabriel is immaterial.
14.   Mental images can be quite vivid.
15.   The mental image Jorge has is quite vivid.

Now, the meanings of 10–15 are as follows:

10m.   Cats are mammals.
11m.   The cat Chichi is a mammal.
12m.   Archangels are immaterial.
13m.   The archangel Gabriel is immaterial.
14m.   Mental images can be quite vivid.
15m.   The mental image Jorge has is quite vivid.

A consideration of meanings 10m–15m leads necessarily to the conclusion that meanings can be universal or individual. Meanings 10m, 12m, and 14m are universal insofar as they do not concern any one individual cat, archangel, or mental image but every cat, archangel, and mental image. By contrast, meanings 11m, 13m, and 15m are individual insofar as they concern only an individual cat, an individual archangel, and an individual mental image. The meanings of 11, 13, and 15 have to do with the noninstantiable instances "Chichi," "Archangel Gabriel," and "the mental image Jorge has." In short, these examples indicate that the meanings of texts can be universal or individual.

One may question this conclusion in several ways. For example, one may want to argue that it appears strange to say that meanings are universal or individual. Moreover, if they are so, why could they not also have the features we ordinarily attribute to things. Why could meanings not be white or blue, sweet or bitter, for example?

I believe this objection is based on the surface grammar of language. My view of textual meaning is that it is what we understand when we understand a text. Thus the meaning of '2 + 2 = 4' is that two plus two equal four, and the meaning of 'The walls of my office are painted white' is that the walls of my office are painted white. In the first I understand something universal, in the second I understand something individual. Indeed, those philosophers who understand propositions as the meaning of certain sentences would want to say that by the first I understand a universal proposition and by the second an individual (or singular) one. And those philosophers who identify meanings with states of affairs would want to say that by the first I understand a universal state of affairs and by the second an individual one. But then, should one not also say concerning the second that I understand something white?

The answer to this question is affirmative to this extent, that what I understand is that the wall is white. Those who accept a propositional view of meaning would want to add that I understand a proposition that describes a white wall. Those who favor states of affairs would want to say that I understand the state of affairs of a wall being white. And so on. But it is a mistake to speak of meanings as having features like color because individuality and universality are not on the same ontological level as color.

I prefer not to get involved in questions that ask whether textual meanings are propositions, state of affairs, referents, uses, or the many other things philosophers identify with meaning, for my limited purposes do not require it. It is sufficient to show that textual meanings can be individual or universal.

Another objection to what has been said concerning the ontological status of textual meaning is to point out that the characterization given provides only a classification of particular textual meanings but does not tell us much about textual meaning itself. Is meaning, considered in itself and thus apart from particular textual meanings, universal or individual?

The answer to this objection is that the mentioned categories do not apply to textual meaning qua textual meaning; they apply only to this or that textual meaning. To try to apply them to textual meaning qua textual meaning would be like trying to apply extensional categories to intensions or vice versa. Let me illustrate the point by referring to the meaning of signs. One may want to argue there are some signs whose meanings are simply the extensions of the terms (Socrates for 'Socrates'); and there are other signs whose meanings are the intensions of the terms (human being for 'human being'). If this is so, then it is not always possible to apply the same categories and procedures to both. For instance, it would make no sense to ask for a definition by genus and *differentia* of Socrates, as it would of human being, because Socrates is not a species that can be defined in that way. Likewise, it would not do to ask someone to point to human being, for the most that one could do would be to point to *a* human being.

This same principle can be applied to the meaning of texts, for not every meaning is of the same sort. The examples provided earlier indicate that some meanings are universal and others individual, regardless of what ultimately one takes meanings to be—propositions, states of affairs, and so forth. For this reason, the most we can say about textual meaning qua textual meaning is that it is neutral with respect to these categories, not in the sense that it can be neither of them but in the sense that it can be both, depending on the particular meaning in question. In this sense we might compare textual meaning to cloth, for just as cloth can be dyed different colors and thus cannot be said to have of itself a particular color but can take on any color, so textual meaning can be of different sorts and thus cannot in itself be identified with one of them to the exclusion of others. If it were in the nature of textual meaning to be one to the exclusion of the others, then it could never be the others. Say that it were in the nature of textual meaning to be universal, then it could not be individual (singular sentences would be meaningless or have universal meanings). Textual meaning, qua textual meaning, must be neutral with respect to these categories in order that particular meanings fit into them.

C.   Individuality and Universality of Texts

Having explained how the ECTs and meanings of texts can be individual and universal, we may now address the original question raised concerning the individuality and universality of texts. In the example mentioned, is the text of *Don Quixote* individual or universal?

The answer depends on what one takes to be the text of *Don Quixote*. First, if one takes the text of *Don Quixote* to be the ECTs, then the answer will depend on whether one is referring to an individual set of ECTs—the ones printed on the copy of *Don Quixote* I own, for example—or to the universal of which the individual set contained in the book I own is an instance. Second, if one takes the text of *Don Quixote* to be the meaning the ECTs, when used as signs, are intended to convey, then the answer will depend on the individuality or universality of the meaning of the text. Because the text is about an individual fictional character, one might be tempted to conclude that the meaning of *Don Quixote* is individual. But the fact is that *Don Quixote* contains many sentences and even paragraphs that mean nothing individual. For example, Don Quixote's musings about life. So it is an oversimplification to classify the meaning of *Don Quixote* as individual. Third, if one takes the text to be the ECTs, whether the individual or the universal set, insofar as they are used to convey meaning, whether such meaning is individual or universal, then the answer is complex for it will depend on the ontological status of the ECTs and the meaning, and these status may not be the same. In the case of the text of *Don Quixote*, we may be referring to a set of universal ECTs, whereas the meaning may be mixed, for example.

To avoid the complications resulting from the third alternative, one may follow the procedure of characterizing texts according to the character of their ECTs. The advantage of adopting this procedure is not only that it avoids complications, but that it is reasonable, for ECTs are the foundation of texts in that texts are those ECTs used as signs to convey meaning. This becomes obvious when one examines the relation of texts, their ECTs, and meaning, as I shall do in Section IV later.

II.   Individuation of Texts

Because texts can be individual, the question comes up as to what causes their individuality. This is what is generally referred to as "the problem of the individuation" of texts. The solution to this problem is no different from the solution to the problem of individuation of other entities. Nothing is so idiosyncratic about texts that it makes their principle of individuation different from that of other entities. And because I have discussed this problem elsewhere at length, I will simply present my position in abbreviated form. Before I do that, however, I should make clear that I distinguish between the problem of individuation properly speaking and the problem of individual discernibility. The problem of individuation does not concern the necessary and sufficient conditions of our knowledge of individuals as such—that is the epistemic problem of discernibility—but rather the necessary and sufficient conditions of the individuality of individuals: the metaphysical account of individuation.[14] I discuss the problem of discernibility under two headings: identification and re-identification, in Chapter 2.

That texts can be individual means that they can be noninstantiable instances. And to ask for the source or "principle" of the individuality of individual texts is to ask for the necessary and sufficient conditions of their individuality. What we are seeking, then, are those conditions that as a whole are responsible for the individuality of a text, that is, the conditions under which an instantiable text becomes a noninstantiable instance.

Elsewhere I have defended the view that there is only one necessary and sufficient condition of individuality: existence.[15] If this view is applied to texts, it turns out that any text that exists is individual and only individual texts exist. But existence, if this view is to work, must not be considered to be a feature, for if it were a feature it would in turn require individuation. Now, no thing that exists can exist without features, so features of some kind or another are also required for individuation. For something to be individual it is necessary that it be some kind of thing. There is no text without features. But those features, although necessary for a text's existence and thus indirectly for its individuality, are not sufficient conditions of its individuality. Only existence is both a necessary and sufficient condition of the individuality of texts, because existence implies features but not vice versa.

This view has both general and specific advantages. Its general advantages are that it avoids the problems that plague other views. The existential view of individuation does not have to worry about the logical possibility of two things having exactly the same features, for existence is considered not to be a feature; it does not have to worry about the principle of individuation being accidental and extrinsic, for existence is fundamentally tied to things even if not, strictly speaking, essential to them; and it does not need to be concerned with the decharacterized nature of the principle of individuation, for although existence is not supposed to be a feature, it is a matter of experience to everyone.

III.   Are Texts Physical or Nonphysical?

To answer this question we must make clear two things. First, the category of nonphysical is not equivalent to the category of mental. I understand the categories of physical and mental in such a way that they are mutually exclusive but not jointly exhaustive. If X is something physical, it cannot be something mental, but not everything is either physical or mental. There may be, for example, nonmental nonphysical entities, such as God, angels, and the like. Although I am not prepared to argue for the existence or nonexistence of these entities here, I want to leave open the possibility of their existence because many philosophers have argued for it. Considering our limited purposes, however, there is no need for us to consider nonmental nonphysical categories. Texts must be constituted by epistemically accessible entities, and it is not easy to argue for the epistemic accessibility of nonphysical nonmental entities. If there are such entities and they are epistemically accessible, then it is altogether possible, other things being equal, that there be nonmental nonphysical texts.

Second, we must remember that texts are ECTs used to convey meaning and therefore are not identical with ECTs or meaning. For this reason, prima facie it would appear best to begin our discussion by asking separately whether

ECTs and meaning can be physical or nonphysical and if the latter, mental or nonmental. But, in ordinary discourse, conclusions about the physical or nonphysical character of texts seem to be derived exclusively from the physical or nonphysical character of their ECTs. When one speaks of an oral text, for example, one refers to spoken ECTs. So, upon reflection and to simplify matters I will address the question of the physical or mental character of texts in terms of the physical or mental character of the ECTs.[16]

A.   Physical Texts

Physical texts are texts whose ECTs are physical.[17] Texts constituted by pebbles arranged in certain ways on a beach, by lines and figures drawn on a piece of paper, or by pixels on a computer screen are physical because the entities that constitute them, that is, the pebbles, lines, figures, and pixels, are physical. Indeed, our ordinary paradigms of texts are physical, and of physical texts it is written and oral texts that we have in mind when we think about texts at all.

One way in which physical texts may be classified is according to the senses with which we have access to them. In this way, physical texts can be said to be visual, auditory, tactile, gustatory, and olfactory, depending on whether we perceive them through sight, hearing, touch, taste, or smell.[18] From the fact that texts must be epistemically accessible, it follows that physical entities not subject to perception through at least one sense (e.g., matter) cannot constitute texts. This is the reason why physical texts can be exhaustively classified according to the senses through which we perceive them.

The most obvious case of a visual text is writing, but texts can also be composed of nonscript designs, figures, pictures, and so on. Nor is it necessary that the essential factor in a visual text be shape. Color could very well, and in fact does, function in some instances as conveyor of meaning. For example, red is often used in East Asia to mean happiness.

A less frequently acknowledged type of visual text consists of physical actions. The deaf, of course, are quite used to thinking about actions—particularly the movements of hand and face—as texts, for many of the signs they use to communicate when they do not use written signs are actions of this sort. But the rest of us tend to ignore this type of text.

All this appears fairly straightforward, and something similar could be said about auditory texts. Just as there can be written texts like the ones mentioned, so can there be oral texts.[19] In this case, instead of the written marks on a piece of paper or other writing material, there would be certain sounds uttered by a speaker or made in some other way by a subject. Consider the written text '2 + 2 = 4.' When I read aloud this text, I produce an auditory text. The sound I make when I read the text is in fact the sound counterpart of the written text, but is not to be identified with the written text. The sounds that a person utters in speech or makes when transmitting through telegraph indicate a type of text that is auditory.

Another type of text that functions in our culture but we seldom take into account is the tactile text. It is the blind who most frequently use this sort of physical text.

None of the types of physical texts mentioned is particularly controversial. When we come to the possibility of gustatory and olfatory texts, however, matters are different, for at least in our culture no compositions of tastes or smells seem to have been used as texts. It is true that in some sense we speak of some smells and tastes as signs of this or that. But even if we were to take that use of 'sign' to imply that the taste or smell in question has a meaning conventionally assigned to it, that would not be sufficient to call it a text.

Generally, when we speak of tastes and smells as signs, we are thinking of them as causally related to something else rather than as signs properly speaking. Thus, for example, a sour taste in wine is a sign the wine has spoiled. But these are not the sorts of signs that make up texts, because they are not conventionally attached to their meaning. Of course, there are cases in which a certain smell is clearly a conventional sign. Take the foul smell that is added to natural gas so that it can be easily and quickly recognized. This smell is certainly used as a sign of the presence of gas, but this sort of case is not very common and applies only to signs and not to texts.

At least two reasons may be given why tastes and smells are not used as texts. The first is a reason that goes back to Augustine.[20] He noted that taste and smell are private in the sense that the experience of a smell or a taste involves the destruction of that which has been smelled or tasted and, therefore, precludes its being smelled or tasted by anyone else; indeed, strictly speaking it would preclude the repetition of the same experience by even the person who experienced the taste or smell in the first place. It is true, of course, that if I smell bread being baked, this does not entail that the bread has been destroyed and I cannot smell it again. Most likely I will continue to smell it until I, or someone else, has eaten it all and the room where the bread was baking has been aired. The point made by Augustine, however, is that the individual particles of the bread I have smelled cannot be smelled again, because the process of smelling implies their modification by our olfatory organs. I continue to smell the bread because new particles of the bread arrive at my nostrils, not because I can have repeated contact with the same individual particles. And the same could be said about taste and food.

The problem with this argument is that sounds may be characterized to a certain extent in the same way. One could argue, for example, that just as bread is destroyed when it is smelled or tasted and cannot be smelled or tasted again, so a sound wave cannot be heard again by the same person or anyone else. One may argue that, just as the bread, which has parts that can taste alike, the wave has parts that are heard alike. Nor can it be argued that sounds, unlike food, can be recorded and thus preserved. The recording of a sound is no more than the preparation of a device that causes a sound of the same type as the individual sound being recorded, not the preservation of the individual sound. In this sound is no different from bread, because a good recipe will ensure that the same type of bread can be produced. However, one difference has some relevance in the case of taste. In tasting a food one may consume all of it. I can drink all the wine there is, for example, but I cannot hear all the sound there is. If there is sound, it can be heard by everyone who has the right aural equipment. And this does not apply to smells.

In short, there do seem to be differences in the way in which sounds and tastes function that could justify an explanation of why tastes are not used as texts whereas sounds are. But the differences are not so great that the explanation can be considered satisfactory. Moreover, the differences between smells and sounds are even less compelling. For this reason we must look for the explanation elsewhere.

A second reason why tastes and smells have not been used as texts is that they tend to be both simple and vague, lacking the complexity that would be required of them if they were to serve as texts and the precision necessary to serve their function unambiguously. How could a Ciceronian period, for example, be produced in taste? Perhaps I am being parochial here, displaying indirectly the lack of sophistication in the area of tastes and smells that pervades contemporary society in North America. All the same, I do not think that even the French or the Chinese, peoples highly skilled in the art of cooking, have come up with texts composed of tastes and smells, and least of all with texts having the sort of complexity and precision of which Cicero was capable in writing and speaking. Logically, however, such possibility must be admitted. One could think of a society that, owing to extraordinary technical advances, would be able to control the homogeneity, composition, and consistency of gases so that the production of specific smells could be produced at will and thus be used to communicate complex meanings. And the same could be imagined concerning taste. It is certainly possible to combine tastes and smells and to arrange them in such ways that meaning would be conveyed as long as one were aware of the meaning of the tastes and smells in question.

Although we tend to separate texts belonging to different types—say, written and oral—this separation is by no means necessary. In some cultures oral texts are used regularly together with visual texts. That this is not as frequent in English-speaking cultures is merely an accident of history. In Mediterranean cultures, for example, it is customary to accompany certain words and expressions with particular movements of the body to convey specific meanings.

Each of the types of physical texts we have examined could be further subdivided according to the various physical features they have. For example, they could be classified by color, size, texture, and so on. But these subclassifications do not readily raise intriguing philosophical issues and therefore need not concern us here. Two subclasses of texts, however, display an interesting relation, which needs to be taken into account to clarify certain problems that come up with respect to texts. One is a subclass of visual texts, namely, written texts, and the other is a subclass of auditory texts, that is, oral texts.[21] The important fact for us about these subclasses of texts is that they are frequently related as signs of each other.[22] Written texts are frequently intended as visual signs of oral texts.[23] Indeed, when someone dictates and someone else writes, what is being written is accepted as a sign of what is being said. The reverse relation is also true, moreover, for oral texts are often intended as signs of written texts. When I read aloud a text, I am presenting an oral sign of the written text.

The origin of this peculiar relation is the fact that writing seems to have developed as a codification of speech.[24] For this reason, written signs often function as signs of oral texts. Naturally, the character of this relation allows not only the use of written texts as signs of oral texts, but also makes possible the reverse relation in which oral texts are used as signs of written texts.

The peculiar relation between written and oral texts raises two interesting questions. The first concerns identity and may be formulated as follows: Can an oral text and a written text be the same text, particularly when one functions as a sign of the other and both have the same meaning? Because I devote Chapter 2 to questions of identity, I shall postpone discussion of this question until that chapter.

The second question is as follows: Can a written text be considered to be a meaning of an oral text, and vice versa, when both texts also have some other common meaning? Consider both the oral text I utter when I read aloud the written text 'No smoking is permitted here' and the written text mentioned. Both the oral and written texts mean that no smoking is allowed here, but it is also the case that the oral text may mean the written text; that is, what is understood by the oral text is the written text. Indeed, the oral text may prompt someone to think about the written text and the written text may prompt someone to think about the oral text, because that is what they understand by them. It looks, then, as if, in addition to the common meaning that the texts have, they also mean each other.

If the difficulty under consideration is not with signs and texts being signs of signs and texts, but with the fact that those signs and texts have two different meanings, that should not be considered very serious. For, in the first place, every sign and every text has at least two meanings. One is itself and the other is whatever other meaning it has. Thus *cat* means both the sign 'cat' and "cat."[25]

And *No smoking is permitted* means both the text 'No smoking is permitted' and "No smoking is permitted."

The fact that signs and texts appear to have different meanings and even functions poses no serious difficulty for understanding, for in general the context makes clear which meaning is involved. When I produce the oral text corresponding to the written text 'No smoking is permitted' and I am dictating to a class, the students will write on their notebooks the written text meant by the oral text without giving much thought to any other meaning of the oral text. But if someone is smoking in the classroom and, addressing that person, I say "No smoking is permitted," her reaction is quite different. Most likely she will put out her cigarette or make a nasty remark, rather than write down on a piece of paper the written text that corresponds to the oral text I utter. Indeed, if she did the last, we would think she was confused. Thus, neither having more than one meaning nor having the special relation that written and oral texts have poses any serious difficulties for the notion of a physical text.[26]

B. Mental Texts

In contrast with the physical character of the entities that constitute physical texts, the entities that constitute mental texts are mental. A mental text is not composed of physical entities but of mental phenomena. The mental text is constituted by images or thoughts that someone, say a psychologist interested in the nature of mental phenomena, investigates or thinks about while carrying on research. Consider the following written text, '2 + 2 = 4,' and further consider the image I can form of that written text after I close my eyes and imagine it. The image I form of the text after I close my eyes is a mental text, and the image I form when, after an interruption, I again think about it, is also a mental text. Perhaps the distinction between the mental and the physical text can be illustrated by noting that the two texts cannot share all features. For example, a feature of the physical text, '2 + 2 = 4,' is that it is capable of being visually perceived, but the corresponding mental text lacks this capability; I can use my eyes to see the first, but I cannot do so for the second.[27]

The question that arises at this point is whether a distinction can be made between mental texts, on the one hand, and what subjects think about when they are said to understand texts, on the other. This question arises because it seems difficult to distinguish between a mental text and the meaning the text conveys, for the meaning of a text does not prima facie appear to be something physical, which seems to imply in turn that it must be something mental and identical with the mental text. The question is important because, if there is no difference between a mental text and the meaning the text is supposed to convey, then, for there to be some difference between a text and its meaning, the text must always be physical, and this contradicts much of what has been said before.

The following observations should help clarify this matter. The same thing that is said concerning written texts vis-à-vis their meaning may be said also about mental texts and their meaning. For example, let us suppose that a mental text is constituted by a mental image of the written text '2 + 2 = 4.' We can think of the meaning of the mental text without thinking about the mental image that constitutes the text. And yet, to think of the text would seem to require thinking both about the mental image and its meaning, because the text is in fact that image considered as conveyor of the meaning. Note that I am not arguing that all mental texts have as ECTs images of written texts. They could certainly be constituted by images of oral texts, for example. Indeed, they may not be constituted by images at all, although about that I am not at all sure. But that is a question that does not directly concern us here. The pertinent points are that, first, a mental text is different from a physical text (whether written or spoken or whatever else), and second, the mental text is not the same thing as the meaning of a mental text, just as the physical text is not the same thing as the meaning of the physical text.

The meaning of a text consists of what we understand when we understand the text, so that it may turn out that the meanings of mental and physical texts are the same, even if the texts are not the same. Thus, for example, the meaning of the written text 'The cat is black,' of the oral text 'The cat is black,' and of the mental text (the image) 'The cat is black' are the same, namely, that the cat is black, even though the texts are different because their ECTs are different. The first is a visual object; the second is an auditory object; and the third is an imaginary object. From this we see, then, that the distinction between the meaning of a physical text and the text also applies to mental texts.

Next we might raise the question of the kind and order of priority between physical and mental texts. On the one hand, it would seem that, if mental texts can be constituted by images and images are mental reproductions of the objects we perceive, then the physical text has priority over the mental text insofar as an image of an object presupposes the object. Realists have been harping on this point for many years. On the other hand, it looks as if some authors compose texts in their minds before they commit them to writing, thus showing that the mental text has priority over the physical one. Indeed, the example of Mozart, who seems to have composed and carried the score of his musical works in his mind for varying periods of time before writing them down, may be cited to support this intuition.

Both of these positions are partly right and partly wrong. It is true that, at least for those of us who do not accept innate ideas of any sort, whatever is found in the mind is the result of experience. The mind has powers of combining and separating, so that what is in it does not have to be an exact replica of what has been perceived. One can hold that, indeed, the mental text, provided it is constituted by images, is in fact derivative and secondary in the sense that those images or their components are traceable to perception. Nevertheless, because the mind modifies what it perceives in various ways, there is no requirement that a mental text be an exact replica of a physical text. Authors may use images that are not derived from written texts, say, to make up mental texts. In that case, the mental text is not derivative or secondary; it is not the mental reproduction of a physical text, but an original text. Indeed, if the author then goes on to reproduce physically the mental text, the physical text is derived from the mental.

Still someone may wish to argue that even when authors produce original written or oral texts, they do not have prior images of what the texts are going to look like before they actually produce them. Thus, while I am writing these words, I may not be thinking of the physical shape of these words and their components. Perhaps I think of their sounds before I write them. But when I speak, producing a physical sound-text, it does not seem that I produce mental images of those sounds before I actually produce them. So, can it be argued that the mental text precedes the physical text?

I believe one can argue that in some cases the mental text does precede the physical text. There is no reason why one cannot hold that some authors do compose not only short texts but the texts of long and complex works in the mind, which they commit to memory before they reproduce them physically. This may have been so in the case of Mozart. I say "may" because it is altogether possible to argue that Mozart and others like him do not have in their minds the text but rather an understanding of the work. That is to say, they may have in their minds an understanding of the meaning which the text is supposed to express rather than the group of signs they are going to use to convey that meaning. Whether this is the case or not, however, I still wish to maintain that at least in some cases a mental text—not just an understanding of its meaning—could precede the physical text, and I base this conclusion on experience. We can, if we wish, picture in our minds the signs we are going to use to convey a certain meaning to an audience before we produce them extramentally, even though we seldom, or perhaps never, as a matter of ordinary practice, do so.

On the other hand, cases like that of Mozart are unusual. Most authors of texts do not seem to think of a text first and then produce it whether orally, visually, or otherwise. The processes of physical production and mental composition do not seem to be separate. Our mind works very much like a computer where a certain event—say, pressure on a key—brings about another event—say, the appearance of a letter on a screen. Just as in a computer, where the pressure is not an image of the letter, so in our experience, whatever causes the sounds to come out of our mouths or the hand and finger to move in a certain way is not an image of those sounds produced by the mouth or that shape formed by the hand.

Two further questions may arise in connection with mental texts. The first asks for that which distinguishes a mental text from a physical one beyond the distinctions already pointed out. If there can be mental reproductions of physical texts and some physical texts are copies of mental texts, the general question of what sets the mental apart from the physical, and not just the specific question of what sets mental texts and physical texts apart, becomes important. This is an interesting philosophical question, but one that is not unique to texts and therefore need not be taken up here, although the way one answers it will affect what has been said here about physical and mental texts. The impossibility of answering it in passing, however, forces me to leave the matter as is.[28]

The second question asks how the texts I have classified as mental can be considered texts when texts must be intended to convey meaning to an audience and mental texts are accessible only to their authors. This question may be answered in a variety of ways. For example, it may be pointed out that many mental texts are merely trial runs for physical and perceptible ones, which sometimes get produced and sometimes not. Also, it is often the case that authors talk mentally to themselves—indeed they do so physically as well—in an effort to coordinate their thoughts, formulate their views, or preserve their views in their memory with the intention of later using them to communicate with others at a propitious time. Moreover, as we shall see, the function of author includes that of audience, so it should not be surprising to find that there are texts which have no audience but the author, thus eliminating difficulties arising from that quarter against the notion of a mental text.

IV.   Relation of Texts to Meanings and ECTs

The meaning of each of the noninstantiable instances of an instantiable text and the meaning of the instantiable text, that is, the meaning of each of the individual texts that fall under a universal text and the meaning of the universal text under which they fall, are the same.[29] Consider two texts cited earlier:

1. $2 + 2 = 4$
2. $2 + 2 = 4$

It would make no sense to say that the meanings of 1 and 2 are not the same or that the meaning of 1, or of 2, is different from the meaning of the universal text of which 1 and 2 are instances. Naturally, to say that 1 and 2 are instances of the same universal requires that the conditions of their identity be specified, which is precisely what will be done in the next chapter. For the moment, however, I shall assume that indeed 1 and 2 are instances of the same universal text. The point that is pertinent here is simply that instances of the same universal text have the same meaning as that text.

A text is a group of entities (ECTs) considered in relation to a specific meaning.[30] The relation involved is not natural because it is the result of intention and design; nor is it real in the sense that there may be something in the ECTs or the meaning to which the relation refers other than the features of the ECTs and their meaning. Indeed, neither the ECTs nor the meaning undergo change as a result of the transformation of the ECTs into a text. What changes is the use to which those ECTs are put or are intended to be put, and that is the result of the way they are conceived; namely, as bearers of the meaning. There is no indication in the ECTs of their function as bearers of meaning when they are taken by themselves, because the connection between them and the meaning exists only in the mind of those who use or intend to use them to convey meaning. The relation between ECTs and their meaning, then, is purely mental, even if the ECTs themselves may not be.

The ECTs of texts 1 and 2 earlier are physical, but the relation between the ECTs of 1, for example, and the meaning of 1 is a purely mental affair resulting from an author's intention to use the ECTs of 1 to convey the meaning of 1. Does this entail that texts are always mental? No, they are not always mental insofar as they have the ontological status of the entities that constitute them, and that status may not be mental, even if they always have an added mental relation to a certain meaning. The way this relation is added to the ECTs may be gathered from the following two illustrations. Consider the case in which an author uses physical, written ECTs to convey some universal meaning:

A = an individual author
'2 + 2 = 4' = individual ECTs
"2 + 2 = 4" = universal ECTs
two and two make four = universal meaning
+acts of understanding of A+ = individual acts

A's function as author is to tie *two and two make four* to "2 + 2 = 4," but A does this only by tying *two and two make four* to '2 + 2 = 4,' through the +acts of understanding of A+. Neither "2 + 2 = 4" nor *two and two make four* can be said to exist or to be in any place. The first because it is a type text and the second because it is a universal meaning. It does not make sense to say that either one qua universal is in a mind, be it A's mind or the mind of God, as some have believed. If they were in minds they would be individual and therefore could not be in any other mind at the same time, although we know they are, because two or more persons can think of the same universal at the same time. And the same could be said about existence. It makes no sense to say that universals, whether meanings or texts, exist or do not exist for similar reasons. It is, therefore, a mistake to try to find a place and a mode of existence for universal meanings. *Two and two make four* does not exist anywhere because neither existence nor nonexistence applies to it. (More on the existence and nonexistence of texts later.)

Now consider the case in which an author uses physical written ECTs to convey some individual meaning:

A' = an individual author
'The image Jorge has of Minina is quite vivid' = individual ECTs
"The image Jorge has of Minina is quite vivid" = universal ECTs
[The image Jorge has of Minina is quite vivid] = individual meaning
+acts of understanding of A'+ = individual acts

In this case, as in the previous one, the author A' connects the meaning [The image Jorge has of Minina is quite vivid] to "The image Jorge has of Minina is quite vivid" through 'The image Jorge has of Minina is quite vivid.' The difference is that the meaning in question is individual. Therefore, what A' understands is something individual rather than something universal. What we have is a physical-type text with an individual meaning that is the result of a mental and conventional relation established by an author (on the basis of social precedents, and so on) between the individual ECTs of the text and an individual meaning.

What has been said about authors also applies to any audience of the text an author has composed. Just as an author thinks of the universal meaning through the individual acts of understanding in the author's mind, so any member of the audience with access to the individual ECTs may also understand the universal meaning of a text.

An individual text, then, is a noninstantiable instance of a universal text and constituted by individual ECTs that are themselves noninstantiable instances of universal ECTs. Moreover, it is intended by its author to convey a specific meaning to an audience; that is, to cause an understanding on the part of the audience. The universal text, by contrast, is constituted by universal ECTs, but its meaning is the same as that of the individual text.

Because texts are artifacts and depend on convention, however, we cannot say that certain universal ECTs are tied to meanings naturally or independently of a subject's intention and design. But subjects have access to universals only through individuals. It follows, then, that universal texts in a sense depend on individual texts; for in individual texts, individual ECTs are in fact tied to meaning through the intention and design of an author.

Texts have a peculiar status. Universal texts are constituted by universal ECTs and as such, as we shall see later, are neutral with respect to existence and location, but their meanings can be universal or individual. Individual texts, on the other hand, are constituted by individual ECTs although their meanings, as with universal texts, can be universal. Thus neither universal nor individual texts can be considered purely universal or individual in all cases. Strictly speaking, they have a divided sort of ontological status and location depending on the ontological status and location of their ECTs and meanings. The most convenient way to describe them, however, as I did before, is to give priority to the entities that constitute them (ECTs) and thus to identify the ontological status and location of the text with the ontological status and location of those entities. For texts are those entities with an added mental relation to a specific meaning. If the entities are physical, the text has a physical location; if they are mental, the text has a mental location; and if they are universal, the text is neutral with respect to location.

V. Are Texts Substances or Features?

The most controversial ontological issues with respect to texts have to do with their individuality or universality and physical or mental character, but no consensus has been reached on several other issues as well. Two about which something should be said in passing are the questions of the substantiality and aggregate character of texts. The first involves determining whether texts are substances, features, or both, considered either separately or in combination.

Before one can determine the status of texts with respect to these categories, however, something needs to be said about the categories themselves. The definition of these categories is by no means easy. Indeed, it poses so many problems that many philosophers have opted for rejecting altogether the notions of substance and feature. I do not wish to get bogged down here in a discussion of substances and features or in a defense of the substance-feature distinction. Rather, I propose to argue that, were one to accept this distinction in the way I shall explain it presently, certain conclusions would follow concerning texts.

Following the procedure I adopted in passing earlier, I propose to understand a substance in the traditional Aristotelian sense in which something is a substance provided it is neither predicable of nor present in something else.[31] And I propose to understand a feature as anything that is either predicable of or present in something else. Peter, my cat Chichi, and the desk on which I am writing these words are substances, but the color of Peter's eyes, Chichi's temperament, and the shape of the desk are not; rather, they are features of those substances. The determining factor on whether something is or is not a substance is not based on whether it can have features but on whether it is or is not a feature. Features can have features—as a color may have a particular intensity or a temperament may have a certain character—but that does not make them substances, for they are still predicable of or present in something else. The misunderstanding of this fact leads to frequent confusions in discussions of substantiality.

The understanding of feature presented here is very broad. It includes what Aristotelians refer to as generic and specific characteristics such as "animal" and "human," specific differences such as "rational," properties such as the "capacity to laugh," accidents such as "white" and "three-feet long," and parts, such as a finger.[32] Within accidents would be included not only qualities such as "white" and quantities such as "three-feet long" but also relations such as "fatherhood," times such as "three o'clock," actions such as "moving the hands," and so on. All of these can be said in some sense of other things, even if they do not intrinsically characterize them. I understand this notion so broadly for the sake of convenience and brevity. I do not mean to rule out the possibility, for example, that such things as relations may be what are called in contemporary philosophy, monadic properties. The exact ontological status of relations and the like is not the topic of this book and thus I intend to leave such questions open.

Having understood substances and features in the stated way, we may return to the question of whether texts are substances, features, both, or a combination of both. From the understanding of texts adopted in the Introduction, it would appear prima facie that they could be both. The reason is that the entities used as the signs of which a text is constituted can be anything. Yet, when one looks at the situation more carefully, texts cannot be substances exclusively if by that one means that they are composed of substances, whether of one or more than one, considered apart from their features.[33] Two reasons may be given for this. The first is that substances are always characterized; that is, they always have features. Peter is a man and short; Chichi is a black cat. This is, of course, the way Aristotle, the scholastics, and many contemporary authors understand substance. But those authors who conceive substance as decharacterized—as some early modern philosophers did and some proponents of bare particulars do in this century—would not be impressed by this reason.

The second reason is that texts must always be composed of more than one sign and thus a single substance without features would lack the complexity required of texts. Hence, even if one were to conceive substances as decharacterized, a single such substance could not function as a text—I shall consider the case of several decharacterized substances later.

A substance can be a text only when the features of the substance function as signs that, taken together in the arrangement in which they appear in the substance, are used to convey a certain meaning by an author to an audience. For example, consider the case of a person P who wants to communicate a message to another person P′ at some future time when they would not have direct access to each other. And suppose furthermore that the only way they could communicate would be through a third person P″ who is supposed to be kept in the dark as to the meaning of the message he is conveying. Under these conditions, it would be possible for P to send some object as a gift to P′ by means of

P″ in which the object and its features function as a text. P and P′ might agree, for example, that if P sends a brown wallet it means that P′ is to deposit the money P has entrusted to P′ in the bank. If the wallet is black, however, the money is to be given to a certain charity. On the other hand, if instead of a wallet, P sends a purse, that means that P′ is to keep for himself the money that belongs to P, and so on. In these cases, the object and its features would act as a text. Moreover, because the object is neither predicable nor part of something else, the text would be the substance considered together with its features.

Still, there is another possibility that may be explored. Let us suppose that, instead of one substance, we have several substances that function as signs to express a specific meaning and that the text is composed only of the substances considered apart from their features. Does this make sense? No, because for the substances in question to function as signs that express the complex meaning of the text they need to have either certain arrangement, or certain distinguishing features, or both.

Consider, for example, the case of three billiard balls that together are used as a text whose meaning is "X is Y." If the billiard balls are similar in all discernible features, we could not possibly use them to say that X is Y, for we could not know which of the balls functions as "X," which as "Y," and which as "is." We need to have recourse to, say, their color—the black ball functions as "X," the white ball as "is," and the red ball as "Y"—or their arrangement—the first ball functions as "X," the second ball as "is," and the third ball as "Y." But both color and arrangement, or whatever else we may use to distinguish the balls, are considered features in the ontology we are using. The result is that, even in cases of texts composed of multiple substances, we have no purely substantial texts. The conclusion of all this is that there can be no texts composed only of substances, even several substances, considered apart from their features.

Note that it would not do to say against this argument that it confuses ontology and epistemology because it gives as a reason against the notion of a text composed of substances considered apart from their features that the substances in question cannot be discerned. We have accepted that texts are epistemic entities in the sense that they must be subject to acquaintance. Hence, if this objection is to be effective, it would be necessary first to do away with the epistemic requirement.

If texts cannot be composed exclusively of substances considered apart from their features, however, we may ask: Can they be composed of features and nothing but features, that is, can texts be composed exclusively of signs that are predicable of or present in other things? In one of the examples given earlier, would it be possible for P to send a message to P′ solely on the basis of some features of an object rather than on the object considered together with its features? It seems possible. Indeed, P and P′ might have agreed that P would send an object as a gift and agreed beforehand that the color and shapes displayed on the surface of the object would be the conveyor of P's message. If the color is red and the shapes are stars, P is to deposit a certain amount of money in the bank; if the color is black and the shapes are stars, he is to give the amount of money to charity; and so on. In these cases, not the substance but some features of it, namely, the colors and shapes on its surface, constitutes the text.

Most texts with which we are acquainted appear to be of the feature variety. For example, the very text I am putting down on paper at this moment appears to be related to the paper as a feature or set of features of it, for it is composed of black marks that characterize the paper in a certain way.

The view that texts can be features and that most of the texts with which we are acquainted are features and nothing but features, does face some difficulties that need to be addressed, however. For example, it is not quite clear that the black marks to which I referred as a text are features of the paper. In the first place, the marks do not seem to be a part of the paper in the way a hand is a part of a human being or a side is a part of a triangle. Moreover, the marks do not seem to characterize the paper in the way color does. For the marks can be considered to be dried patches of ink stuck to the paper in the way a piece of gum is stuck to the underside of a chair, and so they would appear to be, like the gum, substances rather than features.

The first part of this objection is quite sensible. The black marks on the sheet of paper that constitute the text in question are not parts of the paper in the way the lower half of the sheet of paper is a part of the sheet or the molecules that make up the sheet of paper are parts of it. But the second part of the objection is not to be granted so easily, for the marks, unlike the piece of gum, may be considered to be features of the paper insofar as they are dependent upon it both logically and ontologically. Logically, the notion of a mark is related to the notion of something else on which it is a mark; ontologically, marks do not exist independently of the things they mark. Whether what they mark is a sheet of paper or not is irrelevant; what is pertinent is that marks have no independent existence apart from other things. This is precisely what it means to be a feature rather than a substance as agreed upon here, and what distinguishes marks from pieces of gum and other substances.

Still, one may want to counterargue that the marks are made up of ink, which in turn is made up of molecules that are neither parts of the sheet of paper nor characterize it. In that case it would seem that the text made up of ink marks is not a feature of the paper after all, but rather a collection of substances (molecules) arranged in a certain way on the surface of the paper (another substance), in the way that a group of pebbles, for example, rests on a beach.

This counterargument may be answered by drawing a distinction between a text that consists of marks on a page and a text composed of the molecules that make up ink. The text consisting of marks is a feature because marks are features and dependent on other things for their existence. However, when one speaks of a text as composed of the molecules that make up ink arranged in a certain way, one is not speaking about marks, but about ink and its parts. In that case it is true that the text is not a feature, but rather an aggregate substance; that is, an aggregate of molecules. Indeed, even if under normal conditions the arrangement of such molecules could not be maintained, one could always freeze ink and carve a text out of it. Frozen liquids can certainly make up texts, and such texts would have to be considered substantial—winter carnivals are full of texts composed of blocks of frozen water. But marks on a sheet of paper can be nothing but features of the sheet in question regardless of what the marks are made of.

I am not arguing that one thing is both a substance and a feature of a substance. I am arguing that the texts we are speaking of in each of the cases described is different and, therefore, can have different ontological status. A mark, qua mark, is a feature, whereas ink, qua ink, is a substance composed of molecules. The complication arises because the marks in question are produced by ink and ink is a substance, which raises the question of whether substances can function as features of other substances. As the example discussed illustrates, they cannot *function* as features, but they can *cause* features. Ink produces a mark on the sheet of paper, but that mark, considered qua mark, is no longer ink, although it is produced by ink. Hence, it can be said without contradiction that the mark is a feature of the paper whereas ink is not. Nor does it make any difference that we speak of "ink marks," for in such cases what is meant is precisely that the marks are produced by ink. The situation is not very different from the one that exists between an object and the shadow it casts. The object is not the shadow, but nonetheless it is the cause of the shadow.

From all this we may conclude that texts can be composed exclusively of features or can be composed of substances and their features but they cannot be composed exclusively of substances considered apart from their features. Because in the discussion of the supposed substantiality of texts examples of substance-feature texts were provided, there is no need to dwell any further in this category.

The view I have presented here is by no means widely accepted. Although not much attention has been given to the ontology of texts in contemporary circles, the prevalent tendency these days is to conceive texts as forms of action.[34] The background of this position is to be found in the uses to which Austin's work has been put. Austin's discussion of speech acts has led some to the view that texts are in fact acts and nothing but acts, although it is not always clear which of the acts to which Austin referred (locutionary, illocutionary, or perlocutionary) they have in mind.[35]

This position rests on a confusion between the act that produces a text and the text itself. That I engage in the act of writing or speaking to produce a written or spoken text does not warrant identifying the act in question with the resulting text.[36] Nor does it make sense to identify the locutionary act of uttering a text with the text itself; that is, with the sounds being uttered. The case with the sign language used by the deaf is different, because in that language some signs consist precisely in the act of moving the fingers, the hand, and other parts of the body in certain ways. And something similar could be said about so-called body language. Of course, some of the signs of the sign language used by the deaf and the body language used by most cultures are not acts but positions of the fingers or expressions of the face, and in those cases the texts do not consist of acts either. In short, texts can consist of acts and be composed of signs that consist of acts, but they need not be so.[37]

VI.   Are Texts Aggregates or Nonaggregates?

Something is an aggregate if it is a collection, set, or group of entities that constitute a whole. Something is not an aggregate if it lacks the multiplicity characteristic of aggregates. Aggregates are necessarily complex, whereas nonaggregates are necessarily simple. These conceptions of aggregate and nonaggregate are very broad. They include homogeneous substances in which the members of the group may be related extrinsically only and also arrangements of ontologically diverse entities more closely related, such as substances and their features.

From the understanding of texts as complex artifacts composed of groups of entities used as signs adopted in the Introduction and what has been said in the previous section, we should expect that such complexity be reflected in their ontological makeup. The fact that the most obvious cases of texts with which we are acquainted are aggregates of one sort or another supports this point. Consider the script I am putting down on this paper at this moment. It is certainly an aggregate of features, for it consists of certain marks on the page that have certain shapes and so on. The script could in fact be analyzed in terms of various features such as color or shape and the relationships among them. Putting together the feature character of the text that I am now writing with its aggregate character, we could classify the text as a feature-aggregate type of text.

A second possibility might result when a text is considered as a whole composed of a substance and its features. In this case the relevant aspects of the text are both the substance and its features. Consider the case of the text composed of a wallet of a certain color discussed earlier. In this case the meaning of the text depends not only on the wallet (substance or substance cum features, depending on one's view of substance), but also on its color (feature). Thus we have a mixed sort of text, which may be called substance- or feature-aggregate text. There is no reason why this type of text may not be composed of multiple substances and their features. A text composed of pebbles of different colors arranged in a certain way on the beach is composed of several substances (the pebbles) and their features (colors, arrangement, etc.).

So far we have seen how an aggregate conception of texts fits the conception of texts we have adopted, but is it possible for texts not to be aggregates? An affirmative answer to this question is not viable because of the necessary complexity of texts. Indeed, in our experience texts always are aggregates. The most likely case of a nonaggregate text would be that of one consisting of a simple substance. But texts cannot be composed of substances considered apart from their features, let alone one simple substance. A simple substance, without parts or features, a notion in itself difficult to entertain, could not be composed of a group of signs used to convey textual meaning. A substance must be complex in some sense to function as a text, and if it is complex and its parts or features function as signs that make up the text, then the text turns out to be an aggregate after all.

One might still want to argue that in this case the complexity of the substance is not part of the text. If the features of the substance were not considered part of the text, however, the substance in question could not really function as a text. Indeed, it is questionable whether it could function even as a sign, for signs also must be distinguishable from other things to function as signs and thus require features, which would entail complexity. In short, texts always require aggregation.

VII.   Existence and Location of Texts

The answer to the question concerned with the existence and location of texts is closely related both to the universality and the individuality of texts. The theories that deal with this issue may be divided into two sorts, depending on whether they identify the existence of texts with mental existence or with extramental existence. The former locate texts in minds and the latter locate them outside minds. Of those that locate texts in minds, three stand out in particular. The first holds that texts are located in the mind of God; the second, in the mind of the author; and the third, in the mind of the audience. (Of course, it is also possible to hold combinations of these views.)[38] The audience is sometimes identified with one or more particular persons and at other times with the social group considered as a whole.

All these views have important points in their favor. Putting texts in God's mind is convenient, for it solves the problem of where these texts are before any human being thinks of them. Putting texts in the author's mind makes sense because, after all, the author is supposed to have created the text. Finally, putting the text in the mind of the audience helps to explain how audiences can understand texts.

The problem with these views, however, is that they conceive texts as mental phenomena of one sort or another, and texts need not be mental. There can be physical texts, and in fact most texts with which we are acquainted and that function effectively in society are physical insofar as their ECTs are physical. It will not do to restrict texts to a mental sort of existence.

Implicit in the view that texts have only mental existence are two misguided assumptions: The first is the identification of a text with the meaning individual knowers grasp when they understand a text; the second is the conception of all textual meaning as mental. If one assumes that texts are the same as their meanings and meanings are mental, it follows that texts have only mental existence. But texts are not the same as their meaning as already stated and as will be argued in more detail in Chapter 2, and the view that meaning is necessarily mental is certainly a controversial one that cannot be used, without strong support, to argue in favor of some other view.[39] Therefore, the view that a text is always something mental and that a text has only mental existence, based on the mental character of the understanding of that meaning by knowers, is not prima facie viable.

The other sort of theory about the existence and location of texts places texts outside the mind.[40] And here, again, we find at least two opinions. For some authors, texts are to be found in the world as objects with an existence similar to that of other objects. For others, who adopt a Platonic approach, texts are not part of the world but nonetheless are located outside minds in a place of their own, where they have a reality greater than that of the world or of minds.[41]

There is considerable merit in these views. Texts appear to us to have more than mental reality, and in fact most texts we encounter are physical entities insofar as their ECTs are physical entities. Hence, it makes sense to say that texts are part of the extramental world. The advantages of the Platonic position, of course, are related to the causal explanation of the existence of token texts, for the existence of archetypal texts seems to help explain the existence of their copies.

Neither of these views, however, seems adequate insofar as both fail to explain the relation of texts to their understanding. If texts are simply extramental objects of one sort or another, or even archetypal ideas of a Platonic sort, how can they be understood as something different than what they are? For the understanding of texts is not the understanding of what their ECTs are. When I understand the text '2 + 2 = 4' I do not understand certain lines and shapes made up of ink printed on a piece of paper. Rather, I understand that two plus two equal four; that is, I understand the meaning of those lines and shapes. The problem with views that identify texts with extramental realities is that they fail to take account of the full nature of texts; they do not realize that texts are entities endowed with meaning, and not just the entities that constitute them considered apart from meaning. In addition, it should be clear that at least some texts are mental and thus exist in minds, so it makes no sense to put all texts outside minds.

The position that locates texts in the mind and the one that locates texts outside the mind make two mistakes of the same sort, although in different directions. First, those who locate texts in the mind identify texts exclusively with meaning and understand meaning as something mental; those who locate texts outside the mind identify texts exclusively with ECTs and understand ECTs as nonmental. Both positions leave out an essential aspect of textuality: The former leaves out the ECTs and the latter, the meaning. Second, these positions restrict the nature of meaning and ECTs to either the mental or nonmental realm. In order not to fall into the same traps, a different approach is necessary. I shall present my view of the existence and location of texts as a consequence of the fact that texts can be universal and individual, physical and mental. Let me begin with individual physical texts.

Like other physical individuals, individual physical texts are entities that exist at a certain time and in a certain location. This is quite evident in the case of the text of such works as Aristotle's *Metaphysics*. The individual historical text of that work was produced at a certain time and place and as long as it was not destroyed it continued to exist as other individual physical objects do. Likewise, an individual contemporary text of the same work was produced at a certain time and place and endures as long as it is not destroyed. Of course, if no one connects the physical ECTs of the text to the meaning Aristotle gave them, the text enjoys only a limited existence and one could argue that in fact its existence is not as a text at all but merely as ECTs. Still, the fact that the ECTs in question were once related to a meaning cannot be changed.

In addition to the physical text of Aristotle's *Metaphysics* there may also be mental counterparts of it, say the images of the text in Aristotle's mind or in the minds of those who become acquainted with the physical text. These images are also individual texts but they are mental rather than physical; they are noninstantiable instances of a type of mental text existing in individual minds at some particular time. These individual instances exist and are located in time. The question of whether they are also located in space is difficult to answer and depends on the status of mind versus that of physical objects. We will have to leave it unanswered here, because the determination of the nature of mind vis-à-vis physical objects cannot be settled in passing, although from what I said earlier it should be clear that prima facie I do not favor the identification of the mental and the physical. Fortunately for our present purposes, it is not necessary that we answer this question. It suffices to point out that individual mental texts exist in the mind of those individual subjects who think them.

The case of universal texts is quite different from that of individual texts.[42] In this case the matter concerns not the existence and location of, say, the individual historical text of Aristotle's *Metaphysics*, but rather of the type of text of which that individual text is an instance. This raises the very important but difficult question of the ontological status of universals, which, considering the limitations of the current enterprise, cannot be dealt with adequately here. I have, however, provided an extended discussion of this issue elsewhere and, therefore, to save time and space, I shall apply what I concluded there concerning universals in general to the case of universal texts in particular.[43]

My position with respect to the existence of universals is that a category such as existence is not applicable to them. Moreover, because location presupposes existence, location also cannot apply to universals. To try to apply these categories to universals is to fall into what Ryle called a *category mistake*. It is like trying to answer questions about whether geometrical figures have a particular taste or whether pain is colored. Taste does not apply in geometry and color does not function in the world of feelings. It makes no sense to say that triangles taste bitter and circles taste sweet. Although sometimes we use colors to describe moods and feelings, as when I say "I feel blue today," such uses are clearly metaphorical and understood as such by everyone. To try to understand pain in terms of color or geometrical figures in terms of taste leads to conceptual confusions. Likewise, the categories of existence and location do not apply to universals such as cat, good, or table. One may ask whether an individual cat, say Chichi, exists or not or whether she is in my studio with me at the time I am writing these words, but it makes no sense to ask whether "cat" exists or is here or there.

This view should not be identified with the view that universals do not exist.[44] To do that would be to grant that the question "Do universals exist?" or, in a more specific form, "Does cat exist?" is legitimate. And my point is precisely that such questions are illegitimate. My position is that one should not ask this sort of question. Put thus, this is a linguistic claim. But this claim has also an ontological counterpart that I express by saying that universals are neutral with respect to existence and similarly neutral with respect to location.

Of course, if one were to identify universals with concepts in individual minds, then obviously universals would both exist and be located in those minds—understanding 'location' with the provisos mentioned earlier. The concept of cat I am currently entertaining in my mind both exists and is in my mind. But, again, that does not mean that the universal "cat" exists or that it is located somewhere. And my business here is not with the concept of cat in anyone's mind, but with the universal "cat." That these are quite different I have explained elsewhere.[45] Here it should suffice to indicate that "cat" is not the same as "the concept of cat" and that neither is the same as "the concept of cat I have in my mind."

If my view of the ontological status of universals as neutral with respect to existence and location is adopted, then universal texts cannot be said to exist or not exist or to be located or not be located anywhere.[46] Qua universals, texts are neutral with respect to existence and location. Consider two examples of texts mentioned earlier:

1. $2 + 2 = 4$
2. $2 + 2 = 4$

These texts are individual and both exist and have a certain location. That they exist is rather obvious because I am currently perceiving them and whoever reads this book will be able to do the same. And with that goes their location, because I can describe them as being at a certain distance from the top of the page and so on. The universal physical type of text to which they belong, however, is not located in any place where I may perceive it, nor can we say that it exists or does not exist.

I can also say that I have a mental text when I imagine 1 or 2. That text will also exist and be "in" my mind—whatever that 'in' may mean. But that text is not universal, for it is not the instantiable type of which there may be other instances. Indeed, it is an instance of a type and therefore is as individual as 1 or 2. For this reason I may legitimately speak of its existence and location. But I cannot speak of the existence and location of the universal of which it is an instance without getting into serious conceptual muddles. That mental type, just like the physical type of which 1 and 2 are instances, is neutral with respect to existence and location.

At this point we may consider an objection against the view of universal texts I have proposed. From the definition of texts presented in the Introduction, it is clear that among the necessary conditions of texts is that they have authors. But universal texts are neutral with respect to existence and location whereas authorship presupposes both existence and location. Thus universal texts must not be texts.

This objection is based on a misguided understanding of my view and the nature of universality. It assumes that universals are entities of some sort, that is, existents, and therefore distinct in reality from their instances, that is, the individuals that instantiate them. This is why one could ask the question of who their author is apart from the author of the instances. Two things appear to require two authors. Indeed, this is the sort of assumption that drove medievals to posit divine ideas and ask for the causal relation between the divine ideas and God. Once one gets into this kind of dialectic, there is no way out. As I have argued elsewhere, the only way out of this conundrum is to cut the Gordian knot that makes it up, rejecting the assumptions on which it is based.[47] My view is that universals are neutral with respect to existence or nonexistence and thus cannot be considered to be entities other than their instances. Universality, like individuality, is a mode that does not entail an entitative distinction.[48] Thus, there is no need to posit an author of a universal text who is different from the author of the individual text. There is only one author of a text and that author is the author of both the individual and the universal. This, of course, does not explain what the author does vis-à-vis the individual and universal texts, but such a question can be answered only after we know what authorship entails. I will leave its discussion for Chapter 3.

In line with the procedure we are following, where texts are classified according to the character of their ECTs, the location and existence of individual texts has been established on the basis of the existence and location of the ECTs that constitute them. If the ECTs are physical, the texts exist in the world as physical entities; and if they are mental, they exist in the mind as mental entities. And the same procedure has been followed with respect to universal texts. Qua composed of ECTs, texts can still belong to a physical or mental type, but nonetheless they have the neutrality toward existence and location proper to universals. Yet one may wish to inquire whether, because texts are entities that convey meaning, the existence and location of the ECTs of texts is insufficient to determine their existence and location and thus whether the existence and location of their meaning needs to be taken into account for that purpose. It is all very well to classify texts according to the character of their ECTs, for that helps us distinguish among them, but when it comes to their existence and location, it would appear that we need to take into account the status of their meaning as well.

The answer to this issue can be derived from what was said about meanings earlier. Meanings can be individual or universal. If meanings are universal, they are, qua universal, neutral with respect to existence and location. But if they are individual, they have the existence and location appropriate to those individuals. Therefore the answer as to the existence and location of texts depends again upon what one takes texts to be.

VIII.   Historicity of Texts

The fact that universal texts are neutral with respect to existence and location, whereas individual texts are not, raises two sorts of questions. The first concerns identity: How are individual and universal texts the same? This issue will best be left for the next chapter, where textual identity is discussed. The second has to do with the historicity of texts. Can a text be both historical and universal? About this I shall say a word in passing here.

There is no problem about the historicity of individual texts. Qua individual, they are found in a certain place at a certain time if they are physical and in a mind at a certain time if they are mental. The problem surfaces only with universal texts, for I have argued that texts are historical entities and I also claim that they can be universal; and yet universals, qua universals, do not seem to be historical insofar as they do not exist in any place or at any particular time since they are neutral with respect to existence.

Strictly speaking, in the sense of existing at a particular time and place for physical texts and in a particular mind and time for mental texts, it is not possible for universal texts to be historical; only individual, that is, token, texts are historical in this sense. Universal texts, being neutral with respect to existence and location cannot be historical in this sense. If by 'historical,' however, is meant an instantiated rather than an uninstantiated universal, then it is clear that universals can be historical. In this sense, universals that have been instantiated in the world are historical. The universal text of Shakespeare's *Hamlet* can be considered historical in this sense even though, qua universal, it exists nowhere.

XI.   Conclusion

Texts are artifacts, entities endowed with meaning used or intended to be used by authors to convey this meaning to others in order to carry out a diversity of purposes. This fact has important implications for their ontological characterization, for that characterization must include a characterization of the entities that constitute the texts, of the meaning with which they are endowed, and of the relation between them. Because texts are first and foremost the entities of which they are constituted, their ontological characterization must include and begin with the characterization of those entities.

In this chapter I have argued that, if one accepts a distinction between substance and feature, texts can be constituted either by substances and their features or by features alone, but not by substances alone, whether it be one or many, considered apart from their features. From this it follows that texts are always aggregates. Moreover, I have also argued that texts can be universal or individual. Universal texts are texts constituted by entities that are subject to instantiation; individual texts are constituted by entities not subject to instantiation.

Texts may also be physical or mental. This classification is important because we generally think of texts as physical objects of one sort of another that are subject to sense perception. But texts can also be mental entities that are not subject to sense perception. Therefore, it is a mistake to understand textuality as necessarily involving a physical or perceptual aspect.

The distinction between physical and mental texts brings to the fore questions that otherwise might not have been noticed, such as the question of the order of priority between physical and mental texts. Do mental texts always precede physical texts or vice versa? The answer I gave to this question is that there is no set order of priority that can be identified. In some cases physical texts precede their mental counterparts, but in other cases the reverse is true. Questions of priority and relation also arise within the category of physical texts because this category comprises various types of texts depending on the sense with which they are intended to be perceived. In particular this applies to the complex relation between oral and written texts for the ones function at times as signs of the others and vice versa.

This raises interesting questions of textual identity. Indeed, the confusion between physical and mental texts lends support to two positions, both of which turn out to be unacceptable. The first conceives texts as mental entities and tends to identify them with understandings that subjects have of them. This in turn leads to the conclusion that there are as many texts as understandings. The second conceives texts as physical entities and tends to identify them with physical ECTs. This leads to the view that translations are impossible. Thus, the classification of texts into physical and mental and the recognition of their differences have important implications for questions of textual identity. I explore some of these questions in Chapters 3.

The individuality of texts raises the question concerning their principle of individuation. Borrowing from what I have said elsewhere, I claim that the only necessary and suffcient condition of individuation is existence: What makes an individual noninstantiable and, therefore, is the source of its individuality and its distinction from the universal of which it is an instance is the fact that it exists.

The universality and individuality of texts have important implications for the question of their existence and location. Individual texts exist and are located in the same way in which other individuals exist and are located. Moreover, their location is determined by their character. If they are mental entities, they exist only in a mind, but if they are not mental, they exist outside the mind.

With universal texts the situation is different for, qua universal, they are neutral with respect to existence and location in the sense that existence and location do not apply to them. However, their instances can exist and be located in the mind or outside the mind.

So much, then, for the ontology of texts based on the ontological status of the entities that constitute them. Now, with respect to the ontological status of meaning we found that meaning can be universal or individual. Meaning, considered in itself, qua meaning, is neutral insofar as it has no particular ontological status apart from the ontological status of particular meanings. From this it follows that texts of very different sorts can have meanings of different sorts. Individual texts can have universal meanings and universal texts can have individual meanings. This conclusion in turn clarifies the relationship between texts and their meanings. This relationship must be considered as nothing real, being a result merely of an intentional and conventional tie of a meaning to a set of entities that are selected and arranged to constitute a text.

We can also understand from what has been said how texts can be historical. When texts are individual there is no problem in their historicity, for individuals, except those that are actual but not subject to time, are historical entities. The case with universal texts is different, for as universal they are neutral with respect to existence, location, and time. Their historicity, then, is derived from the historicity of their instances; universal texts are historical when they have been instantiated.

These conclusions raise many other questions. Some of these have to do with identity and thus concern the conditions that make texts the same and different. Others have to do with the relation of texts to their authors and audiences. The first set of questions will be taken up in the next chapter and the second in the two that follow it.

2

IDENTITY

The library of the University at Buffalo contains several volumes with the title *Don Quixote* whose author is identified as Cervantes. These volumes are different in important respects: They occupy different spatio-temporal locations; they are printed on different typescripts; the papers of the books have different consistencies; pages vary on the number of words they have; and so on. Nevertheless, ordinary persons regard these volumes as copies of the same text and users of the library have no trouble identifying them as such.[1] So we may ask, what makes them the same? And more generally, what makes texts the same?

This question is not only interesting in its own right but also has important implications for other philosophical issues related to texts. The question of a text's identity is closely tied to issues concerning its completeness or incompleteness and what might be called its boundaries. And answers to these questions in turn will determine both the understanding and the interpretation of texts. Likewise, the answer to the question of textual identity will determine whether a text is new or not, and this will determine such things as the originality of a particular author and the degree to which a text has been plagiarized. Finally, most of what is said about texts in this volume assumes that there is such a thing as textual identity, so we can hardly sidestep the question of what makes texts the same.

Apart from the importance and interest that the question of textual identity may have for other issues involved in textuality, it is in itself puzzling because the basic approaches frequently adopted to answer it pose difficulties. Five of these views suggest themselves.[2] One view identifies a text with the entities used to convey meaning considered separately from that or any other meaning; namely, what I have been calling ECTs. In a text composed of marks made on a piece of paper, the conditions of identity of the marks, apart from the meaning they are supposed to convey, are considered to be the conditions of the identity of the text. This view encounters difficulties, however. Were this view to be accepted, for example, we would lack a way of distinguishing texts from entities that are not texts. Moreover, this view would allow a text to have contradictory meanings, because the same entities can be used to convey such meanings.[3]

A second view identifies a text with the meaning considered independent of the entities (ECTs) used to convey it. In this way, the conditions of identity of a text apply to the meaning only and not to the entities used to convey such meaning. It is not the conditions of identity of the marks made on the paper that determine the identity of a written text, for example, but rather the conditions that determine the identity of what it signifies.[4] The difficulty with this position is that different texts, including texts in different languages that have the same meaning but different ECTs, would have to be considered the same text.

A third possible view holds that texts are to be identified with the entities used to convey meaning (ECTs) considered together with meaning, when meaning is taken in general and not identified with a particular meaning. In this sense, the conditions of identity include meaning but not any meaning in particular. The conditions of identity of a written text represented by marks on paper include the conditions of identity of the marks plus a condition that the marks have meaning, but not that the marks have any meaning in particular.[5] The difficulty with this view is similar to the difficulty mentioned in connection with the first view presented, for in accordance with it the same text could have any meaning whatever, and that does not seem acceptable.

A fourth view identifies texts with certain acts.[6] This view is derivative of Austin's well-known conception of language in terms of speech acts.[7] A text, then, would be a series of acts someone performs. Because Austin distinguished among three different kinds of pertinent speech acts, the question arises as to which of these constitutes a text. The locutionary act, for Austin, is the act of uttering that takes place when someone says, for example, "Pick up the ball, please." It is the act performed when one utters the sounds that constitute an oral text. (This could be applied as well to writing, of course.) The perlocutionary act is the act of getting whoever is asked to pick up the ball to do so. It is the act performed when the locutionary act produces the desired effect. And the illocutionary act in this case is the act of asking someone to pick up the ball. It is the act performed when one says something; that is, when one performs locutionary acts. Within this framework one could identify the text 'Pick up the ball, please,' as a set of locutionary, perlocutionary, or illocutionary acts or as a set composed of all or some of these acts. In any case, the important point is that a text becomes a set of acts performed by a speaker or writer. One of the problems with this position is that it leaves no place for meaning to play a role in textual identity. Moreover, it confuses the use (i.e., an act) of a text with the text, just as it confuses the act of uttering with the utterance. Yet it is not the act of uttering, but the utterance; just as it is not the act of writing, but the writing, through which one communicates meaning. So the text cannot be the act of uttering or writing, even if one were to add to these perlocutionary and illocutionary acts. The text must be the utterance or the writing considered in relation to something else.[8]

Finally, there is the view I shall defend, according to which the conditions of identity of a text include not only the conditions of identity of the entities (ECTs) used to convey its meaning, but also the conditions of identity of the particular meaning they are used to convey. This position is not entirely without difficulty, however. In the first place, the view seems to preclude the possibility that a text may have different meanings depending on its context and how it is used. In the second place, it also seems to preclude the possibility that different audiences understand the same text differently.

In spite of the importance of the issues involved in and related to the identity of texts and the considerable attention that texts are receiving in recent literature, the question of textual identity is seldom explicitly raised by philosophers.[9] Textual critics by contrast are much concerned with this issue. But their concern relates more to the question of the identity conditions of particular texts, rather than of texts in general.[10] I shall have something to say about this in the conclusion of this chapter. In the body of the chapter, I propose to take up the general question of textual identity. My thesis will be that the conditions of textual identity are complex, including not only particular meaning but also syntax and composition.

I. Sameness

For present purposes and following ordinary usage, I shall regard the terms 'identity' and 'sameness' as interchangeable. Indeed, there is very little difference in ordinary discourse between the usage of these terms. 'Identity' is a learned term derived from the late Latin *identitas* (in turn a derivative of *idem*, which means "the same"), whereas 'sameness' comes from an Old Norse common root. In technical discourse there can be differences in the usage of these terms, but as those are idiosyncratic to particular authors, they are irrelevant to my present purposes.

The notion of "sameness" is one of the most versatile in our ordinary conceptual framework. We apply it to all sorts of things, such as colors, persons, times, spaces, relations, essences, experiences, events, concepts, and so on. We speak of persons or their lives as being the same or of the same type; we say that a daughter is the same as her father with respect to this or that characteristic; we refer to the use of the same concepts in discourse; we agree that sometimes we have the same experiences; and we talk about being in places at the same time, being essentially the same, and witnessing the same events. Indeed, a very large number of examples could be given here to illustrate the usefulness and pervasiveness of this notion in ordinary discourse, but for our purposes the examples provided should suffice.

The notion of sameness has obvious relationships to the notion of similarity. It is not unusual to find authors that use the terms 'same' and 'similar' interchangeably. This is so because in ordinary language we do use these terms interchangeably in some occasions. For example, we sometimes say that two objects have similar color when they are both colored red. In this sense, there is no difference between similarity and sameness. But it is likewise true that we often use the notions of similarity and sameness differently, thus justifying the different terms. In this sense, important distinctions are made between the two notions. Perhaps the key distinction is that similarity understood thus occurs always in the context of difference. For two things to be similar, they must also be different in some respect, although the difference in question must refer to aspects other than those on which the similarity is based. Thus one may speak of two persons as being similar provided that they differ in some way. If they do not differ in any way, then they are regarded as the same. The conditions of similarity may be expressed in the following way:

> X is similar to Y if and only if X and Y (1) have at least one feature F that is the same in both and (2) also have at least one feature F_1 that is not the same in both.

Features are understood very broadly in this formulation. They may include anything that may be said of a thing and thus not only qualities, but also relations, position, temporal location, states, actions, and so on. This broad understanding has been adopted both for consistency with what was said in Chapter 1 and to facilitate discussion.

In contrast with similarity, sameness does not require—indeed it precludes—difference. That does not mean that two things could not be regarded as the same with respect to some feature or other and different with respect to something else. A daughter, for example, may be the same as her father with respect to stubbornness while being different with respect to gender. The point is, however, that for the daughter and father to be the same with respect to stubbornness, their stubbornnesses must not involve any difference whatsoever. If there were some difference, say that their stubbornnesses were not exactly the same in every respect so that one were stronger than the other, one would speak instead of a "similarity of stubbornness." We might express this understanding of sameness of things and sameness of their features in the following two propositions:

> X is the same as Y if and only if there is nothing that pertains to X that does not pertain to Y and vice versa.

> X is the same as Y with respect to F if and only if there is nothing that pertains to F of X that does not pertain to F of Y, and vice versa.

The first expresses what might be called *absolute sameness*, because it applies to the whole entity in question; the second, what might be called *relative sameness*, because it applies only to a feature(s) or aspect(s) of an entity.[11]

Part of the reason for the frequent blurring of the distinction between sameness and similarity in English discourse is that the term often used as the opposite of both is 'difference,' even though there exists a term that more properly expresses the opposite of similarity: 'dissimilarity.' Similar-different and same-different are generally regarded as pairs of opposites in English. This usage does not necessarily extend to other languages, however. In the Middle Ages, for example, a concerted effort was made to keep the notions of similarity and sameness separate, and this was supported by the use of different opposite terms for each. 'Difference' (*differentia*) was used, at least in technical philosophical discourse, as the opposite of 'similarity' (*similaritas*), whereas 'diversity' (*diversitas*) was used as the opposite of 'sameness' (*identitas*).[12]

Not all sameness about which we speak is of the same sort. There are at least three fundamental but distinct types of sameness, which I shall respectively call *achronic, synchronic,* and *diachronic. Achronic* sameness is sameness irrespective of time; it may be understood as follows:

X is achronically the same as Y if and only if X is the same as Y.

By contrast, synchronic sameness and diachronic sameness have to do with time. *Synchronic* sameness may be taken thus:

X is synchronically the same as Y if and only if X is the same as Y at time t.

Diachronic sameness may be understood in the following way:

X is diachronically the same as Y if and only if X is the same as Y at times t_n and t_{n+1}.

The distinctions between achronic, synchronic, and diachronic sameness, then, have to do with time. In the first case, sameness has no reference to time at all; in the second case, sameness applies at a particular time; and in the third, it applies at two (or more) different times. These three sorts of sameness generate three different problems for philosophers who wish to account for them. In the case of achronic sameness philosophers will want to determine the necessary and sufficient conditions that make a thing the same irrespective of time. This is another way of asking what makes a thing be the thing it is, and the answer involves identifying its necessary and sufficient conditions. For this reason, I like to call this issue *the problem of identity*. Because of the atemporal character of the inquiry involved, atemporal entities, such as universals, could be included in it. Indeed, this sort of investigation can be applied to anything that may become the subject of philosophical discourse. We may ask about the necessary and sufficient conditions of an individual person, but also of universals, concepts, propositions, events, and so on.

Note that the conditions of achronic sameness may include temporal conditions. This may be the case when the entities in question are temporal in such a way that their sameness is tied to their temporality. For example, one may want to argue that being born at a certain time is part of the sameness conditions of an individual historical figure and so on. To say, however, that the conditions of sameness of X include temporal conditions does not entail that the question of sameness has to be framed in temporal terms. One thing is to ask what makes X to be X and another to ask what makes X to be X at a particular time or what makes X to be X at two or more different times. The conditions of X being X may include temporal conditions but the question is not temporal. This is the difference between achronic sameness, on the one hand, and synchronic and diachronic sameness, on the other.

The case of synchronic sameness is different from that of achronic sameness insofar as what is sought in the former is to account for the necessary and sufficient conditions that make a thing be the thing it is at a particular time. This difference is significant because it restricts the relevant types of things to temporal ones. It would make no sense to ask for an account of the sameness of atemporal entities at a particular time. Thus, for example, questions concerning synchronic sameness could not apply to universals, mathematical entities, or even to God if God is conceived as being outside of time, as in Augustine. Apart from this significant difference, achronic and synchronic sameness are similar because their analyses abstract from the *passage* of time; this abstraction is what distinguishes them both from diachronic sameness.

In diachronic sameness what is at stake is the determination of the necessary and sufficient conditions that make a thing be the same at two (or more) different times. Indeed, it is usual for philosophers to speak of the problem of accounting for diachronic sameness as the problem of accounting for "identity through time" or as the problem of "temporal continuity."[13] Diachronic sameness applies only to those entities to which temporal passage applies. It makes no sense to talk about the diachronic sameness of instantaneous entities or atemporal entities.

In the present context we are dealing with texts, which can be universal or individual, and this will affect the sorts of questions concerning the sameness that can be applied to them. Universal texts are not subject to time, whereas individual texts are temporal not only insofar as they may be located in time, but also insofar as they may be subject to the passage of time—there is no contradiction in the notion of an instantaneous text, but I know of no text that by nature need be instantaneous. Now, because universal texts are not temporal, questions concerning synchronic or diachronic sameness do not apply to them. But certainly one can raise questions concerning their achronic sameness.

The question of what is involved in accounting for the sameness of individual texts is not as clear as it is in the case of universal texts. To answer it, we must point out that the notions of "individual sameness" and "individuality" warrant distinction. We saw in Chapter 1 that "individuality" is to be understood in terms of the notion of "noninstantiability," but "individual sameness" involves two notions, that of "noninstantiability" and that of "sameness" proper. Thus, prima facie it would seem that the problem of *individuation* should not be confused with the problem involved in accounting for *individual sameness*. The first problem has to do with the determination of the necessary and sufficient conditions that make it possible for something to be a noninstantiable instance, apart from whether it is to be considered the same in any sense. The second problem has to do with the establishment of the necessary and sufficient conditions whereby an individual, apart from whatever might make it a noninstantiable instance, is the same.

It may turn out de facto that the conditions in question are the same for both cases and, therefore, that the answer to the problem of individuation turns out to be the answer to the problem of the achronic and synchronic sameness of the individual. But the conditions need not be the same; the conditions for individuation may turn out to be only part of the conditions for sameness. This point becomes clear if we compare what was said concerning individuation in Chapter 1 with what will be said concerning individual sameness later in this chapter.

The case of the diachronic sameness of individuals is different from the cases of achronic and synchronic sameness, for in this instance the conditions that need to be identified are those that make an individual the same at two (or more) times, not the conditions that make an individual be the individual it is apart from time (achronic sameness) or at a particular time (synchronic sameness). I mention this distinction because in the pertinent literature it is not infrequent to find authors who identify individuality with individual diachronic sameness or at least make individual diachronic sameness a necessary condition of individuality and, as a result, consciously identify or unconsciously confuse the problem of accounting for individuation and the problem of accounting for individual diachronic sameness.[14]

Another propaedeutic matter that should be raised here before we proceed concerns the distinction between the problem of accounting for individual sameness and that of accounting for the discernibility of individual sameness. From what we have discussed concerning the distinction between the problem of individuation and the problem of the discernibility of individuals one would surmise also a distinction between individual sameness and the discernibility of such sameness. Indeed, in the case of most things, whether natural or artificial, that distinction seems to hold. The problem of individual sameness is an ontological problem whose solution consists in the identification of the necessary and sufficient conditions of the sameness of individuals. The problem of discernibility is an epistemic issue that involves the identification of the necessary and sufficient conditions of our knowledge of the individual sameness of individuals. In one case the question involves the necessary and sufficient conditions that are responsible for the sameness of X. In the other case, the inquiry concerns the necessary and sufficient conditions that enable a subject to understand X to be the same. To keep these two issues separate and avoid unnecessary complications I prefer to refer to the second issue as *the problem of the identification of individuals*. Moreover, when the identification in question involves the same text at two different times, that is, diachronic sameness, then I refer to the search for its necessary and sufficient conditions as *the problem of the reidentification of individuals*. I discuss identification and reidentification in a separate section of this chapter.

A.   Achronic Sameness of Texts

The problem of achronic sameness has to do with the determination of the necessary and sufficient conditions that make entities the same apart from any consideration of time. The question with regard to texts may be taken to apply to the following: (1) the universal notion of "text" itself; (2) a universal (i.e., type) text of which individual (i.e., token) texts are instances; and (3) individual (i.e., token) texts, whether instantaneous or subject to continuity. Thus, the question of whether texts are achronically the same is complex. If it is applied to the notion of "text" itself, then the question simply raises the issue as to whether something is a text and the conditions that make it so.[15] But the question may also be intended to ask what makes a particular text the same apart from the conditions that make it a text. That is, we could be asking for the conditions that make the text of Cervantes's *Don Quixote*, for example, the text that it is and this is the same as asking for the conditions of the achronic sameness of the universal text of Cervantes's *Don Quixote*. Finally, we may ask for what makes each individual instance of a text, say an individual copy or token of the text of Cervantes's *Don Quixote* found in a certain library, the individual instance it is. This last question is concerned with the determination of the principle of individuation and was discussed in general in Chapter 1.

1.   *Achronic Sameness of Universal Texts*

The second way of interpreting the question concerns the necessary and sufficient conditions that make a universal text the same. What makes the universal text of *Don Quixote* or the universal text of the American Declaration of Independence, for example, the text of *Don Quixote* and the American Declaration of Independence? To bring out the problem more clearly, let us consider a few texts that have been chosen for the facility with which they can be handled. Longer texts could be used to make the same points, but dealing with them would be quite cumbersome.

1. $2 + 2 = 4$
2. $2 + 2 = 4$
3. Two and two make four.
4. Two plus two equals four.
5. Dos y dos son cuatro.
6. Dos mas dos son cuatro.
7. TWO AND TWO MAKE FOUR.
8. Four two and two make.
9. $3 + 3 = 6$

Our ordinary intuitions would seem to dictate that we consider 1 and 2 as two instances of the same universal text and likewise with 3 and 7. When we speak about the text of Okham's *Summa logicae* we make no distinction between the manuscript copies of it written in different medieval hands and those printed on a page. Nor is the color of the ink used relevant, nor the paper or parchment, nor the size of the letters, nor even whether those letters are all capitals or not. We are also quite certain—on the basis of our ordinary intuitions— that 9 is not the same as any of the other members in the group, and the reason given would be most likely that it means something different than the others. Moreover, most people, I believe, would not regard 5 and 6 as the same texts as 1, 2, 3, 4, 7, 8, or 9. They would argue that 5 is a translation of 3, as 6 is of 4 into a different language. The matter of whether 3 and 4 or 5 and 6 are different texts or not would probably elicit some disagreement. Some would argue that, because they mean the same thing, are written in the same language, and contain the same key words ('two' and 'four,' in the English text; 'dos' and 'cuatro' in the Spanish text) or functionally synonymous ones ('and' and 'plus,' 'y' and 'mas,' etc.) they are the same text. But others would argue that they cannot be regarded as the same even under those conditions, because they are composed of different signs even if those signs are synonymous. In addition, they might point out, there are different physical characteristics to contend with as well.

These considerations illustrate that the sameness of universal texts is by no means easy to establish. A list of the necessary and sufficient conditions for the achronic sameness of universal texts does not seem to be readily available. The most likely candidates are the sameness of meaning, author, speech acts, audience, context, arrangement of signs, and signs themselves.

a.   Sameness of Meaning. The condition that appears at first as most obviously necessary in connection with the achronic sameness of universal texts
is sameness of meaning. I take sameness of meaning to indicate at least that two
texts have the same meaning if their truth conditions are the same. Thus, 'Dos
y dos son cuatro' and 'Two and two make four' have the same meaning because
the conditions under which one would be true are the same conditions under
which the other would be true, and the conditions under which one would be
false are also the same conditions under which the other would be false. It is,
of course, common to find texts that have meanings to which truth value cannot apply, such as commands. And there may be other exceptions to this conception of meaning sameness. But the minimal understanding of sameness of
meaning provided here may give a rough idea of what is involved. The presentation of a satisfactory view of meaning identity would require more space than
I can provide for it in a discussion of textual identity, thus I cannot address the
many problems it poses at this point.

One could easily see why it might be argued that sameness of meaning is
both a necessary and sufficient condition of the achronic sameness of universal texts; that is, that universal texts that mean the same are the same text. Indeed, this condition allows us to distinguish 9 from 1–8 previously, for its
meaning is different from that of the other texts on the list. This condition is
particularly attractive, of course, to those who identify a text with its meaning.

There are various ways in which this view may be assailed, however.
Some of these ways are ineffective, but I consider at least one effective against
the view that sameness of meaning is both a necessary and sufficient condition
of textual sameness.

Although sameness of meaning does appear to be a necessary condition
of textual sameness in the sense that texts that do not mean the same could not
possibly be the same texts, it would be difficult to argue that it is also a sufficient condition. That it is a necessary condition can be seen clearly in the reasons why 9, for example, is not the same text as any of the texts 1–8: it does not
share the same meaning. On the other hand, to have the same meaning does not
seem to ensure textual sameness. If that were the case, texts 1–8 would all be
the same text, something very few would be prepared to accept and something
I certainly do not wish to defend. To do so would imply that two texts composed
by different authors in different languages could be regarded as the same text
provided their meanings were the same. It would also suggest that a painting
and a written text would have to be regarded as the same text if their meanings
were the same. But none of this seems acceptable. Therefore, we must conclude
that sameness of meaning is a necessary condition of textual sameness under
the specified strictures, but it is not a sufficient condition of it.[16]

The view that sameness of meaning is a necessary condition of textual
sameness might be suspect in some cases, however. For, although it is obvious

that it applies to the sort of short texts we have been using as examples, one may wish to argue that it does not apply equally to very long texts. Suppose that there is a change in the meaning of one of the thousands of sentences that make up the text of *Don Quixote* and that such a sentence is relatively unimportant in the whole text, so that a change in its meaning does not affect the meaning of any other sentence of the text. Can we really say that one text of *Don Quixote* is not the same as the other? Strictly speaking, it appears to be so, but in practical terms it does not appear to make much difference.[17] How can this difficulty be resolved?

The solution may be given in two steps. According to the first, the issue raised by the change in meaning of the sentence in question does not concern textual identity but meaning identity. The issue is whether the whole meaning of a text is the same when the meaning of part of the text changes but that change is insignificant. Thus, regardless of the answer, one can still maintain that sameness of meaning is a necessary condition of textual sameness. According to the second step, whether the change in the meaning of the sentence makes a difference or not will depend on the function of the text within the culture within which and for which the text was created, for ultimately that culture determines what is essential and what is not essential to the meaning of a text and hence to its identity.[18]

b. Sameness of Author. Apart from sameness of meaning, other ways to account for textual sameness may be explored, although some of these do not seem very promising. Consider the author.[19] It is possible in principle to argue that a universal text is the same whenever it has the same author. But this argument does not make much sense, for it implies that all the texts an author produces are the same universal text regardless of the differences among them. One could, of course, argue that by "the same text" in this case is meant "part of the same text." And, indeed, this sense is sometimes used in discourse. We sometimes speak of everything an author has produced as a single work. But that is something different from saying that every text an author has produced is the same universal text in the sense that it is identical with every other text produced by him or her. Therefore, sameness of author could not be a sufficient condition of sameness of universal texts, for the condition of sameness of meaning would be missing. But, what if that condition were added? Would sameness of meaning and sameness of author combined ensure textual sameness of a universal sort?

The answer is negative, for the same author may create two different universal texts that have the same meaning, say, a poem and an essay. Indeed, the case of St. John of the Cross's *Spiritual Canticle* comes to mind. But simpler examples abound in everyday experience, where we use different sentences to mean the same thing. Texts 1, 3, 4, 5, and 8 could have the same author and yet, in spite of that and the sameness of meaning they share, would not be the same universal text.

So much then for the sufficiency of authors for the identity of universal texts. But what of necessity? Is sameness of author a necessary condition of the sameness of texts? Could there be two instances of the same universal text produced by two different authors? This is one of the puzzling questions that Borges explores in his "Pierre Menard, Author of the *Quixote*." His answer is negative, insofar as Borges ever gives an unambiguous answer. He assumes that the authors in question are separated by important temporal and cultural differences that alter the meaning of the text. Although the ECTs of which the texts are composed are the same, the meanings of those ECTs considered as signs are different because of the cultural distance between the authors.[20] If we are to follow the understanding of Borges, it is clear that sameness of author may be a necessary condition, but only insofar as the author affects sameness of meaning.

What about contemporary authors? Indeed, what about authors who are alike insofar as that is possible, say identical twins raised in the same environment and so on? Could we not say that in that case the authors of the texts are different but the texts are of the same universal type, a universal instantiated in two instances? If this is possible, sameness of texts does not require sameness of author if by "sameness of author" is meant the same individual person.

In short, sameness of author appears to be neither a necessary nor a sufficient condition of the sameness of universal texts. When we say "sameness" of author, we are speaking of numerical sameness. It is altogether possible for two similar, but numerically different authors to produce the same text. This is obvious from the mentioned case of identical twins. But does it make sense to say that persons who are not only different numerically, but also different in other respects, could produce two instances of the same text?

In one way it is obvious that this can happen, for two persons may differ in respects that would have no relevance to their composing a text. For example, they may differ in the fact that one of them has a tiny birthmark on his back and the other does not. But would it make sense to say that two persons could be authors of the same text even though they had substantial differences in outlook, education, and so on?

Logically speaking, I do not see how the question can be answered negatively in all cases. Indeed, when it comes to short, simple texts, it does not seem difficult to think of counterexamples. There is no reason why two authors could not have produced two instances of the text "Please, do not smoke" independently of each other. But it is difficult to accept the real possibility of this happening with long and complicated texts, such as the text of *Don Quixote*. It does not seem possible that anyone but Cervantes could have produced for the first time an instance of the text of *Don Quixote*. And if two persons were to have produced instances of the same universal text, say, *Don Quixote*, independently of each other, then those two persons would have to be similar in respects relevant to the composition of the texts.[21]

Note, however, that in raising this question we have shifted to a different issue. The issue originally posed in this section was whether sameness of author, regardless of whether the author is considered individual or universal (i.e., a type of author), is a necessary or sufficient condition for textual identity. The answer to that question seems to be negative. The question that has been raised now, however, has to do with the conditions of sameness of the author, assuming the identity of the text. That is a different question, which I address in Chapter 3 because to answer it we need to know much more than we presently know about authorship. I should also note that the issue we have been discussing should not be confused with the separate issue of whether authors are necessary or sufficent conditions of there being texts. This issue is addressed, again, in Chapter 3.

There is only one case in which author identity could be considered to be a necessary condition of textual identity. This occurs when the author is somehow tied to the meaning of the text so that the meaning involves something about the author. This can happen, for example, when the author presents himself in the text as a *dramatis persona*. But a *dramatis persona*, as we shall see in Chapter 3, is an author different from the author we have been discussing here. The latter I call the *historical author.* I bring this up here only to preempt a possible objection.

    c. Sameness of Speech Acts. A closely related position to the one just discussed views speech acts as necessary or sufficient conditions (or both) of the identity of a text. To put the matter thus, however, is to leave it obscure, for speech acts come in a great variety. At least three classes of these must be distinguished, as noted earlier.[22] Locutionary, illocutionary, and perlocutionary acts can be, like all other acts, universal or individual. Thus, when we wish to determine whether the sameness of speech acts is a necessary or sufficient condition for the sameness of universal texts, we must distinguish among several possibilities: (1) individual locutionary acts, (2) universal locutionary acts, (3) individual illocutionary acts, (4) universal illocutionary acts, (5) individual perlocutionary acts, and (6) universal perlocutionary acts.

The identity of none of the individual acts mentioned appears to be a necessary or sufficient condition of the identity of universal texts. This should be clear from what was said earlier in the context of author identity. An individual instance of an act of uttering, for example, does not appear to be necessary or sufficient for the identity of a universal text. Two numerically different acts of uttering can result in two different instances of the same type of utterance, which, if they have the same meaning and so on, could be the same text.

And the same could be said about the individual illocutionary and perlocution-ary acts.

The situation with universal speech acts seems to be different, however. Consider the case of locutionary acts. Prima facie, it would seem necessary for a particular universal oral text to be the product of the same type of uttering acts, for the text is constituted by certain types of utterances that are intrinsi-cally tied to the type of acts of uttering them. The act of uttering goes with the utterance and vice versa, so it would appear that the acts of uttering are neces-sary for the utterance and therefore for the text constituted of the utterances. However, this is not certain, for one could argue that uttering the sounds is not really necessary if one were able to produce the same types of sounds in some other way. Moreover, the acts of uttering are certainly not sufficient for the identity of the universal text because the utterances produced by such acts could have different meanings.

Now consider the perlocutionary acts; namely, what we do or accomplish when we say something, say, to get someone to open a door. Is the identity of these universal acts necessary or sufficient for the identity of a universal text? It does not seem necessary, for the perlocutionary acts could in principle be the result of different locutionary acts, and different locutionary acts would give rise to different texts. Nor could they be sufficient because sometimes our lo-cutionary and illocutionary acts are ineffective in producing perlocutionary acts. I can order Peter to open a door, and he may ignore my order.

The case of universal illocutionary acts resembles that of universal locu-tionary acts. Their identity is not sufficient for textual identity, but it appears necessary for it. It is not sufficient because the same illocutionary acts can be performed with different universal locutionary acts. Different sounds can be used to perform the same illocutionary act. I can order Peter to open the door in French or Spanish, for example. And different locutionary acts result in dif-ferent texts because locutionary identity is necessary for textual identity.

But illocutionary identity appears necessary for textual identity, for the illocutionary act is the act of saying something, and what is said in the act is the meaning of the text.[23] But meaning identity is necessary for textual identity. So it turns out that illocutionary identity is necessary for textual identity.

In short, the identity of a universal text requires the identity of universal illocutionary acts, but not of locutionary or perlocutionary acts. None of these acts, however, provides sufficient conditions of the identity of a universal text.

Note that I have been speaking about speech acts in the usual way, as re-ferring to speech. However, what has been said applies, mutatis mutandis, to linguistic acts not involving speech, such as writing, signaling, and so on.

   d.   Sameness of Audience. Another factor that may be used to account for the sameness of a universal text is the audience.[24] Can sameness of audience be a necessary or sufficient condition of the sameness of universal texts? As far as a sufficient condition is concerned, it is clear that it cannot, for the same audience can be the audience of different universal texts. The same person, for example, can be the audience of the text of *Hamlet* and the text of *Don Quixote*, or of "2 + 2 = 4" and "The cat is on the mat." On the other hand, when it comes to being a necessary condition, the situation is more complex and thus not so easily settled. The difference in the situation comes about because the author may have a particular audience in mind for the text and as such that audience may influence in important ways what the author produces. Most texts are elliptical; they contain lacunae meant to be filled by their audiences. The meaning the author intends to convey through the text is incomplete unless what the audience is meant to supply is taken into account. It is not necessary for the audience to be the individual audience the author had in mind; the audience that is pertinent is the type of audience the author had in mind, just as it is not the individual author that is pertinent for the achronic sameness of a universal text but rather the type of author. A certain type of audience can supply the needed elements for the universal text. As a result, although sameness of audience is not a sufficient condition of the sameness of universal texts, it appears indeed to be a necessary condition of it in cases where the text contains lacunae to be filled by the audience.

Now, someone may wish to argue that, if a particular type of audience is a necessary condition of the sameness of a universal text, then the author (or type of author) should also be one. Indeed, it is the author who leaves out, intentionally or unintentionally, the parts of the text missing in the lacunae that the audience must fill. Moreover, the author's subjectivity has much to do with a text and its meaning. So how can the author be left out if the audience is thought to be necessary? Either both are left out or both are put in.

I do not wish to argue that the author is not closely related to the text or not necessary for its existence. Indeed, as we shall see in Chapter 3, the author is not only responsible for the selection and arrangement of signs that compose a text but also for the overall meaning in the sense that will be explained later. Moreover, the author is also responsible for the lacunae that the audience has to fill. But this does not mean that sameness of author is a necessary or sufficient condition of textual identity. Identity conditions are not the same as conditions of existence and thus something may be a condition of existence (in this case, let us assume, the author) of something (the text) that is not a condition of its identity. Moreover, there is an important difference between author and audience; namely, in composing a text, the author, consciously or unconsciously, takes into account the audience and what it is meant to supply. Signs are selected, arrangements are made, and materials are included or excluded with the audience in mind. None of this, however, applies to the author. Thus, the audience intended by the author is in some cases a necessary part of the puzzle that determines the meaning of a text in this special sense, whereas the author is not, and in that way sameness of audience appears to be a necessary condition of the achronic sameness of some texts.

e. Sameness of Context. What applies to the audience in relation to achronic sameness also applies to context: Context is always important for the meaning of texts, for what appears to be the same text may have very different meanings, depending on context, and thus turn out to be different texts.[25] The threat, "Don't touch that or I'll kill you" has quite a different meaning when it is addressed by a mother to a child reaching for a fragile object or when it is said by a police officer to a burglar reaching for a gun. This does not mean that in all cases where the meaning of a text changes in accordance with context the identity of the text also changes. There are texts whose function prescribes for them more than one meaning, or even a range of meanings, and thus cannot be said to be different texts just in virtue of changes among the meanings that constitute their legitimate range. But in other texts a change of meaning implies a change in text. So different contexts may entail different meanings and thus different identities, although sameness of context does not ensure textual sameness. It is obvious from everyday experience that different texts can be and are uttered under the same (in all pertinent respects) conditions.

Moreover, one may want to argue that, unlike the case of the audience, sameness of context can never be a necessary condition of textual sameness, for contexts play no role at all in determining the meaning of some texts.[26] Consider text 1 (2 + 2 = 4) earlier. It would appear that the meaning of this text cannot be altered by the surrounding circumstances, provided that the signs of which it is composed and the arrangement in which they are organized continue to have the determinate meaning we associate with them. The example that has been given, however, is an unusual one, for the texts we normally use in communication are not mathematical. Most frequently we communicate with texts that take for granted the context as a determinant of their meaning. A more sensible view, then, would be to argue that sameness of context is not pertinent for all texts and as such it is not a necessary condition of their sameness, but that it is certainly necessary in the case of texts where it is pertinent for the determination of their meaning. Note again that, in the case of author and audience, the sameness of context that is pertinent is the sameness of type of context not of individual context. In short, sameness of context is not a sufficient condition of textual sameness, but it is a necessary condition whenever the meaning of the text depends on it.

f. Sameness of Sign Arrangement. Another candidate for necessary and sufficient condition of the achronic sameness of universal texts is the arrangement of the signs that compose a text. Sameness of arrangement, however, cannot be a sufficient condition of textual sameness. Syntax is not enough to make two texts the same. This is quite clear from texts 1 $(2 + 2 = 4)$ and 9 $(3 + 3 = 6)$ and from what has been said already concerning other necessary conditions. The same syntactical structure may be common to different texts and therefore cannot ensure textual sameness. But is it a necessary condition? The question concerns, for example, texts 3 (Two and two make four) and 8 (Four two and two make). Can texts that have different arrangements be considered the same texts? If we were to follow our ordinary intuition in this matter, we would answer negatively. Yet the matter is not that simple.

In short texts, it appears that any change in order results in a different text. In some cases the reason is evident: The meaning of the text is destroyed or modified. Consider

1. $2 + 2 = 4$

And let us exchange the '4' for the first '2' that appears in the text. The result is

10. $4 + 2 = 2$

Obviously, the truth value of 10 is different from that of 1, so the texts cannot be the same. Or consider

3.   Two and two make four.

And let us scramble its words thus:

11.   Make and two four two.

The result is gibberish, so 3 and 11 cannot be the same text. There are, however, changes of order that do not change meaning, even though we do seem to regard them as implying a change of text. Consider

8.   Four two and two make.

On the other hand, in very extensive texts, say Kant's text of the *Critique of Pure Reason*, some changes of order may not generally be regarded as sufficient to warrant a change of identity. The reason for this seems to be that the relevance and importance of a change in order has to be seen in a total context. A change that results in a change of meaning clearly will have to be regarded as implying a change in the identity of the text—at least in cases where the change of meaning is significant. If the change of meaning makes little difference to the overall meaning of a text, then the text could be regarded as the same or at least as fundamentally the same. Even when there is no change of meaning, however, modifications in the arrangement of the signs can still be regarded as sufficient to change the identity of the text in cases where those changes alter the nature or function of the text in some sense. The change of text 3 to text 8 is a good example, for that change implies a change in the function of the text. Whereas text 3 is primarily scientific, text 8 appears to be literary. A change in arrangement that implies a change of function, then, implies a change in identity. From this we conclude that sameness of arrangement generally is a necessary condition of textual sameness. However, in cases where that sameness is violated but the changes in arrangement in question are such that neither the substantial meaning of the text nor its function is altered, such sameness may not be a necessary condition of textual sameness. Again, as in the case of meaning, whether it does or does not depends ultimately on what is considered essential by the culture within which and for which the text is produced. Note that, as in other cases examined earlier, I have been speaking of the type of arrangement; that is, instances of universal arrangements do not matter.

   g. Sameness of Signs. Finally, we come to signs, the components of texts. The question we have to answer is whether sameness of signs is a necessary or sufficient condition of the sameness of texts. The first problem we encounter with this question concerns the conditions of the sameness of signs themselves, for it is by no means clear what conditions are involved in it. Interestingly enough, the search for those conditions is surprisingly similar to the search for the conditions of the sameness of texts.

   The main difference between signs and texts is that the meaning of texts is in part the result of the meaning of the signs of which they are composed, whereas the meaning of signs has nothing to do with the meaning of their components.[27] Thus, for example, 'cat' is a sign, but it is not a text; whereas '2 + 2 = 4' is a text and not a sign.

   The fact that some signs may not be composed of signs does not mean that they are necessarily simple. Indeed, the question of whether signs can be simple is not easy to answer. Most signs, like texts, involve complexity and therefore some kind of arrangement, as well as an author, an audience, and a meaning.[28] The relative semantic simplicity of signs makes irrelevant the consideration of authors or audiences as conditions of sameness, however; for two different authors can very well use the same thing or type of thing as a sign of some meaning. The audience is generally irrelevant also, because the relative simplicity of signs diminishes the semantic role played by the audience. On the other hand, context is very important. The "shot" a physician gives to a patient is certainly different from the "shot" a thief receives from a police officer.

   Having said this by way of introduction, let me give a few examples of signs to see if we can determine on what basis they may be regarded as the same:

a.   bear (noun)
b.   bear (noun)
c.   BEAR (noun)
d.   bear (verb)
e.   oso (noun)
f.   bare (adjective)
g.   rbea

On the basis of ordinary custom I would say that a–c are the same sign; d, e, and f are all different from one another and from a–c; and g is not a sign at all, but simply a set of letters, each of which, considered separately, is a sign. Signs a and b have the same physical appearance, the same meaning, and the same grammatical function. Sign c has the same meaning and grammatical function as a and b but a different physical appearance. Sign d has the same physical appearance as a and b but a different meaning and grammatical function. Sign e is the Spanish translation of a, b, and c and has a different physical appearance, even though it has the same meaning and grammatical function.[29] Sign f is different in appearance, meaning, and grammatical function, even though when pronounced it sounds the same as a–d.[30] The difference in pronunciation is irrelevant, however, because sounds that are signs must be regarded as different from written signs although they may be used to convey the same meaning.[31] It is important that f has the same components as a and b but the arrangement is different and that it has a different meaning and grammatical function. Finally, g again has the same components as a–d and f, but it has a different arrangement, which makes it look different, and has no meaning (that it has no meaning entails that it is not a sign at all).

From all this it would seem that the key factors to be considered in the sameness of signs are meaning, function, components, appearance, arrangement, and context. As in the case of texts, sameness of meaning seems to be a necessary condition of the sameness of signs but not a sufficient condition. 'Oso' and 'bear' mean the same thing but are not the same sign. And, although 'bear' (the noun) and 'bear' (the verb) are exactly alike in all physical aspects, they have different meanings and therefore are not instances of the same sign.

Something similar could be said about function, for function is closely related to meaning. The meaning of 'bear' (the animal) and of 'bear' (the action) are different in part at least because 'bear' functions as a noun in some situations and as a verb in others.[32] However, it is also true that different signs with different meanings may have the same function; for example, 'bear' and 'cat' in a sentence such as 'The X is an animal,' where 'X' is replaced by either one of them. Moreover, different signs with the same meaning can have different functions, as is clear in paraphrases and circumlocutions. For these reasons, it would seem that sameness of function does not ensure the sameness of signs and thus that sameness of function is not a sufficient condition of sign identity.

On the other hand, it would appear that sameness of signs requires sameness of function.

The case with appearance is similarly complicated. Indeed, 'bear' and 'bare' have the same appearance in sound, and 'bear' (the noun) and 'bear' (the verb) have the same visual appearance and neither the first pair nor the second are the same signs.[33] Appearance, therefore, cannot be a sufficient condition of the sameness of signs. But is it a necessary condition? Not in all cases, because 'BEAR' and 'bear' are the same sign and yet look different.[34] This indicates that only some aspects of the appearance of a sign are relevant for the identity of a sign; namely, those determined by the author or generally accepted to be so in a particular context by a linguistic community. Color, arrangement, design, size, and so on are all features that can become necessary conditions of the sameness of signs, but they are not sufficient conditions, for sameness of meaning seems also to be necessary.[35]

We may say, then, that the necessary and sufficient conditions of the achronic sameness of signs are three: (1) sameness of meaning, (2) sameness of function, and (3) sameness of features identified by the author or accepted in a particular context by a linguistic community as relevant for meaning. Note that context should not be underestimated. Indeed, the difference between 'bear' (the verb) and 'bear' (the noun) depends on context. The two are different because the first is part of sentences such as "To bear such a burden is a virtue," and the second is part of sentences such as "The bear liked the honey it found in the jar." Their function depends on their sentential context.[36]

Before leaving the discussion of signs I should make explicit what appears to be a rather serious implication of the view presented here. The requirement that signs have the same meaning to be achronically the same implies that words which have different meanings are not the same sign. This seems counterintuitive, for we frequently regard a sign as the same even if it is used to mean different things. Take, for example, the word 'cape.' In a sentence such as "She wore a red cape," the word is used to indicate an article of clothing, but in sentences such as "She spent the weekend on a cape," it is used to mean a piece of land.[37]

I have two answers to this problem at this time, although I have said something more about this matter elsewhere, particularly with respect to texts.[38] First, to preserve this intuition, we would have to give up too much. For giving up the requirement of sameness of meaning in the case of signs and also, as a consequence, in the case of texts creates too many problems, making it very difficult to account for sameness. Second, that 'cape,' meaning an article of clothing, and 'cape,' meaning piece of land, are two different signs does not mean that they are not the same word, if by *word* one refers to a certain artifact developed in a language that is used to convey one or more meanings. By understanding words in this way, we can preserve the theory proposed here concerning signs and texts and the commonsense intuition that 'cape' is the same in some sense in the two sentences just given. We have a case of different signs but the same word.

Having identified the conditions of the sameness or identity of signs, we can return to the topic under discussion: Whether sameness of signs can be a necessary or a sufficient condition of sameness of universal texts. For the reasons already stated in connection with text 3 (Two and two make four) and text 11 (Make and two four two), we see that sameness of signs could not be a sufficient condition. Nonetheless, it would seem that sameness of signs is a necessary condition of the sameness of texts, because a difference of signs may affect both meaning and appearance. Consider the following two sentences:

12.   He was a respectable man.
13.   He was a dignified man.

Clearly these two sentences, although having the same structure, and so on, mean different things if the terms of which they are composed are being used in the ordinary sense. Thus, they constitute not one but two texts. On the other hand, what do we make of the following?

14.   The Philosopher wrote the *Metaphysics*.
15.   Aristotle wrote the *Metaphysics*.

And of the following

16.   He made a contribution to the fund.
17.   He made a donation to the fund.

In texts 14 and 15 we have two sentences that are exactly the same except that text 14 uses an honorific title to refer to Aristotle and text 15 uses his proper name. In texts 16 and 17 we have a similar case except that here the difference concerns the use of two different but synonymous signs, 'contribution' and 'donation.' Is text 15 the same text as text 14 and text 17 the same as text 16? I believe most of us would want to answer negatively because the texts are not composed of the same signs, even if those signs were to be regarded as having the same meaning. Indeed, some authors would find it objectionable if someone were systematically to exchange all instances of 'Aristotle' in their writings by 'the Philosopher.' They might object that, although the referent of the term is the same, they chose 'Aristotle' and not 'the Philosopher' because they wanted to look at Aristotle as an author rather than as a philosopher. Whether this makes sense or not is debatable. For our purposes, however, it is important that authors would object to the exchange of expressions.[39] Similarly, authors would find objectionable the substitution of 'contribution' for 'dona-tion,' even if they could not give a reason why they, in the first place, had not used the former term rather than the latter. Once the question is posed, how-ever, they might object to the exchange because of the differing features of the words, and so on. In a poem, for example, the sound difference between the two words may be important for the intended rhyme. Or it may be that one word is favored over the other because it is more sophisticated, and so on.

Still someone might want to argue that the texts *mean* the same thing and thus there is no reason why text 14 could not be regarded as the same as text 15 and text 16 as the same as text 17. And, indeed, they would be the same if texts were identical to their meanings or sameness of meaning were a sufficient con-dition of textual identity. But if texts are not their meanings, but are groups of entities, used as signs, which are selected, arranged, and intended by authors to convey specific meanings to audiences in certain contexts, and meaning is not a sufficient condition of textual sameness, then texts 14 and 15 cannot be the same nor can texts 16 and 17. They are clearly composed of different signs. That texts 14 and 15, or texts 16 and 17, may actually do the same job does not change the fact that they are different texts, just as some of the signs of which they are composed are different signs having the same meaning and even the same function. Of course, sameness of signs in turn depends on what is re-garded as semantically significant or significant in a particular context.

In short, then, we have examined various conditions that appeared to be good requirements of the achronic sameness of universal texts, but we found that none of them taken by itself constitutes a sufficient condition of textual sameness. Moreover, we found that the author, speech acts, audience, and con-text are related to the sameness of universal texts only insofar as they affect meaning. Sameness of meaning, then, incorporates these conditions when they are pertinent, and thus there is no need to list them as conditions separate from the sameness of meaning. This is not the case, however, with the sameness of arrangement and sameness of sign composition. We found that universal texts with the same meaning but composed of different type signs, or of the same type signs arranged differently, cannot be considered the same universal text. Thus arrangement and sign composition, although not sufficient conditions of textual sameness, may become independently necessary conditions of it. The reason is quite simple. Texts are mixed entities. They are entities with meaning. Their conditions of sameness must include conditions of entitative sameness (arrangement and composition) and meaning. All these conditions together constitute the necessary and sufficient conditions of their achronic sameness. We may formulate those conditions thus:

A universal text X is achronically the same as a universal text Y if and only if (1) X has the same meaning as Y, (2) X and Y have the same type of syntactical arrangement, and (3) X and Y are composed of the same type signs.

These conditions should be taken with the provisos noted throughout the discussion. Although it is cleaner to apply them strictly, in fact our practices show that some changes are not considered sufficiently important to alter identity. We might, then, speak of absolute identity when these conditions are applied without qualification, and of relative identity when these conditions are relaxed on the basis of communal practices concerning what is considered sameness of meaning, syntactical arrangement, and signs.[40]

2. Achronic Sameness of Individual Texts

An individual text is an instance of a universal text. The copy of the text of *Don Quixote* that I read when I was in high school, for example, is an individual text, an instance of the universal text of *Don Quixote*. The question before us concerns the necessary and sufficient conditions of its sameness apart from temporal considerations.

As an instance of a universal text, an individual text shares all the features of the universal except for the universal text's instantiability. Consequently, the conditions of achronic sameness that apply to the universal text must also apply to the individual text. But those conditions alone would not be sufficient for achronic individual sameness, because the conditions of universal sameness apply to all the instances of the universal. What condition or conditions, then, must be added to the conditions for the achronic sameness of the universal (of which the individual is an instance) that, taken together with them, would account for the achronic sameness of the individual? In short, what makes an individual text the individual text it is?

Put thus, it might appear that the issue we are raising here is the same as the issue discussed in Chapter 1 under the rubric "the problem of individuation." However, there are differences between the two that should not be overlooked. The problem of individuation involves the necessary and sufficient conditions of the individuality of texts. And I proposed that those conditions reduced to one: existence. The problem of the achronic sameness of individual texts concerns the determination of the necessary and sufficient conditions of an individual text, not just of its individuality. Thus, the conditions for the achronic sameness of individual texts includes the conditions of individuality and also the conditions of the type of text the text is; namely, the conditions of the universal text. Hence, the necessary and sufficient conditions of the achronic sameness of individual texts are the necessary and sufficient conditions of the achronic sameness of the universals of which the texts are instances, taken together with the conditions of their individuality (i.e., existence). For what makes an individual text what it is, is both what makes it the type of text it is together with what makes it the individual it is. Thus,

An individual text X is achronically the same as an individual text Y if and only if (1) X is an instance of the same universal text of which Y is an instance and (2) X's existence is the same as Y's existence.

This conclusion applies to all individual texts. Now let us turn to synchronic sameness.

B.   Synchronic Sameness of Texts

Unlike achronic sameness, synchronic sameness applies only to temporal entities. It makes no sense, then, to speak of the synchronic sameness of universals. Synchronic sameness applies only to individuals, for only individuals can be subject to time. For all intents and purposes, there is no difference between the conditions of the achronic sameness of individual texts and their synchronic sameness. Synchronic sameness is the same as achronic sameness except that it is taken at a certain time. The time restriction only eliminates entities not subject to time and makes no difference for those that are temporal. Hence, there is no need for us to dwell on this issue. I shall turn, then, to diachronic sameness, in which time plays a more significant role.

C.   Diachronic Sameness of Texts

Diachronic sameness applies only to individual texts that are subject to the passage of time. These texts may be divided into feature aggregates and substance/feature aggregates. Accordingly, I shall divide the discussion between the diachronic sameness of feature-aggregate and substance-feature-aggregate texts.

1.   *Diachronic Sameness of Individual Feature-Aggregate Texts*

Two basic views seek to account for the diachronic sameness of individual texts that are feature aggregates, a substantial view and a feature view.

   a.   Substantial View. According to the substantial view, the diachronic sameness of individual texts that are features of substances is accounted for in terms of the substances of which they are features.[41] This view may be formulated as follows:

An individual feature-aggregate text X at time t_n is the same as an individual feature-aggregate text Y at time t_{n+1} if and only if there is a S such that (1) S is an individual substance, (2) both X and Y are features of S, (3) X and Y belong to the same type, and (4) S is the same at t_n and t_{n+1}.

Thus, the diachronic sameness of an individual text carved on a rock is accounted for by the diachronic sameness of the rock on which the text is carved. The text at t_n is the same as the text at t_{n+1} because the text is an aggregate set of features that belongs to an individual substance that is the same at t_n and t_{n+1}.

This view seems to make sense for at least two reasons. In the first place, because in a substance-feature ontology the features are ontologically dependent on the substance, it makes sense to argue that the substance accounts for both the existence and the identity of its features. If the destruction of the substance results in the destruction of its features, one would expect that the persistence of the substance would result in the persistence of its features. Second, we seem to become aware of the diachronic sameness of features on the basis of the diachronic sameness of the substance of which they are features. I know that the individual text of a certain sort I see carved on an individual stone at t_n is the same as an individual text of the same sort I see carved on an individual stone at t_{n+1} because I know they are carved on the same stone. Indeed, if I knew that the stones were not the same I would probably conclude that the texts are not the same individual text even if they were instances of the same type of text.

When one examines these reasons further, however, they are not as compelling as they first seem. Let us take the first one, according to which the diachronic sameness of the individual substance seems to account for the diachronic sameness of the individual text because the text is ontologically dependent on the substance. It is far from clear that this is so, for a text can change while the substance on which it is found remains fundamentally the same. The diachronic sameness of an individual substance is not a sufficient condition for the diachronic sameness of its features. One can imagine, for example, that a stone on which a text is carved persists while the text is eroded or erased. It is true that in such a case the stone would have undergone some change, but the change could be regarded as minor. Perhaps the text in question is merely and superficially scratched on the stone. In that situation, the text could be easily destroyed with a bit of sanding although the stone would for all intents and purposes be the same and would certainly be substantially the same.

Perhaps, even if substantial diachronic sameness is not a sufficient condition of the diachronic sameness of features, it may be argued that it is a necessary condition of their diachronic sameness, because the features of a substance do not seem to be able to exist unless the substance exists. Take the case of the carved text on a stone. It appears that unless the stone exists and persists there can be no text that persists, for the destruction of the stone would automatically result in the destruction of the text.

The matter is not so simple, however. Let us suppose that the stone about which we are speaking does not cease to exist all of a sudden but is subjected to a process, of say electrolysis, whereby its molecules are replaced by molecules of some metal, so that after a certain period of time the original stone has become a piece of metal. If under those conditions one regards the piece of metal as the same as the original stone, even though all its features (weight, color, consistency, etc.) except for its shape and texture have changed, one could still argue that the diachronic sameness of the substance is a necessary condition of the diachronic sameness of the text. But if the piece of metal is regarded as a different entity from the original, which seems a more reasonable view, then no substantial diachronic sameness underlies the textual diachronic sameness. Of course, one could always question whether there is a textual diachronic sameness under those conditions. But can we really argue that there is not? Whether there is or not depends in fact on what is regarded as essential for the text. If only the shape of the carving is involved, then it is clear that the text is the same, for the particular shape of the carved text on the stone has not changed with the substantial changes that the stone has undergone. On the other hand, if it is not shape alone that is regarded as essential to the text, and say, color is also of the essence, then the substantial change has entailed a change in the text and the diachronic sameness of the text has been interrupted.

In short, substantial diachronic sameness can be considered neither a necessary nor a sufficient condition of the diachronic sameness of individual feature-aggregate texts. It is possible to have individual feature texts that persist even though the individual substances on which they depend undergo substantial change and it is also possible to have individual feature texts that do not persist in spite of the diachronic sameness of the individual substances on which they depend. This objection undermines the substantial view of diachronic sameness of individual texts that are features of other entities.

Part of what has been said also applies to the other reason used to justify the substantial view; namely, that we become aware of the diachronic sameness of such texts through the diachronic sameness of their substances. For even if I know that a substance has not changed substantially, this does not translate into knowledge about the diachronic sameness of its features. For example, take a piece of wax that has a text imprinted on it. We could subject the wax to some heat—enough to make the imprinted text disappear—and then reimprint a text of a similar type. In this case we have the same piece of wax and yet we have two different instances of the same type text; that is, we have two individual texts rather than one. Under these circumstances, knowledge of the diachronic sameness of the wax would not ensure knowledge of the diachronic sameness of the individual text. Indeed, on the basis of the appearance of the piece of wax (i.e., the substance), the text seems to be the same, whereas in fact it is not. Thus, knowledge of substantial diachronic sameness cannot be a sufficient condition of knowledge of the diachronic sameness of individual feature texts.

Likewise, knowledge of substantial diachronic sameness is not a necessary condition of knowledge of the diachronic sameness of individual feature texts. Here we can go back to the example of the stone that has been replaced by metal. One could argue that in this case we have two substances, known as such, and yet the text is the same, because what is essential to it as a text is its shape, which has not changed, rather than any of the features of the substance that changed when the substance changed. Considerations such as these pave the way for a second theory of the diachronic sameness of individual texts based on features rather than substance.

   b.   Feature View. According to the feature view, the diachronic sameness of individual texts that are features of other entities is accounted for in terms not of the sameness of the individual substance of which they are features, but rather in terms of the sameness of the features of the substance that are not constitutive of the substance. And here two possibilities suggest themselves. One identifies the features that account for diachronic sameness with features other than the aggregate of features that constitute a text. The other identifies the features that account for diachronic sameness precisely with the aggregate of features that constitute the text. The first possibility could be expressed as follows:

> An individual feature-aggregate text X at time t_n is the same as an individual feature-aggregate text Y at time t_{n+1} if and only if there is a S such that (1) S is a set of one or more features, (2) S contains no features that are part of X or Y, (3) X and Y belong to the same type, and (4) S is the same at t_n and t_{n+1}.

The second alternative may be understood thus:

> An individual feature-aggregate text X at time t_n is the same as an individual feature-aggregate text Y at time t_{n+1} if and only if there is a S such that (1) S is a set of one or more features, (2) S contains those and only those features that constitute X and Y, (3) X and Y belong to the same type, and (4) S is the same at t_n and t_{n+1}.

   If this position is taken in the first sense, then not much can be said in its favor. Indeed, it has the disadvantages of the substance view and none of its advantages. For how could one argue that the diachronic sameness of an individual text is to be accounted for by features that are constitutive neither of the substance that sustains the text nor of the text itself? Take the case of the text carved on a stone. Let us assume that the stone is porous and has been stained red. Let us further assume that color is not essential to the text carved on it. Then, we may ask, how can color explain the diachronic sameness of the text carved on the stone? One could argue that it might explain the diachronic sameness of the stone (something quite debatable but that I will accept at the moment for the sake of argument) and that in turn the diachronic sameness of the stone accounts for the diachronic sameness of the text carved on it. But this is not to say that the color accounts for the diachronic sameness of the text. On the contrary, what accounts for the diachronic sameness of the text is the diachronic sameness of the stone. That is, we are back to the substance view. For features to account for the diachronic sameness of a text they must do so directly, not mediately. In short, no features can account for the diachronic sameness of an individual text as long as the features in question are not constitutive of the text.

The other possibility is to argue that the features that account for the diachronic sameness of an individual text are those that constitute the text, such as a certain depth in the carving of a certain shape, and whatever is established by convention to be essential for a particular set of features to be used as the text. This view also seems reasonable prima facie, for what could better account for the diachronic sameness of something than its constitutive features? It would appear quite sensible to argue that if X and Y have the same features, they are the same thing.

The problem with this answer is twofold: First, the sameness of a type of features does not entail the sameness of individual features. That an individual text at a particular time has the same type of shape and depth as another at some other time does not necessarily mean that they are the same individual text; that is, one individual text is diachronically the same as the other. Sameness of type of features is a necessary condition of the individual diachronic sameness of texts, but it does not appear to be a sufficient condition of it.

Second, if by this answer is meant that sameness of individual features is what accounts for the individual sameness of the text through time, this again will not do, for the explanation begs the question. What is needed is the identification of the necessary and sufficient conditions of a lack of change in individual features, not a statement to the effect that change has not occurred. An explanation of how the individual features of an individual text are diachronically the same is still wanting.

In short, the view that attempts to account for the diachronic sameness of individual feature-aggregate texts in terms of features does not seem promising. I turn next to the diachronic sameness of individual texts that are substance/feature aggregates.

2.   *Diachronic Sameness of Individual Substance/Feature-Aggregate Texts*

In the case of individual texts that are substance/feature aggregates, the issue of diachronic sameness is simplified by the fact that in our experience these texts are always physical objects. (Mental texts are always feature aggregates and we have ruled out discussing nonmental nonphysical texts in this book.) The problem, then, of accounting for the diachronic sameness of individual texts that are substance/feature aggregates is very similar to that of accounting for the diachronic sameness of such individual things as trees and cats. One important difference should be kept in mind, however: Texts, unlike trees and cats, are the result of convention, and therefore, their diachronic sameness is subjected to epistemic conditions that are not operative in the case of other objects.

Many views can be used to account for the diachronic sameness of individual texts of the substance/feature-aggregate type. But I shall deal with only three of the most important of these: the bundle view, the feature view, and the bare continuant view. Some of these views are obviously very similar to the views used to account for individuality, but they should not be confused with them, for their aim is quite different.[42]

   a.   Bundle View. The bundle view argues that the complete set of features characterizing a substance/feature-aggregate text makes it the same individual text at different times; that is, accounts for its diachronic sameness. In the example of the text composed of pebbles lying on the beach, the color of the pebbles, their size, shape, texture, relative position, and so on ensure the diachronic sameness of the individual text. This view may be put as follows:

An individual substance/feature-aggregate text X at time t_n is the same as an individual substance/feature-aggregate text Y at time t_{n+1} if and only if (1) X and Y belong to the same type and (2) the complete set of features of the individual substance(s) used to make up X at t_n is the same set of features of the individual substance(s) used to make up Y at t_{n+1}.

At the outset this position seems quite viable. First of all, it would seem that in fact the features of an individual text make us aware of it being the same text, thus accounting for its diachronic sameness; we recognize individual texts by their features. Moreover, an individual text does not seem prima facie to be anything more than the features that make it up, and so it stands to reason that those features ensure its diachronic sameness.

Yet, a bit of reflection reveals serious weaknesses in the bundle view as well as in the two arguments used to support it. In the first place, if texts are epistemic entities insofar as what they are depends on certain known conventions, it is clear that only elements that are epistemically accessible can be considered essential to texts.[43] But not all the features of substances that are used as texts are or can be known in the circumstances where they function as texts. For example, the internal consistency of the pebbles that compose a text on the beach is generally beyond the observational horizon of the author who composed the text and the audience that is supposed to understand it. Therefore, such consistency cannot play a role in the reidentification of the text. And the same could be said concerning many other features of the substances that constitute substantial texts. It makes no sense to argue for the bundle view based on the claim that we become aware of the diachronic sameness of individual texts through the features of texts.

It is possible, however, to interpret the bundle view in a different way. The bundle theorist might argue that it is not the bundles of features of the substances that constitutes texts that account for the diachronic sameness of substance/feature-aggregate texts, but rather the bundles of features that constitute the texts themselves. The formulation of this view, then, would have to be changed to something like this:

> An individual substance/feature-aggregate text X at t_n is the same as an individual substance/feature-aggregate text Y at time t_{n+1} if and only if (1) X and Y belong to the same type and (2) the complete set of pertinent features that constitutes X at t_1 is the same set of features that constitutes Y at t_{n+1}.

It is not, for example, all the features of the pebbles that constitute the text on the beach, such as their internal consistency, weight, and so on, that account for the diachronic sameness of the individual text. It is rather the semantically significant features of the pebbles, which qua textual features have been conventionally selected as essential to the text and are thus epistemically accessible. We have two bundles: the bundle of features of the substances used to make up the text and the bundle of features that constitute the text. Some of the features are surely common to both bundles say, the shape of the pebbles, but others are not. The internal consistency of a particular pebble need not be a part of the features of the text, and the arrangement of the pebbles, which is part of the text, is not a characteristic of any one of the pebbles that constitute the text. It may be that the pebbles are arranged in the shape of a triangle. Triangularity is a characteristic of all the pebbles taken as a group but not of each of the pebbles, for none of the pebbles need be triangular in shape to be arranged triangularly with other pebbles.

In short, then, the objection we have considered is compelling against only the first formulation of the bundle view, not the second. This does not mean, however, that the account of the diachronic sameness of individual substance/feature-aggregate texts in terms of bundles of features is out of the woods. Two other objections undermine it. The first is that, even if we consider only the features of a text qua text, excluding any feature of the substances that compose it but are not semantically significant, the diachronic sameness of all the features are not necessary or sufficient conditions for the diachronic sameness of individual texts. For example, in the text on the beach we know that the number and arrangement of the pebbles are features of the text and thus part of the bundle of features that presumably would account for the diachronic sameness of the text. But I believe that in a text originally composed of thousands of letters displayed on a computer screen, the loss of one or two letters would not generally (there are exceptions, of course, depending on the place occupied by the letters, etc.) result in a fundamentally different text. So some features of texts seem not to be essential to their diachronic sameness, and this seriously undermines the view that the bundle of *all* of a text's features account for that sameness, even when such features have semantic significance.

In a similar way it can be argued that even all the features of a text do not constitute a sufficient condition of the diachronic sameness of an individual text. The reason is simple. The features of a text, even if individual, do not entail diachronic sameness. To be an individual feature is not to be the same individual feature at two (or more) different times. Thus, even if we had two sets of individual features, that is, of noninstantiable instances of the features, and even if those individual instances belonged to the same type, still that would not make them the same individual features and hence would not ensure their diachronic sameness.

To illustrate the point, take a set of individual features S_1 that constitutes a text at time t_n. At time t_{n+1} we also have a set of individual features S_2 that is in fact like S_1 because it is a set of individual features and features of the same type as the features that make up S_1. The question we need to answer is how S_1 at t_n is the same as S_2 at t_{n+1}, but this cannot be done on the basis merely of the fact that they are sets of individual features that belong to the same type.

The point of these two objections is twofold: (1) We can have the same individual text at two different times even though the text changes some of its features; and (2) having no difference in features, that is, in their type, individuality, and number, does not ensure individual diachronic sameness. For these reasons, the bundle view does not adequately account for the individual diachronic sameness of texts that are substance/feature aggregates.

b. Selected Feature Views. The failure of the bundle view may prompt other proposals. A natural response, particularly to make up for the first deficiency indicated concerning the bundle view, is to say that not *all* the features of an individual text of the substance/feature-aggregate variety make up the conditions of its diachronic sameness, but only *certain* features of it. Thus we might say that

> An individual substance/feature-aggregate text X at time t_n is the same as an individual substance/feature-aggregate text Y at time t_{n+1} if and only if (1) X and Y belong to the same type and (2) one or more features of X at t_n are the same as one or more features of Y at t_{n+1}.

Among the many features of physical texts, materiality, quantity, and spatio-temporal location stand out as those that might appear best able to account for diachronic sameness. Materiality, for example, would seem to be a prime candidate. After all, going as far back as Aristotle, matter has been conceived as the subject of change, the substratum that ensures sameness within the process of change. Thus, it is the stuff out of which a substance/feature-aggregate text is made that ensures its diachronic sameness in spite of changes in other features of the text such as color, texture, and the like.

Yet, matter seems hardly a good candidate to ensure diachronic sameness for, even if in fact it could ensure diachronic sameness, it does not meet the epistemic requirement to be identified as a necessary and sufficient condition of a text. Matter is not something with which observers can be acquainted. We perceive extension, color, and so on but not matter. Although it could be argued that matter functions as the necessary and sufficient condition of the diachronic sameness of the physical substance or substances that constitute a text, it would not then function as the necessary and sufficient condition of the diachronic sameness of the text.

The problems with quantity are different from those faced by the material view, for quantity (say dimensions or weight) seems perceptual. Thus in principle quantity could function as the basis of the diachronic sameness of individual substance/feature-aggregate texts. To do so, however, quantity must be selected as a necessary and sufficient condition of the text in question, for it is conceivable that a text may be preserved while its size is shrunk and its weight undercut. Suppose that the text on the beach about which we have been speaking is composed of balloons rather than pebbles. Even if we let some air out of the balloons, thus shrinking them in size, we would still regard the text as the same unless, of course, we had stipulated that the size of the balloons were semantically significant. And something similar would be the case if we cut the number of pixels that constitute a text displayed on a computer screen.

More important than these considerations, however, is the objection already raised against the bundle view, which applies not only to that position but to any feature view. It argued that, even if a feature or set of features (including quantity, of course) is a necessary condition for the diachronic sameness of an individual text, it cannot function as a sufficient condition of it because it does not account for the *individual* sameness of those features. In other words, that text X at t_n and text Y at t_{n+1} are of such and such a type or have such and such type of features, is not a sufficient condition to say that X is individually the same as Y.

The analysis of relational features follows along similar lines. Consider spatio-temporal location. It would seem at first that, for physical texts that are substance/feature aggregates, spatio-temporal location would not only be a necessary but also a sufficient condition of diachronic sameness. Upon reflection, however, it is clear that, although spatio-temporal location might be a necessary condition of the diachronic sameness of individual texts of this sort, it is certainly not a sufficient condition of it. A text does not continue being the same individual text through time simply because it is located in time and space. A text can be located in time and space and yet be replaced by another, either instantaneously or through a slow process in which its semantically significant features are changed.

A more sensible view is to argue that, not just spatio-temporal location, but spatio-temporal diachronic sameness is what accounts for the diachronic sameness of individual physical texts of the substance/feature-aggregate sort. Here again, matters are not so simple. First of all, we must be clear as to what spatio-temporal diachronic sameness means. One thing that it should not necessarily mean is that texts occupy the same space throughout a determined period of time. For the same text can certainly change places and remain the same. Spatio-temporal diachronic sameness should be understood to mean that there are no spatio-temporal gaps between one spatio-temporal location and another. That is, it should mean that there are no interruptions in the space or spaces occupied by a text at various times. If we have a text, say, X, located at space s_n at time t_n, and we have a text Y located at space s_{n+1} at time t_{n+1}, we can say that X is spatio-temporally continuous with Y if there are no interruptions between s_n and s_{n+1} in the times represented by t_n and t_{n+1}. Now, this position argues that if X is spatio-temporally continuous with Y then X is the same text as Y and therefore there is diachronic sameness between X and Y.

The flaw in this argument is that, although it makes considerable sense to argue that spatio-temporal diachronic sameness is a necessary condition of the diachronic sameness of individual physical texts, it does not seem plausible to argue that it is also a sufficient condition of it. Indeed, we could have cases in which there have been no spatio-temporal interruptions and yet the features deemed necessary for the identity of the text have been changed. Consider the case of a text that is composed of white marble balls arranged in a particular way, in which the spatio-temporal arrangement of the balls means that philosophers are liars but the color of the balls stands for the negation of whatever the arrangement of the balls conveys. Thus, the meaning of the text is that philosophers are not liars. Now let us suppose that we alter the color of the balls to red, which means emphatic affirmation, without changing the arrangement of the balls. Under such conditions it would certainly make sense to say that the red balls are spatio-temporally continuous with the white balls, but it would not make sense to say that the text composed of the red balls is the same as the text composed of the white balls. Indeed, one text contradicts the other, so one could not very well argue that they are the same individual text. Hence, as in the case of the nonrelational features of texts, relational ones, such as spatio-temporal location, are not sufficient conditions of the diachronic sameness of individual texts.

c.   Bare Continuant View. The bare continuant view is a dialectical response to the difficulties of views that are tied to features. If none of the features of a text, taken singly or in conjunction with others, is necessary and sufficient to account for the diachronic sameness of a text, what accounts for diachronic sameness must be a bare continuant; that is, an entity whose function is to ensure continuity but that has no features in itself other than the features that are perceived as features of the text. Many pre-Kantian views of substance fall into this category and so do some contemporary views of individuation. The view may be formulated as follows:

> An individual substance/feature-aggregate text X at t_n is the same as an individual substance/feature-aggregate text Y at t_{n+1} if and only if (1) X and Y belong to the same type and (2) there is an individual entity E such that (i) E has no features other than the features of X and Y, (ii) E is common to X and Y, and (iii) E is the same at t_n and t_{n+1}.

Note that there are similarities between this position and the substantial view, but the differences are striking. Most important among the latter is that the continuant neither is a substance in the Aristotelian sense nor has any features of its own.

The strength of this sort of position lies both in the recognition that a principle to account for the diachronic sameness of individual texts is required and also that no theory based on the features of texts seems to account for sameness. The problems with the view stem from the same source that undermines all theories identifying decharacterized entities as principles of something else. In the case of texts, in particular, this is a devastating flaw, for texts are epistemic entities, and therefore, their constituents must be subject to acquaintance. When it comes to diachronic sameness, something we are or can be acquainted with must serve as both necessary and sufficient conditions of that sameness. An entity whose existence is posited only on theoretical bases will not do.

One line of defense against this argument is to say that we are somehow acquainted with bare continuants. But this line of argumentation is unconvincing. I have dealt with this sort of argument elsewhere, so I do not see the need to repeat my objections against it here.[44]

Another line of defense is to argue that we are actually acquainted with the bare continuant through the features of the text. This line of defense also is flawed insofar as those features do not provide a proper basis for diachronic sameness. The diachronic sameness of the bare continuant remains mysterious and can hardly account for the diachronic sameness of individual texts.

3. Conditions for the Diachronic Sameness of Individual Texts

Even though we have not found in the views so far discussed any one that would account satisfactorily for the diachronic sameness of individual texts, we have not wasted our time. The discussion has revealed the most important flaws of the views examined and in so doing has indirectly established certain requirements that a viable view should fulfill. These requirements are four. The first of these is that, whatever conditions are identified, they must be necessary conditions of the individual text whose diachronic sameness is being accounted for. This does not mean that they must be necessary to the substance of which the text is a feature aggregate when the text is of that sort or to the substances and features that constitute the text in substance/feature-aggregate texts. There are features of substances that are not necessary to the texts that are themselves features of those substances. On the other hand, there are features of substances that are not necessary for the substances but are necessary for the texts. And there are features of substances that are not necessary for texts constituted of those substances. What is important is not the status of the condition with respect to the substance of which an aggregate text is a feature but that the conditions be constitutive of the text, whether the texts are feature aggregates or substance/feature aggregates.

The second requirement has to do with the epistemic character of texts. Nothing that is not subject to acquaintance can function as a condition of the diachronic sameness of individual texts, for texts are epistemically accessible entities.

Third, diachronic sameness cannot be accounted for in terms of features qua features alone, even if those features are necessary for it. The reason is that features are not by themselves individual.

Finally, the conditions of the diachronic sameness of individual texts must be both necessary and sufficient. Part of the problem with the theories discussed earlier rested on the identification of only some conditions, particularly necessary ones, rather than all conditions. An appropriate theory, then, must take care to include all conditions both necessary and sufficient.

The view I propose is that two conditions, when taken together, are necessary and sufficient for the diachronic sameness of individual texts. This view could be formulated as follows:

An individual text X at t_n is the same as an individual text Y at t_{n+1} if and only if (1) X and Y belong to the same type and (2) the existence of Y is continuous with the existence of X.

Condition (1) is meant to gather the conditions of the achronic sameness of universal texts that as such also apply to the instances of those texts.

Condition (2) is meant to indicate that the continuous existence of the individual text is a necessary condition of its diachronic sameness. Continuity is necessary because it is possible to have two individual texts exactly alike in all respects at two different times that are not the same individual text; only continuity between them will ensure their individual identity. The two conditions taken together form the sufficient condition of diachronic sameness. Moreover, these conditions apply both to feature-aggregate and substance/feature-aggregate texts.

II.   Difference

From what has been said concerning sameness we can learn much about difference, for difference is the opposite of sameness. Indeed, I would claim that the two notions, as I have understood them here, are mutually exclusive.

Corresponding to the two understandings of sameness that were given earlier, we may present two understandings of difference as follows:

X is different from Y if and only if there is something that pertains to X that does not pertain to Y or vice versa.

X is different from Y with respect to F if and only if there is something that pertains to F of X that does not pertain to F of Y or vice versa.

Likewise, just as sameness may be taken achronically, synchronically, or diachronically, so can difference:

X is achronically different from Y if and only if X is different from Y.

X is synchronically different from Y if and only if X is different from Y at time t.

X is diachronically different from Y if and only if X at time t_n is different from Y at time t_{n+1}.

Our concern in this chapter has been with the sameness and difference of texts. And we have found that texts can be achronically, synchronically, and diachronically the same. Moreover, just as texts may be achronically, synchronically, and diachronically the same, so they may be, mutatis mutandis, different in the same ways. For our purposes, however, only two cases of difference merit examination; namely, the achronic difference of the universal text and the diachronic difference of the individual text.

The question of the achronic difference of universal texts has to do with the identification of the necessary and sufficient conditions that make texts different irrespective of time. For example, we may ask what the necessary and sufficient conditions are for some text not to be the text of *Don Quixote*. The answer is not difficult: It is necessary only that at least one of the conditions specified above for achronic sameness be missing. The conditions were sameness of meaning, syntactical arrangement, and sign composition. If one or more of these is missing, then a text is not the same as the text with which it is being compared, and is therefore, different from it.

Likewise, for the diachronic sameness of individual texts, three conditions were identified in addition to the just mentioned ones: individuality, sameness of type, and continuous existence. If any one of these is missing, then the texts in question are not the same and must be different.

III.   Identification and Reidentification of Texts

To *identify* something means to single it out and to *reidentify* it means to identify it as the same. I identify the sheet of paper on which I am writing when I am able to single it out, separating it from those things that surround it, say the table on which it rests, the pen with which I am making marks on it, and the sheet of paper next to it on the table. To reidentify involves more than identification, it involves singling out something at two or more times and regarding it as the same. Reidentification requires three logical stages: the singling out of a thing at one time, say a sheet of paper; the singling out of a thing at another time, say a sheet of paper; and the identification of the two as the same, the same sheet of paper.

The interest that identification and reidentification have for philosophers centers around the question of the proper criteria for identification and reidentification. The term 'criteria' underscores the epistemological nature of the issues, for criteria refer to the marks that allow us to identify or reidentify something. In both cases it involves knowledge: In the first, it is knowledge of something as being itself and also distinct from other things; and in the second, it is knowledge of something as being itself and the same at two or more times. Both issues concern the explanation of how knowers know, rather than of the way things that knowers know are.

The problems of identification and reidentification are to a great extent the epistemological counterparts of the ontological problems of identity discussed earlier. So far we have discussed what makes universal texts achronically the same and what makes individual texts achronically, synchronically, and diachronically the same. The issues of synchronic and diachronic identity do not apply to universal texts because they are not subject to time and its passage; only individual texts can be synchronically the same because only they are subject to time, and similarly only they can be diachronically the same because only they are subject to the passage of time.

Putting these issues epistemically, then, we may ask for the necessary and sufficient conditions of knowing that universal and individual texts are achronically the same and the necessary and sufficient conditions of knowing that individual texts to which appropriate temporal qualifications apply are synchronically and diachronically the same. The problem of identification is the epistemological counterpart of the ontological problems of determining the necessary and sufficient conditions of the achronic sameness of universal and individual texts, as well as the necessary and sufficient conditions of the synchronic sameness of individual texts. The problem of reidentification is the epistemological counterpart of the ontological problem of determining the necessary and sufficient conditions of the diachronic sameness of individual texts.

It is altogether possible that the necessary and sufficient conditions that solve ontological problems also apply to their epistemological counterparts. There is no reason why the causes that explain the sameness of a sheet of paper through time cannot be the reason why we know it as the same sheet of paper at different times. One might want to argue that the features of the sheet of paper account for both its sameness through time and our understanding of that sameness. However, although the necessary and sufficient conditions that solve ontological problems may be the same as those that solve epistemological ones, they need not be so, for they are not meant to account for the same thing. Therefore, it is advisable that ontological and epistemological problems in general be treated separately to avoid confusion, and I have done so with regard to the problems that concern texts. I will discuss the epistemological problems of identification and reidentification very briefly here, however, for most of what was said earlier concerning the ontological problems of sameness applies here as well, and it would be superfluous to repeat it.

The questions we have to address under identification are three: (1) What are the necessary and sufficient conditions for identifying a universal text? (2) What are the necessary and sufficient conditions for identifying an individual text considered apart from time? (3) What are the necessary and sufficient conditions for identifying an individual text at a particular time? Although questions 2 and 3 are logically different, in this epistemological context, just as in ontology, they amount to the same and therefore can be conflated. Concerning reidentification only one question needs to be addressed: What are the necessary and sufficient conditions for reidentifying an individual text; that is, identifying the individual text as the same at two or more times?

From what has been said earlier we know the conditions of the achronic ontological identity of universal texts: sameness of meaning, sameness of syntactical arrangement, and sameness of type-sign composition. These conditions, of course, do not ensure epistemological identity; for that we need to have knowledge of these conditions. In short, the conditions of the epistemological identification of a universal text amount to the knowledge of the conditions of ontological identity of the universal text: knowledge of the sameness of meaning, knowledge of the sameness of syntactical arrangement, and knowledge of the sameness of type-sign composition.

From what has been said concerning ontology and epistemology, it follows, however, that it is prima facie possible that knowledge of all the conditions of ontological identity will not be necessary for epistemic identification. Indeed, it is possible that the knowledge in question be of conditions other than those for ontological identity. But this possibility is not available in the case of the achronic identification of universal texts, for nothing is in a universal text but the ontological conditions, and unless we know they are all fulfilled, we cannot know whether the text is the same. To know that something is the text of *Don Quixote* I have to know that the text has the same meaning, the same syntactical arrangements, and the same type-signs as the text of *Don Quixote*, otherwise I cannot be sure that the text is indeed the text of *Don Quixote*. Therefore, the ontological formula developed earlier should be modified to read:

A universal text X is known to be achronically the same as a universal text Y if and only if it is known that (1) X has the same meaning as Y, (2) X and Y have the same syntactical arrangement, and (3) X and Y are composed of the same type signs.

The adaptation of this formula to individual texts will not yield achronic and synchronic sameness in the case of those texts, however. The formula would look as follows for the case of achronic sameness of individual texts:

An individual text X is known to be achronically the same as an individual text Y if and only if it is known that (1) X has the same meaning as Y, (2) X and Y have the same syntactical arrangement, and (3) X and Y are composed of the same type signs.

And the formula would look as follows in the case of synchronic sameness:

An individual text X is known to be synchronically the same as an individual text Y at t if and only if it is known that (1) X has the same meaning as Y, (2) X and Y have the same syntactical arrangement, and (3) X and Y are composed of the same type signs.

The reason that these formulas are not effective in yielding achronic and synchronic sameness of individual texts is that they specify only conditions of universal sameness. Thus, although X and Y are, in accordance with those conditions, of the same type, they need not be individually the same. Conditions of individual sameness must be added. This means that for individual texts the problem of achronic and synchronic identity is the epistemological counterpart of the ontological problem of individuation; that is, it is concerned with how we know that a text, over and above being a text and the type of text it is, is also an individual text.

The necessary and sufficient conditions that serve to identify or discern individuals can be quite different from the conditions that individuate.[45] Nor do they necessarily differ only insofar as the conditions for epistemological identification involve knowledge of the conditions of ontological identification, whereas the conditions of ontological identification involve no such knowledge, as we saw in the case of universal texts. The case of individual texts is different from that of universal texts. The root of the difference is that individual texts are immersed in circumstances that make possible their identification in various ways. For example, color in certain contexts may be sufficient to identify a physical text, even if it is neither a necessary nor a sufficient condition in another set of circumstances. This problem is not parochial to texts but affects all individuals, and because I have dealt with it in detail elsewhere, we need not dwell on it here to any great extent.[46] Let it suffice to say that we become acquainted with individuals, whether texts or not, in a variety of ways, depending on the different features they have and the circumstances that surround them. In cases where those features appear to be similar, however ultimately temporal and spatio-temporal coordinates based on the absolute point of view represented by a subject individuate epistemologically; that is, identify an individual.

Something similar to what has been said concerning identification and individuation can be said concerning the issue of reidentification and diachronic sameness. The diachronic sameness of texts involves the necessary and sufficient conditions of the sameness of an individual text through time. It entails explaining, for example, what makes an individual text the same at two different times, determining as well under what circumstances and on the basis of what factors a text could not be the same. This is all very different from the issue involved in reidentification. The latter has to do with the determination of the necessary and sufficient conditions of our identification of the text as the same at two or more different times. It involves, therefore, the necessary and sufficient conditions of the knowledge that a subject may have of a text with which one is acquainted at one time as the same as a text with which one is acquainted at other times. Sameness through time has to do with the causes of a feature of the world, whereas reidentification has to do with the causes of a feature of a knower's knowledge about the world.

Note that the ultimate status of "the world" does not affect this distinction as long as the world is not identified with a knower's knowledge of the world. The world may be, for all we know, ideal. Or it may be, as some post-Kantian philosophers claim, consciousness, or part of consciousness, or even phenomenal. None of this makes any difference as long as what is understood by 'the world' is not identified with "knowledge of the world." As long as this distinction is preserved, there can be a difference between the causes of the world, or what happens in it, and the causes of the knowledge a knower has of the world.

A similar procedure to the one followed to establish the necessary and sufficient conditions of identification can be followed to establish the conditions of reidentification of an individual text. Earlier in this chapter, I presented the necessary and sufficient conditions of the diachronic sameness of individual texts in the following formula:

> An individual text X at t_n is the same as an individual text Y at t_{n+1} if and only if (1) X and Y belong to the same type and (2) the existence of Y is continuous with the existence of X.

Converting this formula into an epistemic mode, we could say, then, that

> An individual text X at t_n is known to be the same as an individual text Y at t_{n+1} if and only if it is known that (1) X and Y belong to the same type and (2) the existence of Y is continuous with the existence of X.

Clearly, if these conditions are satisfied, we know that the individual text X is the same as the individual text Y, but as in the case of the identity of individual texts, it is sometimes possible successfully to reidentify individual texts on the basis of conditions other than these. For example, in a world where the only red thing is an individual text, the text can be reidentified by its red color and we need not know anything about continuous existence. But in our world, matters are quite different.

IV. Conclusion

I began this chapter by noting that in the library of the University at Buffalo there are several volumes with the title *Don Quixote* that, although different in many ways, users of the library regard as the same. This raises the particular question of what makes them the same and in a more general way of what makes texts the same.

After posing the question, we saw that five different answers suggest themselves. These answers were based on conceptions of texts as (1) the entities that constitute them, (2) their meaning, (3) the entities that constitute them considered together with meaning, (4) certain acts, and (5) the entities that constitute texts considered as having not just meaning but a particular meaning. Accordingly, the identity of texts was conceived in five different ways.

Unfortunately, all five encounter difficulties, but the least objectionable way is the fifth, so I set out to explain its advantages. To carry out that task, however, I had to clarify the nature of the question, for its apparent simplicity hides considerable complexity. This complexity comes from two sources: first, the notion of sameness itself and, second, the object to which the sameness is supposed to apply. Sameness is to be distinguished from similarity and may be taken achronically (i.e., irrespective of time), synchronically (i.e., in terms of time but irrespective of the passage of time), and diachronically (i.e., in terms of the passage of time).

Achronic sameness may apply to anything whatever. Therefore, in relation to texts, we found that it could be used to refer to (1) texts qua texts, (2) universal texts (whether of the substance/feature-aggregate variety or the feature-aggregate variety), and (3) individual texts. When applied to texts qua texts, the question of achronic sameness amounts to the question of what makes a text be a text. This question was already answered in the Introduction, where the definition of *texts* was presented. Only when the question refers to universal or individual texts does it become significantly different from the question of definition. In that sense we want to know, first, what makes achronically the same different copies of the text of, say, *Don Quixote* found in the university library and, second, the conditions of achronic sameness of each individual copy of the text of *Don Quixote*.

The attempt to answer the first question led us to a consideration of the basic elements that play roles in textuality: meaning, author, speech acts, audience, context, sign arrangement, and signs. The conclusion reached was that universal texts are achronically the same when they have the same meaning, display the same syntactical arrangements, and are composed of the same type signs. This explains how all copies of the text of *Don Quixote* in the library are achronically the same universal text, for they fulfill these conditions even though they occupy different locations, are printed in different typescripts on papers of different consistencies, have varying numbers of words per page, display different colors of ink, and so on.

So much, then, for the achronic sameness of universal texts. We still had to consider each of those copies of the text of *Don Quixote*, for the conditions of the achronic sameness of individual texts cannot be the same as those of universal texts, otherwise individual copies of a text would be universal texts and vice versa.

The answer to this question was gathered in part from the answer given in Chapter 1 concerning the individuation of texts and in part from what was said in the earlier part of this chapter concerning the achronic identity of universal texts. In Chapter 1, I concluded that the only necessary and sufficient condition of a text being individual is its existence. So I only needed to add to this the conditions that apply to the universal of which the individual is an instance. Thus, the conditions of the achronic sameness of an individual text are the conditions that make the universal of which it is an instance achronically the same plus existence. This explains both how the copies of *Don Quixote* in the library are copies of the universal text of *Don Quixote* and how they are individual copies of it.

The question of synchronic sameness did not need separate attention. Synchronic sameness applies only to temporal individuals but its conditions do not differ from the conditions of achronic sameness when applied to individuals. Hence, no extensive discussion of it was given.

The situation with diachronic sameness is different, however, insofar as the conditions that apply to it are quite different from those that apply to synchronic sameness. Like synchronic sameness, diachronic sameness applies only to individuals, but it applies to individuals subject to the passage of time. These conditions establish what makes the individual text of, say, *Don Quixote* I read yesterday in the library the same I am reading today. Note that this question does not concern the epistemic question of how I know they are the same. The latter question was answered later in the chapter.

Naturally, complications arise from the fact that some texts are substance/feature aggregates and others are feature aggregates. We discussed several of the views to which these complications give rise. The conclusion reached, however, was that such complications do not affect the issue substantially and that a single set of conditions applies to all individual texts subject to diachronic sameness. These conditions are such that two individual texts are the same diachronically when the texts belong to the same type and there is a continuity of existence between them.

The other side of sameness is difference, and so something had to be said about it. As a correlative of sameness, the same thing that applies to sameness applies, mutatis mutandis, to difference. Texts are different if and only if they violate any of the specified conditions of sameness; they are achronically different if and only if they do not have the same meaning or they do not display the same syntactical arrangement and so forth. And they are diachronically different if and only if they do not belong to the same type and so on.

With respect to the issues of identification and reidentification, it was established that much that needed to be said about them could be derived from what had been said earlier with appropiate modification. Thus, the question concerned with the necessary and sufficient conditions of the identification of a universal text amounts to a question concerning the necessary and sufficient conditions of identity taken in an epistemic context; that is, the knowledge of the conditions of the identity of the universal text: meaning, syntactical arrangement, and type-sign composition.

The case of individual texts is somewhat different insofar as the identity of individual texts can be determined in a variety of ways, depending on the circumstances in which they are found. Ultimately, however, spatio-temporal coordinates, based on an absolute point of view represented by a subject, serve this purpose in the case of texts subject to space and time.

Finally, with respect to the reidentification of individual texts at two or more times, knowledge of the text's sameness of type and continuous existence would ensure effective identification. But there are conditions under which other factors may also be effective.

Having summarized the results at which we arrived, I would like to turn now to some of the implications of the view of textual identity presented here. Consider the case of the various volumes in the library with the title *Don Quixote*. In what sense are these texts the same and in what sense are they different? From what has been said, it follows that they are instances of the same universal text. Only one universal text is involved as long as the copies in question have the same meaning, syntactical arrangement, and type signs. As instances, however, these copies are different. There is, therefore, nothing puzzling about the identity of the various texts of *Don Quixote* currently in the library.

If the texts in question did not have the same meaning, syntactical arrangement, or type signs, then they would have to be considered different, not only as individuals, but also as universals. An English translation of *Don Quixote* is not the same type text as the Spanish text even if the translation has the same meaning. This example brings back the distinction between a text and a work.[47] The conditions of identity of a text and a work are not the same. The conditions of identity of a text include sameness of meaning, but the conditions of identity of most works include only sameness of meaning, for works are the meanings of certain texts. English and Spanish texts may have the same meaning and thus represent the same work, but they are not the same type of text because they differ in syntactical arrangements and are not composed of the same type signs.

In a similar way, one may argue that oral and written texts are necessarily different types of texts even when one is taken as a sign of the other and both have an additional common meaning. The sounds "The cat is on the mat" I utter and the written marks 'The cat is on the mat' are two different texts, even though they are related in such a way that one may mean the other in addition to meaning that the cat is on the mat. The question of the identity of oral vs. written texts raised earlier may be confidently answered now. Note that what has been said concerning the identity of oral and written texts also applies to mental texts.

Another question raised at the beginning of this chapter had to do with the novelty of a text and the corresponding originality of an author. When and to what degree is an author original? This clearly depends on the novelty of the text he or she produces. But what determines novelty? According to what has been said here, novelty has to do with difference, specifically the introduction of difference in a text. Novelty, therefore, will depend on the violation of the conditions of textual sameness.

Any difference displayed by a text makes it and its author original to that extent. Now, we know that texts are artifacts constituted by entities endowed with meaning by an author to convey meaning to an audience under certain circumstances. Thus any aspect of the entities or their meaning that sets the text apart from other texts is an element of novelty. The element of novelty may be the use of an entity already in use to express a meaning that is different from the one the entity has been previously used to express. Sentences in a language, for example, may be given new meaning. Likewise there is an element of novelty in the use of a new entity for the expression of a meaning that is not new. Sentences of an artificial language, for instance, are new texts in this sense even when their meaning is not anything new. Finally, there may be a new meaning for a new entity. Here the novelty is much higher than the novelty in the cases just discussed. When someone, for example, not only creates a new entity but also endows the entity with a new meaning, the circle of textual novelty and author originality is complete. An original work written in Esperanto by the inventor of that language would be a case in point. This does not mean, of course, that such a text would be more valuable than the text of *Don Quixote*. Textual value is not a result of originality alone but has to do with, among other things, the cultural function of the text.

The requirement of sameness of meaning for textual identity has an important implication. If sameness of meaning is a requirement of textual identity, then when two or more persons understand a text differently it cannot be said that they understand the same text. Suppose that two persons, P_1 and P_2, hear the same sound, "Fire!", uttered by a third person, P_3, and that P_1 understands it to mean that there is a fire and P_2 understands it to mean that she is to shoot. In this case, the two persons do not understand the same text, because two meanings are attached to the sound. Yet, there is only one sound. And the author presumably produced only one text, so is there one or two texts?

The answer to this problem is that we must keep in mind that the conditions of identity of the entities used to constitute a text are different from the conditions of identity of the text, just as the conditions of the identity of works are different from the identity conditions of texts. Texts are artifacts constituted by entities with meaning and thus their conditions of identity come from the semantically significant features of the entities that compose them and from their meaning. If these points are kept in mind, then we can see that the same entity can be used at the same time by different persons to convey different meanings and thus as different texts. The sound "Fire!" uttered by P_3 and heard by P_1 and P_2 is one sound. But, because the meaning attached to it by P_1 is different from the meaning attached to it by P_2, we have two different texts. Whether they are the same text P_3 produced is altogether a different matter. It is possible that P_3 produced the text understood by P_1, or the one understood by P_2, or neither. In fact, it is possible that P_3 produced no text at all, but simply made a sound because she was trying out her vocal cords.

Does this mean, then, that whenever one understands a text differently, one understands a different text? This seems to be counterintuitive, for we frequently allow for different understandings and interpretations of the same text. The answer to these questions depends on the nature of understanding and interpretation, so I have discussed them elsewhere in some detail.[48] For our present purposes it is sufficient to say that the limits of meaning of a text depend on the cultural function of the text. A text whose function is religious has different limits to its meaning than a text whose function is literary or legal. The cultural function determines the limits of the meaning and therefore the identity of the text.

This brings me to the issue that concerns editors. What are the identity conditions of particular texts, say the text of *Don Quixote*, both of the universal and the individual? The answer that I have provided to the question of identity answers this question only in a general way; that is, I identify the conditions of identity of all universal and individual texts. But I do not say anything about the particular conditions that apply to a particular universal text and its instances, say, the universal text of *Don Quixote* and the copies of it we have in the library. To say, for example, that the conditions of diachronic identity of it include sameness of meaning, of type of syntactical arrangement, and of type of signs does not help the editor. For the editor wishes to know which physical features of the text, for example, are identity conditions so that they can be preserved or discarded in the edition of the text being produced. Should one take into account earlier drafts of *Don Quixote* made by Cervantes? Should one prefer a revised version of the text produced by Cervantes but never published?

The scheme I have presented here does not answer these questions. The reason is not that the questions are not important or interesting. They are. The reason is that they are not the questions a philosopher can or should answer. Remember, the limits of textual meaning are established by the cultural function of a text and that function is not determined by philosophers but by the culture that uses the text. The culture, then, determines the function and, therefore, the conditions of textual identity of particular texts. Editors will receive no concrete help from me. They have a job to do, and only they can do it effectively. Of course, differences of opinion occur, but that is precisely part of the process. Which text editors edit and which modifications they make in it will depend on the function of the text and the purpose of the edition, and they are better equipped to do that job than philosophers.

3

AUTHOR

In most periods of the history of philosophy, philosophers have had very little to say about authors of texts in general. After all, it seems a matter of common sense that the author of a text is the person or persons who composed it.[1] What can there be that is controversial in this? Yet, upon closer scrutiny a host of questions can be raised concerning authors and their relations to texts. One may ask, for example, about the identity of the author, for, upon reflection, it becomes clear that most often texts are not the result of one person only, but of multiple persons who through time have contributed to the text. Which of these persons is to be considered the author, then? The person who first produced a historical text that no longer exists but is an ancestor of the contemporary text we have? Or are the editors who choose among various textual readings the ones they think are the best to be considered the authors of the text? And what roles do the audience and society at large play in this process? If most texts are elliptical and require completion by audiences, does the audience not play an authorial role as well in this respect? Finally, we know that societies are responsible for natural languages and most texts are composed of natural languages, so we may ask: Is society at large not to be considered somehow responsible for texts and in some sense their author?[2]

Other questions that may be examined concern the exact function of the author: What is it that authors do? Are they responsible only for the arrangement of the signs that compose texts or are they also responsible for the meanings of the texts? In many ways they do not seem to be responsible for either of them, because they create neither, using most often signs and meanings already available. What do authors create, then, if anything? Or is the function of authors other than creation?

There are also questions concerning whether there can be texts without authors. Consider, for instance, the case of a text that, like so-called found-art, appears to be the result of no intentional design—say, a group of pebbles on the beach that spell some words which have a well-known meaning and whose arrangement and position is the result of tides and wind. In this case we seem to have a text that has no author. Yet, the whole idea of an entity having meaning without being the product of intentional design seems not only preposterous but also contrary to the definition of texts adopted in the Introduction.

One may also ask questions concerning the limitations that knowledge of an author of a text may place on an audience's understanding of the text. Consider the Bible. Those who believe it is the word of God see the precepts for human conduct it contains as divine commands to be followed by all human beings. But those who believe the Bible to be a purely human product consider its precepts mere records of the beliefs of a certain society at a certain time with no prescriptive force for any other society. Clearly, knowledge of an author by an audience may alter the way the audience understands a text. To what extent, then, we may ask, is knowledge of the authors required for the understanding of a text and to what extent does such knowledge influence an audience's understanding of the text?

Finally, questions may be raised as well concerning the inner subjective states of authors and their relations to the meanings of texts of which they are authors. Is the meaning of texts to be found in that subjectivity, which always remains somehow private and idiosyncratic, or does the meaning of texts transcend the subjectivity of authors? The answers to these questions are important, for upon them depend a host of other issues related to the understanding, interpretation, and discernibility of texts.[3]

Obviously, many interesting issues can be raised concerning authors and their relation to texts. In this chapter I propose to concentrate on five such issues: the identity of the author, the function of the author, the need for an author, the repressive character of the author, and the nature and implications of the author's subjectivity. I begin with the issue of the author's identity, for understanding the author's identity facilitates the clarification and solution of other problems that surround the notion of author.

Note that the authors of texts need not be restricted to human beings. Any being capable of both intentional action and understanding texts, whether human or not, can produce texts. Certainly, if there are beings such as God and angels, they must be capable of producing texts. But recent studies show that nonhuman animals too may be capable not only of using signs, and even perhaps texts, but also of instituting them. For our purposes, it is irrelevant whether the authors of texts are divine, angelic, human, or merely animal, although such questions are relevant in an investigation of intentional behavior. Because I am not concerned with intentional behavior per se here, however, I need not dwell on this matter any further. It should be kept in mind, then, that, although the discussion of authorship here centers on human authors, what is said about them may apply also, mutatis mutandis, to nonhuman authors.

I.   Identity of the Author

In accordance with the definition of texts given in the Introduction, it would seem that if there is a text there is an author, for the author is the one who is supposed to select and arrange the entities, used as signs, that compose the text to convey a specific meaning to an audience in a certain context. But a text may turn out to be more than one, so correspondingly, there may not be just one author. Indeed, in *A Theory of Textuality*, several different texts were identified: the actual (itself divided into historical, contemporary, and intermediary), the intended, and the ideal. Moreover, there are also universal and individual texts as noted earlier in Chapter 1. This raises the problem of identifying and characterizing the various authors that give rise to those different texts. I would like to distinguish four different authors: the historical author, the pseudo-historical author, the composite author, and the interpretative author.

A.   Historical Author

The historical author is the subject who produced the historical text, that is, the historical artifact we call a text and that consists in certain entities used as signs and intended to convey a specific meaning to an audience in a certain context.[4] This subject may in fact turn out to be several subjects, for it is not unusual to have several persons cooperate in the composition of a text either in the process of selection and arrangement of signs or in the process of determining the meaning that is to be conveyed. This procedure is quite frequent in science, for instance, but it is also sometimes followed in literature. The case of the voluntary cooperation of several subjects in the production of a text should be kept separate from cases where a text is subjected to modifications by subjects other than the original author without the knowledge and consent of that author. In these cases those who modify the original text are also "historical authors," but they are not the authors of the original historical text—only of modified versions of the original historical text. For the consideration of such cases, then, it is useful to introduce a distinction between *the original historical text* and what might be called *derivative historical texts*. The author of the former in turn could be called *the original historical author* and the authors of the latter *subsequent historical authors*. It should be clear, however, that, based on what was established in Chapters 1 and 2, the original historical text and its modified versions cannot be considered the same unless the modifications made on the original historical text that result in the modified versions of it are not such that they change the conditions of textual identity established in Chapter 2.

Although the historical author (I shall refer to this person in the masculine singular throughout the chapter to avoid confusion) may turn out to be a group of subjects rather than a single subject, he is not to be confused with the composite author that will be discussed shortly; the historical author is only one of the authors or group of authors that make up the composite author. The historical author is, then, the author of the historical text. Note that this author existed—he was an actual subject who lived at a certain time in history. Although he actually lived, however, we do not know him exactly as he was for various reasons.

First of all, there is much about him we do not know at all, a fact that gives rise to historical controversy. Take Aristotle, for example: Do we know how he felt about Alexander? Do we know of all the experiences during his childhood which influenced his point of view? What sorts of tastes did he have? And so on. Moreover, what we do know about him has been filtered through much speculation and lore. It is also colored by the ideas we have about his thought. He may appear to us more commonsensical and approachable than Plato, but was he really that way? Is not our perception of him and his character shaped in a way by an interpretational tradition that began even during his lifetime? I do not mean to suggest that we know nothing about Aristotle or that all we know is a matter of conjecture. Least of all am I suggesting that such conclusions apply to all authors. What I am suggesting is that the author of what I have called the *historical text* is the real historical figure, but our knowledge of that historical figure is at best an approximation of what the author in fact was. The composite figure that we know or think we know is what I call the *pseudo-historical author*. The historical author is presented to us only in the persona of the pseudo-historical author.

Before we leave the historical author to turn to the pseudo-historical author there is a question which is of some interest. When we consider the historical author, do we consider the person in question throughout his life or do we consider that person at only a certain point in his life, say at the moment of composing the text or at that moment and before, excluding the future? The question is interesting because persons change throughout their lives and those changes suggest that the author who composed a text may not be the same author several years hence. Is the author of the *Tractatus* the same as the author of the *Philosophical Investigations*?

This question is not only interesting but also difficult to answer, because it involves issues of personal identity, issues that have been a focus of philosophical controversy for centuries.[5] I believe, however, that we may deal with this question here in a way that sidesteps those issues. What I propose is to distinguish between two questions: the question of personal identity through time and the question of authorial identity through time. Note that I shall assume, for present purposes and in order to facilitate the discussion, that authors of texts are always persons, although it is altogether possible, as earlier, that some animals not only understand but also produce simple texts. This difficulty could be avoided either by positing some kind of rudimentary personhood in such animals or by speaking of subjects rather than persons in this context, as I did earlier. What will be said here would apply either way, and so I will ignore the issue.

Returning to the question of authorial identity, my claim is that one need not treat the question of personal identity and the question of authorial identity as the same. The first involves determining whether person P_1 at t_1 is the same as P_2 at t_2; for instance, whether the person Wittgenstein at the time the *Tractatus* was written is the same person as the person Wittgenstein at the time the *Philosophical Investigations* was written. To answer this sort of question one would have to discuss the nature of persons and the conditions that would ensure personal identity through time.

Now, as we shall see, the function of authors has to do with the creation of texts. This means that the identity conditions of authors are related to the identity conditions of texts. Thus, if a person created a text at a certain time but could not have created it at some later time because he had changed in any significant way, then the person of the later time cannot be considered the author of the earlier text, even if, qua person, he were the same. In short, conditions of personal identity in general are not sufficient conditions of authorial identity. The person Wittgenstein at t_1 and at t_2 may be the same person according to personal identity criteria. But the author of the *Tractatus* may not be the author of the *Philosophical Investigations* insofar as the first author could not have produced the second book, and the author of the second book could not have produced the first.[6] The historical author, then, is only that person, at that juncture of history, who produced the historical text in question or that same person at some other juncture of history where he could produce the same text.

In conclusion, if what we mean by *historical author* is the *person* who happens to have composed a particular text, then we need not restrict that person to a historical time, place, or conditions. But if what we mean by *author* is the *composer* of a text, then we cannot say that the author is the same when the conditions that make possible the authorial function that produced the text in question are missing. From this it follows that personal identity is presupposed by authorial identity, so that if the author of a text at two different times is the same, necessarily the person is the same. If Wittgenstein, the author of the *Tractatus* and the *Investigations*, is the same, then the person who composed the two books is the same, but not vice versa. The reason for this is that there are aspects of a person that are essential to authorial identity but not to personal identity.[7] For example, a certain view may be essential for someone to be the author of a text in which that view is defended, but views are not essential to the identity of persons, because persons can change their views without changing their identity.

This position does not entail that two different texts cannot ever have the same author. For what makes an author the same is the capacity to produce a text and having an additional capacity to produce some other text does not necessarily conflict with it. Say that a person produces texts T_1 and T_2. According to what has been said, the author of T_1 and T_2 can be the same as long as, at the time of producing T_1, the author of T_1 could also have produced T_2 and, at the time of producing T_2, the author of T_2 could also have produced T_1. Nor should one conclude from this that some other person with the capacity to produce T_2 is also the author of T_1 and vice versa simply in virtue of that capacity. For that other person is not the same person, and personal identity is a necessary condition of authorial identity.

This position entails what appears to be an undesirable consequence; namely, that there cannot be significant developments in the same author. For an author who changes significantly, presumably could not be said to be the same author he was before that change because he could not, after the change, produce the text he produced before the change. Indeed, one may want to push this point further and say that any changes that occur in a person that would preclude the person from having the capacity to produce the same text would result in a change of authorship.

Consider the fact that it would be hard for anyone to argue that the three-year-old child Aristotle was the author of the text of the *Categories*. What we mean by the author of the text of the *Categories* is the mature Aristotle, who in fact produced the book, or alternatively we mean the person Aristotle, who at some point in his life produced the book. The point of the distinction between author and person I propose is not to do away with ordinary and perfectly understandable ways of speaking. The point is to introduce a technical meaning of 'author' that captures the unique relation an author has to a text and the implications of that relation. It is my claim that such a technical sense of 'author' is in fact embedded in some things we say about authors even if it is not so embedded in everything we say about them. Therefore, it is helpful to bring the notion out into the open and use it to clarify the notion of authorship and its relation to the notion of a text.

From what has been said it follows further that the identity of the historical author, as distinct from that of the person who is the author, is contingent on the identity of the text and not vice versa. We already saw that the identity of a text does not depend on the identity of the historical author, even though it may depend on that of the pseudo-historical author when this is a dramatis persona. In the case of the historical author, the identity of the text and the conditions of such an identity play an important role. This brings me to the point I want to make; namely, that the type of text in question plays a role in the historical author's identity. The conditions of identity of the historical author of a diary, then, might be different from the conditions of identity of the author of a novel, or of a sign such as 'No smoking.' This helps solve many problems raised by what appear to be counterexamples to this view.

Having proposed a technical distinction between the historical author of a text and the person who is the author of that text, let me propose that for the sake of simplicity I continue to speak, unless otherwise noted, of the historical author as the person who plays the role of historical author. This will facilitate later discussions. For example, it will facilitate the discussion of the category of author as audience I introduce in Chapter 4. Strictly speaking, in accordance with what has been said here, this category should be that of the person who is the historical author and also plays the role of audience. But this way of speaking is cumbersome, even if precise, and so, for convenience's sake, I shall not adopt it.

B. Pseudo-Historical Author

The pseudo-historical author may be understood in two ways. In one way, he is simply a composite of what we know or think we know about a historical author independent of what the historical author wishes others to think concerning the composer of the text.[8] In another way, the pseudo-historical author is the persona whom the historical author wishes others to think composed the text.[9] In either case, the pseudo-historical author, unlike the historical author, never existed as a real person. Let me take up the former of these two ways of understanding the pseudo-historical author first.

Many historiographers would rather refer to the pseudo-historical author understood in this way as the *historical author.* They do this because they wish to restrict the meaning of history to an account of events and eliminate the notion of history as the events of which an account may be given. However, this is a contradictory position that confuses the issue.[10] If we maintain the distinction between history as a series of events and history as the account the historian provides of those events, then we can speak of the historical author as the figure who is part of history in the first sense and of the pseudo-historical author as the figure who is part of history in the second sense. The pseudo-historical author is the author we think produced the historical text. We know him from the descriptions that his contemporaries and other historians have left us as well as from the clues we find about him in the text he is thought to have composed. It is altogether possible that the historical author fits all or most of the descriptions that make up the pseudo-historical author, although in fact there would always be something left out—say, the thoughts he did not express but that influenced his choice of words at the moment he wrote the word *saraballae* in his treatise *De magistro.* It is also possible that the historical author does not fit most or even any of the descriptions we have of him except for the attribution to him of the authorship of the text in question. Indeed, even that may be questionable.[11]

The term I use for this category of authorship is intended to underscore that the pseudo-historical author is a view of the historical author rather than the historical author himself. It does not necessarily entail that the pseudo-historical author is always inaccurate. It is logically possible that a particular pseudo-historical author is a completely accurate view of a particular historical author, but this is a mere possibility. In fact, although pseudo-historical authors may not contain any inaccuracies, they are always incomplete, imprecise, and frequently do contain inaccuracies.

A good example of the sort of case that raises the issues to which I have been referring is that of the notorious Pseudo-Dionysius. 'Pseudo-Dionysius' is the name historians have given to the author of a group of four important treatises written in the early part of the Middle Ages: *On the Divine Names*, *On Mystical Theology*, *On the Celestial Hierarchy*, and *On the Earthly Hierarchy*. Throughout the Middle Ages he was identified with Dionysius, whom St. Paul is supposed to have converted to Christianity in Athens according to Acts 13:34. Indeed, it was not until the Renaissance that the identity of Dionysius was questioned by Lorenzo Valla. Today we know that he could not have been the man converted by St. Paul, because his works depend on Proclus, dating him to at least 400 years after his conversion was supposed to have taken place in Athens. Who is the author of the mentioned texts, then? For over a thousand years it was Dionysius, but today it is believed it was probably an ecclesiastic from Syria who lived around the fifth century A.D. The medieval persona is clearly a pseudo-historical author, but even the picture we have of him today must be considered only remotely like the actual historical figure who wrote the mentioned texts and called himself *Dionysius* to give his works the weight of authority necessary to ensure their survival and influence. Indeed, the historical author of the treatises must have had a keen sense of the importance of the pseudo-historical persona.

The import that a pseudo-historical persona has is well demonstrated by the author of the Book of Daniel of the Hebrew Scriptures. In this case, the historical author of the book identified Daniel as its author to make the statements in the book appear as credible predictions of the future, whereas in fact the events predicted had already passed.

These examples also illustrate the notion of the pseudo-historical author understood in the second sense given earlier. In this sense, Dionysius and Daniel are the personas that the historical authors of the treatises in question wanted others to believe were the authors of the treatises. Obviously, there are many reasons why a historical author will use a pseudonym rather than his own name. Sometimes these reasons have to do with the dangerous character of the opinions expressed in a text, at other times with certain advantages that the author may draw from anonymity, and still at other occasions with a certain effect and understanding that the historical author may wish to produce in the audience by the use of a pseudonym. These need not be the only reasons, of course; others may be available, but there is no need for us to go through them here.

The second sense in which we have understood the pseudo-historical author, namely, as the *persona* whom the historical author wishes us to think composed the text, is not exhausted by the use of pseudonyms. An even more frequent use of a persona occurs when an author puts himself in a text in some way, that is, when he becomes a dramatis persona, as happens when Chaucer assumes the roles of both author and pilgrim in *The Canterbury Tales*.[12] This may be done in many ways: as a signer of a Preface or Introduction, as one of the characters in the text, as the narrator or composer of the text, as one of the persons to whom characters in the text refer even when that person plays no direct role in the events described in the text, as an autobiographical I, and so on. In all these cases we have a persona that plays a direct or indirect role in the text. This dramatis persona is a pseudo-historical author, because he is always presented as representing the historical author, disclosing parts of his identity. It is not important, by the way, whether the persona adopted by the historical author in this context is or is not a result of a conscious effort on the part of the historical author to deceive or influence the audience. Whether it is or not, it is nonetheless presented in a certain light, in a certain context, and only partially. We must be careful, then, to distinguish between the author *of* a text and the author *in* the text, for they play different roles and have different functions.

Discussion of the various descriptions that make up the pseudo-historical author in the first sense given brings me to four points. The first is that I take the descriptions that make up the pseudo-historical author to be generally intended by the historians who propose them in good faith to communicate information concerning the historical author; only through occasional bad faith or because of unintended mistakes made by historians do they not describe accurately the historical author. It is the historical Voltaire that historians wish to describe when they describe the author of *Candide*, even though they might make mistakes in those descriptions owing to incomplete or faulty information or to faulty historical methodology. Of course, not infrequently, historians willfully distort the historical record for nonhistorical reasons to present a figure in a good or bad light. For example, the picture of Stalin painted by many North American historians is hardly flattering, whereas Russian historians until recently tended to whitewash many of Stalin's actions and look at them as minor pecadillos. Such willful distortions produce as effective pseudo-historical authors as the descriptions presented by historians who act in good faith do. Indeed, sometimes they are more effective, because the historians who produce them take advantage of certain desires and aspirations in the audience for which they produce the historical account. But that should not obscure the point that in most cases historians act in good faith. In contrast, the authors who intentionally use a pseudonym for their texts do not have the same motives—their purpose is most often to deceive the audience. And those authors who put themselves in the text may or may not have deception in mind concerning their true identity.

This brings me to the second point, that there are constraints on the pseudo-historical author. The pseudo-historical author is not, as may be suggested by some critics, who identify it with the historical author, a fiction on the interpreter's mind resulting from freewheeling fancy.[13] The pseudo-historical author is always posited as the historical author of the text and thus as a historical person who actually produced the historical text. This implies that the figure of the pseudo-historical author must be historically credible. The author of the text of *Don Quixote* cannot be, for example, a pharaoh of ancient Egypt—he must be someone Spanish, living in the sixteenth century, and so on. Moreover, as author of the text, the figure of the pseudo-historical author must be concordant with what the text reveals, either directly or indirectly, about its author. I say directly or indirectly because authors sometimes explicitly reveal themselves in various ways in texts, but even if they do not, texts tell us something about them. It is a well-known principle that effects tell us something about their causes, and so we should expect for texts to tell us something about their authors. The figure of the pseudo-historical author, then, must be credible as author of the text. We cannot impute the text of Augustine's *De magistro* to Voltaire or the text of *Candide* to Augustine. But we must resist the view that posits what the text tells us about an author as clear and subject to strict rules. Texts are complex artifacts composed of entities that are used to convey meaning, and it is by no means easy to establish the features of the person who produced a text based on an examination of the text alone. Thus the notion of implication suggested by some to explain what texts tell us about their authors is too strong.[14]

The third point that I wish to bring up is that, strictly speaking, there are as many pseudo-historical authors understood in the first sense as there are versions of the historical author entertained by audiences. Each member of the audience of a text who has an idea of who Stalin or Voltaire were, has constructed a pseudo-historical author that may or may not be the same as the picture constructed by someone else. It is not only possible but in fact frequent for even the same person to hold different views about the same historical figure at different times. The number of pseudo-historical authors, then, is potentially infinite.

Fourth, because it is doubtful that the pseudo-historical author, whether understood in the first or second sense, ever existed, it is also doubtful that he could have produced any of the texts that may be attributed to him. It is doubtful that he could have produced either the contemporary or the historical texts. And he could not be considered the author of the intended text, for that text, as I argued in Chapter 3 of *A Theory of Textuality*, is little more than a phantom posited by those interpreters who find certain mistakes or infelicities in the texts with which they are dealing.[15] Of course, sometimes on the basis of the idea they have of the historical author, namely, the pseudo-historical author, interpreters will argue for one particular understanding of a text rather than another, in their attempt to discover the intention of the author from an analysis of their idea of that author. But that is all a construction based on conjecture in which interpreters may be mistaken. So it cannot really be argued convincingly that the pseudo-historical author is the author of the intended text.

Nor can it be argued convincingly that the pseudo-historical author is the author of the ideal text, for the ideal text is the text that the historical author should have produced, whereas the pseudo-historical author is the interpreters' own conception of who the historical author actually was. The ideal text cannot be the product of an author that is supposed to be historical and is actually taken to have produced the historical text. The pseudo-historical author, then, is not the author of any text, in fact; he is only the author posited by someone as author of the historical text.

C.   Composite Author

The composite author is the author of the contemporary text. The contemporary text is the version or versions of the historical text that we have, resulting from the vicissitudes to which the historical text has been subjected. The players in the composition of the contemporary text are three: the historical author who produced the historical text; the various scribes or typesetters involved in the transmission of the historical text from the moment of its production to the present; and the editors who have tried to put together a definitive or at least historically accurate version of the historical text. Each of these players or groups of players has an important role in the formation of the contemporary text and, therefore, must be considered partial authors of that text. The contemporary text is the result of the cumulative efforts of all those who had a hand in producing it.

The role of the historical author is to produce the historical text, whether original or derivative, but that is just the beginning of the process that gives us the contemporary text. The different scribes or typesetters that copied the historical text from which other scribes and typesetters made other copies, and so on, are also responsible for part of the shape the contemporary text has. In the process of copying scribes make mistakes; they miss words; they misread expressions; they add or eliminate punctuation, and in some cases even add clarifications and glosses. This sort of thing was more frequent before the use of the printing press (in fact it was standard procedure then), when texts were copied by hand and each process of copying involved the potential of substantial changes. But even after the invention of the printing press, typesetters continue to make frequent mistakes and some authors do not have the opportunity, patience, inclination, or even the expertise to correct them.[16]

Even in the case of recent texts, the distinction between the historical text and the contemporary text is significant and, thus, the distinction between the historical author and the author of the contemporary text is as well. It is because of the mistakes and changes that occur in various versions of the text that the need arises for the work of an editor, who plays the role of third author component of the composite author. The role of editors is to make decisions among various readings of a text, collating the various versions and choosing what they consider the best, measured by criteria established by themselves or by the editorial tradition within which they work.[17]

The editorial labor involved in the modern production of ancient and medieval texts is extraordinarily important because only seldom does the autograph version of a text survive. In most cases, what we have are many manuscripts that contain widely differing readings of a particular passage. In these circumstances, the editor constructs the family tree (stemma) of manuscripts, determining which branch is the best, with the ultimate goal in mind of reconstructing the best possible version of the text. This involves not only enormous knowledge of the language, thought, and style of the author in question, but also knowledge of the subject matter discussed by the author. The editor will be called upon to choose among various readings of a text, to correct mistakes, to straighten out unintelligible or corrupt passages, and in general to give us a sensible and credible version of a text. To do this, the editor will have to act in many instances as the author of the text, thinking through what he or she takes to be the proper reading and phrasing. The editorial role is particularly important in cases where there is only one extant manuscript, for then the editor becomes the sole arbiter of how the text is to be read.[18] All this indicates that, of the three authors who make up the composite author, the editor is second in importance only to the historical author.[19]

D.   Interpretative Author

The interpretative author may be understood in two different ways. In one way this author is simply an audience (one or more persons) that is trying to understand a text and in so doing ends up with an understanding that differs from the understanding of the meaning of the historical text. In this sense, by changing the conditions of identity of the text, the audience creates a new text of which it becomes the author, although the audience may think it is dealing with the historical text. Naturally, this does not entail that the audience has selected and arranged the entities that constitute the text and that it uses as signs. Thus its authorial role is somewhat diminished, but it is still there insofar as the new text is its creation, even if unintended.[20]

The text created by the interpretative author is ideal in the sense that it exists only in the mind of the audience, that is, the person (or persons) who reconstructs the text. The ideal text, then, is a construct in someone's mind, and it is that mind that is its author, because that mind produces the ideal text while it scans the ECTs of the contemporary text it examines.

The interpretative author, taken in this sense of audience, however, does not always have in mind the construction of an ideal text. Most often his aim (in case he is a single person) is simply to understand the historical text. Often, however, he ends up constructing an ideal text rather than understanding the historical one.

Platonists will want to argue, no doubt, that it is not interpreters of texts taken in the stated sense that create the ideal text. Interpreters merely avail themselves of the ideal; they do not create it, but simply discover it through a kind of mental dialectic. I have no prima facie objection to conceiving the ideal text in this way and holding that the interpreter is not the author of the ideal text but a kind of conveyor of it. If that is the case, then the question arises as to the identity of the author of the ideal text and whether in fact such a text requires an author. Plato would have the text without the author; Augustine would have God as the author of the text; and others would follow other paths. But all this, although interesting and in need of an answer, is immaterial to us at present.

The interpretative author may also be understood in a second sense, however. In this sense, his function is to make it possible for an audience, separated from the historical text by various circumstances, to understand the text. This is done by adding something to the text, namely, another text, such as a commentary.[21] The interpretative author understood in this second sense is the author of an interpretation.

What has been said about the various types of authors we have discussed suggests that the historical author is in many ways paradigmatic of authorship; for this author is responsible for the historical text, without which no other text and no other author is possible. Moreover, as we shall see when we come to the next section of this chapter, the function of the historical author determines and controls to a great extent the functions of the other authors. For these reasons, generally, when one speaks of an author of a text, one refers to the historical author. The honorific title of *author* is usually accorded only to the historical author. This is in line with the very etymology of the term 'author,' from *auctor*, which in Latin means "he that brings about the existence of an object, or promotes the increase or prosperity of it, whether he first originates it, or by his efforts gives greater permanence or continuance to it."[22] It is also in line with ordinary usage, as any dictionary will bear. This view, however, is quite different from the position espoused by some contemporary philosophers, for whom the *pseudo-historical author* functions paradigmatically.[23]

Another collorary of what has been said about the various categories of authors examined is that some of them may overlap. We already noted that the historical author is part of the composite author insofar as he is the author of the historical text. But, moreover, it is also possible in principle, although seldom in fact, for a historical author to become a composite author in the sense in which he is responsible for the reconstruction of the version of the historical text we have at a particular time and place. To this it must be added that the composite author frequently overlaps with the first way in which we understood the interpretative author. Indeed, I am tempted to say that no composite author is possible without that author playing also the role of interpreter, since the construction of a text that is different from the historical text but is taken to be the same as it, seems to imply an understanding of the text different from the understanding its historical author had. This is not quite right, however, for there are situations in which the composite author is merely a scribe who makes an inaccurate copy of the historical text, and scribes can do this without paying any attention to the meaning of the text they are copying—indeed, that is frequently the reason why they make mistakes in the first place.

Having discussed the identity of the author, we must now deal with the question of the author's function. This question is not as simple as it appears at first sight.

II.　Function of the Author

The function of an author varies, depending on the author in question. The function of the historical author is to act as the primary cause of the historical text insofar as he is in charge of selecting and arranging the signs that compose a text to convey a specific meaning to an audience in a certain context. The function of the composite author is similar to that of the historical author insofar as this author also seeks to produce a text. The difference between the two is that, in the case of the historical author, this production is not subject to any constraints imposed by the preexistence of a whole text or any of its parts, except of course for the signs belonging to the language in which the text is produced when the author is not the creator of those signs. In the case of the composite author, however, the author seeks to reconstruct the historical text as it was first created by the historical author. What is common between these two authors is that their causal relationship is directed toward the text.

The reconstruction the composite author carries out concerns both the reconstruction of the entities that constitute the historical text and the recognition of the mental relation of these entities to a certain meaning. It involves, therefore, the reconstruction of the entities that constitute the text and the under-standing of the meaning of the text.

By contrast, the primary function of both the pseudo-historical and the interpretative authors is epistemological, although they can also have other functions. Their primary function is not to produce the text but to disclose its meaning to an audience; that is, to make possible the understanding of a text by an audience. In the case of most pseudo-historical authors, what we have is a certain picture of the historical author—whether intended by the historical au-thor or not, correct or not, or posited by the historical author or put together by others—that influences the way audiences understand the text. This author has no causal relation to the historical text; its causal relation is to the understand-ing of that text or its contemporary versions that audiences may have. In cases where the pseudo-historical author functions as a *dramatis persona* in the text, however, its function goes beyond epistemology because it is a constitutive part of the text. The author is represented in the text by signs and plays a character role in the work.

The function of the interpretative author depends on how this author is conceived. If the interpretative author is conceived as someone who develops an understanding of the text via certain criteria, then the author is instrumental in causing that understanding. But if what the interpretative author does is to produce an interpretation of the text to facilitate its understanding by an audi-ence that has difficulty in doing so because of its contextual distance from the historical text, then the interpretative author functions directly as a cause of the interpretation and indirectly as a cause of the understanding the interpretation produces in the audience. The function of this author with respect to the text, then, is epistemological, because its aim is understanding even if it may be con-sidered metaphysical, that is, causal, with respect to the interpretation.

Let me now take up the functions of each of these authors and explore them in further detail. I begin with the function of the historical author.

A.   Function of the Historical Author

The task of the historical author is to select and arrange the signs that compose a text to convey a specific meaning to an audience in a certain con-text. At least two important elements must be considered for the understanding of the function of a historical author. The first is the activity in which the au-thor engages; the second is the object toward which that activity is directed.

Beginning with the second, we know that a text is a group of entities, used as signs, selected and arranged by an author to convey a specific mean-ing to an audience. We also know that the meaning is not the signs that are se-lected and arranged to express it. Finally, we know that the connection between the entities used as a text and the meaning of the text is conventional. So we may ask, For which of these is the historical author responsible? Is he responsible for the meaning? Is he responsible for the entities that compose the text? Is he responsible for the connection between entities and meaning? Or should we say that he is responsible for two of the three or for all three? With respect to the first, we may ask, What is entailed by the "selection and arrangement" of the signs and how is this to be related to the creativity generally attributed to historical authors? Our inquiry in fact amounts to the identification of what makes someone a historical author, that is, the necessary and sufficient conditions of a historical author, and thus entails further unpacking the general description that we have been using thus far of a historical author. Moreover, since the notion of historical author is a functional one, vis-à-vis texts, our inquiry will be restricted to a functional interpretation of that notion. In this sense, what follows complements rather than duplicates what was said earlier about the historical author.

Let me begin with the notion of creation. This notion has been and still is much contested and discussed in philosophy.[24] Within the Judaeo-Christian theological context that stands behind Western discussions of this notion, creation is generally understood to involve both the production of something separate (*ad extra*) and also the production of something from nothing (*ex nihilo*). In the Western tradition, only the divinity is regarded as being able to create in this way. Human authors of texts, then, could not be taken to be creators in this sense. But there is also a secondary and less stringent understanding of creation. In this sense, to create is simply to produce something new (*de novo*) and separate, even if the production involves preexisting materials. It is in the sense of creation *de novo* and *ad extra*, but not *ex nihilo*, that artists are said to create art objects; and it is in this sense that an author can be said to create a text. The historical author of a text produces something new and separate out of preexisting materials.

That a text is something separate from the historical author appears to pose no serious difficulties at the outset. Most texts are objects that enjoy an existence independent of their historical authors and often exist long after their historical authors have ceased to exist. There is a category of texts, however, whose separateness is not as clear; namely, mental texts. For mental texts appear to depend on the author for their existence, and furthermore, they seem to be part of the author in some way.

I would like to argue, however, that in spite of the relation of dependence a mental text may have on the mind of the historical author or anyone else who might be able to think it, it also has an objective status that distinguishes it from the author's mind and thus may be considered separate from it in this sense. Historical authors are related to texts, including texts that have never left their minds, as subjects are related to objects, and as such texts are something other than subjects even if they depend on subjects for their existence. This is all that is needed to maintain that a text is separate from its historical author and thus that it is produced *ad extra*. For, although there may not be any physical separation between the two, indeed if we are dealing with a mind and a mental text there could not be one, a text and its historical author are still distinct entities. That this is so may be easily illustrated by considering that one can imagine the transference of a mental text from one mind into another. If we think of minds as TV monitors and of mental texts as the images they reproduce, it is obvious that several minds can have the same image simultaneously or at different times.[25]

The novelty of a text is more difficult to explain than its separateness. The first thing that needs to be said is that, although there may be some merit in the view that creation *ex nihilo* entails creation *de novo*, there is no merit in the contrary position: Novelty does not require production out of nothing. But if creation *de novo* does not entail creation *ex nihilo*, what does it entail? It need entail no more than the creation of something different from what was already there, so that novelty involves a kind of difference.[26]

Differences come in a wide variety and not all of them need be regarded as pertinent to the novelty of a text. As we saw in Chapter 2, only some of them are sufficient for a text not to be the same as some other text. Moreover, the ways in which difference is measured depend in turn on whether the text in question is universal, say, the universal text of *Don Quixote*, or instances of that universal, say, copies of the text of *Don Quixote*. The differences that count as far as the universal text is concerned are differences of meaning, syntactical arrangement, and type-sign composition. Some changes in audience and author are sufficiently significant to allow us to speak of "a new text." But these modifications have to be of the sort that change the meaning of the text. These conditions have been discussed at length in Chapter 2, so there is no need to repeat them here.

The differences that count as far as an individual text is concerned are the differences relevant for the universal text of which the individual is an instance in addition to conditions of individuality and continuous existence. A new individual text is either one belonging to a different type from that of all other individual texts, or one that belongs to the same type as others but does not fulfill the condition of continuous existence.

Having established the conditions that make a text different and, therefore, new, we can now see in what sense a historical author is the creator of a text: To create a text is to produce a new text; thus a historical author is a creator of a text insofar as he produces a different text according to the specified ways.[27]

Strictly speaking, to be an author of a text, then, entails that the author has created a new universal or a new individual text.[28] But the element of novelty can appear in various areas. In the case of universal texts, it is in the meaning, syntactical arrangement of the signs which compose the text, and the type-sign composition. In the case of individual texts, it is in those mentioned with regard to universal texts and those that affect individual identities such as individuality and continuous existence. An author may create a new universal text by giving new meaning to signs and arrangements already in use or by expressing an already known meaning with new signs or the new arrangements of signs already in use. This entails that the author of a text need not be regarded as creator of the meaning of a text or even of the relation between that meaning and the entities that constitute the text. Qua author, he need be considered creator only insofar as he is responsible for a text that is different from all other texts. Thus, an author of a text understood in the sense of creator of the text need not be considered the author of the work in cases where the meaning of the text is a work.[29] The work may be something already known. In this sense, for example, translators are the authors of the texts we call translations because they put together signs in new arrangements even though they express meanings already expressed by other signs. What has been said concerning universal texts and their relation to authors applies, mutatis mutandis, to individual texts.

At this point we encounter a difficulty, for we have been speaking of universal texts as well as their instances and of novelty in both. But, if universal texts neither exist nor are located in time or space, as was argued in Chapter 1, it is not clear how historical authors can function as creators of universal texts. It would seem to make sense to speak of historical authors as creators of individual texts, for both are historical entities that exist in a temporal or spatial dimension. But does it make sense to speak of historical authors as creators of universal texts that are neither historical nor spatio-temporal in any sense? Yet, we do want to say, for example, that Cervantes created the text of *Don Quixote*, even though that text can be multiply instantiated and thus must be considered universal. The same problem arises with artistic and culinary creations; we want to say that a chef created a new soup if he created a new kind of soup or recipe for a soup.[30]

To answer this question we must go back to something that was said in Chapter 1. A universal text, that is, the universal of the instances of a text, is not an entity distinct in reality from those instances. A universal and an instance of it are not two distinct things that require two distinct authors. The question of the authorship of a universal text as distinct from that of its instances should not come up if one keeps in mind the ontological character of universals. There is only one author of a text—of the universal and of its instances. There is one complication, however, for it is not the author of every instance of a text that is considered to be the author of a text. Indeed, if that were so there would be many authors of the same text, because different people may produce different instances of it. Only the agent who produced the first historical instance of a text (more on this later) is considered its author. The notion of historical author is a historical designation that refers to the relation of one historical phenomenon to other historical phenomena. There is a distinction between the agent who first produces an instance of a universal text and those agents who produce subsequent instances, and this distinction gives rise to the view that universal texts have historical authors. In this sense, a historical author is the author of a universal text when he is the first one who considered the type of text of which he produced an instance. The others are not historical authors, because they are reproducing what someone else had already considered.[31]

Having stated that historical authors create texts *de novo* and *ad extra*, but not *ex nihilo*, and that authors create universal texts only insofar as they produce instances of them, one may want to ask whether in fact historical authors should be described as discoverers rather than creators of universal texts. Is their function not in fact to find something that was in a sense available all the time but that had never been noticed before? In this sense the author is only a person who reveals or discloses what was hidden or had gone unnoticed.

This conclusion does not follow from the understanding of authorship that has been presented here. It is true that considered from my position universal texts are neither created nor not created, because temporality, location, existence, and their contraries are not categories that apply to them. It makes no sense to speak of the creation of something that neither can exist nor cannot exist, and likewise with the other categories mentioned, for creation involves the notion of causing to exist at a certain time or location. In that sense historical authors cannot be creators of universal texts. But in that sense they cannot be discoverers of texts either, for the notion of discovery, just like the notion of creation, involves the notions of existence, temporality, or location. To discover something is to make known or display at a particular time or place something that already existed. But according to the view defended in Chapter 1, these categories do not apply to universal texts considered in themselves, so it makes as little sense to say that authors discover them as it does to say that authors create them. From this standpoint, universal texts do not seem to be created or discovered.

From another standpoint, however, matters look different. I have already argued that universal texts have authors and can be considered to be the creation of authors insofar as their instances have authors and have been created by them. So our question amounts to the question of whether the authors of the instances of universal texts are better described as discoverers rather than as creators. Hence, we need to determine which categories apply to those authors.

The situation with respect to instances of universal texts is quite different from the situation with respect to universal texts, for the categories of existence, temporality, and location apply to all of them, except mental texts, to which only the first two apply. In principle, individual texts can, therefore, be created and discovered insofar as the categories mentioned apply to them. The question, then, is whether their historical authors are best described as their creators or discoverers. To say that they are their creators is to say that they have produced something different that did not exist as such before; to say that they are discoverers is to say that they have uncovered something that existed before but was not known. The argument for discovery is based on the fact that individual texts are instances of universals and thus are preceded by them. But existence and temporality do not apply to universal texts and thus the precedence in question cannot be temporal or existential. It is not possible to argue that the existence of individual texts is preceded by the existence of the universal texts of which they are instances. Under these conditions the only alternative is to hold that the first historical instance of a universal text has not been discovered but, rather, has been created by its historical author. Now we can go back to universal texts and see that they too cannot be described as being discovered, for their instances are not discovered.

The understanding of the function of historical authors presented here makes room for the important distinction between author and user. To explain this distinction, let me go back to the main point of the discussion and note that the historical author of a text is the person responsible for the features that make a text different from other texts. The historical author creates a text insofar as he produces a textual artifact that is different from all other textual artifacts either in meaning, syntactical arrangement, or sign-type composition. By contrast, those persons who use the text are not responsible for the features that make a text different from other texts. The user of a text does not create a different text, but merely employs a text of which there is at least one previous instance.

Historical authors may also be users, since they are responsible for the differences in texts precisely because they wish to use the texts to convey some meaning. Very often texts are created and used simultaneously, as when someone uses an expression for the first time; but it is not the case that the creation of a text implies its use. Someone may, for example, create a text and not use it, as when a woman writes a poem for the man she loves and never gives it to him. Authors may also at times use texts after they have produced them, say, that the woman does after all give the poem to her lover. Finally, authors may be considered partial users insofar as most times the texts they produce are composed of linguistic signs and formulas already in use. A long novel may be composed of sentences and expressions, many of which are commonly used, even though the complete text of the novel is different from all other texts produced until the time such a text was created. Clearly, historical authors may be, and often are, users, but users need not be historical authors.

Note that I have restricted the discussion of author vs. user to universal texts, but something similar can be said concerning individual texts. Nothing philosophically interesting results from such a discussion, so I have omitted it.

Some philosophers want to reserve the notion of author of a text for those persons who also produce works, thus eliminating the creators of clever phrases and the like from the category.[32] I find this unacceptable, because the matter of what is or is not a work is a purely historical affair dependent on cultural conventions, and authorial creativity can be evident as much in a text of a work as in one that does not have a work.

It is also misleading to identify what I have called here the *historical author* with the writer of a text.[33] The notion of writer, like the notions of speaker and imaginer, are closer to the notion of user than to the notion of author. A writer is simply someone who produces a written text, and this need not imply that the text is original in any sense and therefore that the writer is its author. And the same can be said of speakers or imaginers of texts. At the same time, it is not the case that writers, speakers, and imaginers need be merely users, since the production of an original written text implies an author. The scrambling of these categories so typical of some of the literature on textuality is unfortunate, often resulting in confusion rather than enlightenment. Let me go back now to authors.

There is the possibility that more than one person may create instances of the same text, either simultaneously or at different times, independent of each other. In such a case, the question arises as to whether each of the persons in question is to be considered a historical author or only one of them, the others being users. Let me separate the two and restrict the number of persons and instances of texts to two for the sake of simplicity, although the principles involved may also apply, with appropriate modifications, to cases of more than two instances and persons.

Case 1. Two and only two instances of the same text are produced, and they are produced simultaneously by two persons independent of each other.

Case 2. Two and only two instances of the same text are produced, and they are produced at two different times by two persons independent of each other.

In Case 1 both persons fulfill the criteria of authorship; they have created a different and therefore new text. Both persons are authors of the text and both of them are equally and rightly so. This is not very different from what happens with scientific discoveries made simultaneously by scientists working independently of each other.[34] This means that in principle there can be many historical authors of the same text. By the "same" text is meant, of course, the "same type" of text, for the individual texts, the instances, are numerically different in each case. The condition of there being more than one author of the same text is that the authors in question be the first ones to have selected and arranged the group of signs that constitute the text to convey the specific meaning in question to the same type of audience in the same type of context. I say the "same type" of audience and context because it is sameness of type and not numerical sameness in these categories that is relevant for the preservation of meaning.

Thus, it is possible in principle, for example, that there be many historical authors of the text of *Don Quixote*, and I do not mean many collectively, in the way in which the American Declaration of Independence has many authors, but many authors distributively, in the way in which Cervantes is the historical author of the text of *Don Quixote* and Shakespeare is the author of the text of *Hamlet*.[35] But this possibility is merely logical. If it were to be realized, there would have to be not only sameness of signs and syntactical arrangement, but also sameness of type of context and audience insofar as these may affect the meaning of the text, and the fulfillment of all these conditions does not seem likely. Indeed, the different historical authors who would compose the text of *Don Quixote*, for example, would themselves most likely have different features that might affect the way they view the meaning of the text they compose. For different persons to be authors of the same type of text, they would have to have the same relevant types of features themselves as well as be placed in the same types of circumstances, even though they would not have to be numerically the same. And such requirements seem to be very difficult—indeed impossible from the practical standpoint—to meet. For all intents and purposes, then, it would seem that each text has only one historical author, although this applies only to long and complicated texts. The possibility of having many authors of the same text increases proportionally as their length and complexity decrease. It is altogether possible that many instances of the text "Please do not smoke" were first produced independently by many historical authors at the same time. Several persons may have reacted that way at the English Court when someone first brought tobacco to England from the Americas via Spain.

Case 1 suggests the logical possibility of there being more than one simultaneous historical author of a text, but our discussion illustrates the difficulties of actualizing such a possibility. Case 2 raises a similar point but in a situation where the production of the text by two different authors working independently of each other is not simultaneous. Do we have one or two authors, then? If two persons at two different times produce two instances of the same text independently and the text is different from all other texts, it would seem reasonable to conclude that they both are authors of the same text. Indeed, if this is possible for all texts and even likely for short and simple ones (as in Case 1), it would seem even more obvious in Case 2, where the persons in question work separately not only in terms of space but also of time.

Yet, something seems to be wrong with regarding someone as a historical author of a text when another instance of the text has already been produced previously by someone else, even if such production is carried out without knowledge of the existence of that instance. Let us take an example from the arts and suppose that someone, unacquainted with Picasso's *The Old*

Guitarist, were to produce a painting exactly like that of Picasso. Would we call the second *The Old Guitarist* an original painting? Would we value it as we value Picasso's painting? Most of us would be inclined to answer negatively. But why, and how are we to reconcile this answer with the claim of authorship by both persons?

The point, of course, is that someone who produces an instance of a text of which other instances have been produced without knowledge of those instances is a creator of the text insofar as he has produced something new within his experience, but cannot be considered its historical author because he has not produced something new within a larger collective experience. Someone else has prior claim to novelty in the larger context. This indicates that authorship is historical and contextual. To be a historical author entails the creation of something new at a certain time in history and within a particular set of circumstances. Novelty, within or without the realm of textuality, is a historical phenomenon.[36]

Moreover, there is another reason on the basis of which one may doubt there can be two authors of the same text under the conditions specified in Case 2: when the text is long and complex. History does not repeat itself and, for as long and as complicated a text to be produced at two different times, such repetition would be required because textual identity would presuppose identity in context, audience, and so on. This does not appear to be logically impossible, but the factual impossibility at least in the case of long and complicated texts appears to be quite an obstacle.

In conclusion, the function of the historical author of a text, qua historical author, is to produce a text that differs, qua text, from all others. There may be more than one historical author of a text distributively, although it is unlikely that long and complicated texts have more than one historical author. On the other hand, there is no reason why the historical author of a text may not be more than one person. Certainly the text of the American Declaration of Independence was the result of the work of several persons who produced it and thus cannot be considered to have only one author. Nor are historical authors prevented from also being users of texts, including those they compose.

A text, indeed, may have many users. Every time we quote a poet or use a cliché we are using texts whose historical authors are other than ourselves. But that is something that does not need further explanation. Perhaps, however, it may be in order to add here the rather obvious point that to use a text does not necessarily imply plagiarism. Plagiarism involves the misrepresentation of ourselves as authors of texts. Users of texts are not plagiarists unless they represent themselves as the historical authors of the texts in question.

Moreover, with respect to quoting, perhaps we should make clear that in some circumstances, quoting involves the kind of creativity characteristic of authors rather than users. If a text is taken out of context and its meaning changed, then the person who quotes the text is acting as an interpretative author rather than as a mere user of the text, for the result is not an instance of the universal historical text but rather an instance of a new text that happens to have in common with the historical text the same type of constituting entities (ECTs). Some of the implications of this point are discussed in the next chapter.

Finally, let me also draw attention to the distinction between historical author and translator. This distinction had been generally well respected until recently, when the suggestion has been made that translators are in some sense authors. This view is concordant in many ways with the position I have defended, according to which the historical author of a text is the person responsible for creating a new (universal) text. Thus, translators, insofar as they produce a different composition and arrangement of signs from the original one, even if the meaning of the text is the same, are historical authors. They are historical authors of the translation of the text, which of course is also a text; but they are historical authors neither of the historical text nor of the work. They are not historical authors of the historical text because they are not responsible for the type of artifact used by the historical author to convey the meaning he intended to convey. And they are not historical authors of the work for two reasons: first, because the work is the meaning of the text and that is supposed to be the same for the historical text and its translation; second, because whether the person responsible for that meaning is the author of the historical text or not, the historical author of the translation is not the author of that meaning.

A translation itself is a historical text, for it has a historical author and was produced at some point in time. But the historical text that is the translation should not be confused with the historical text of the work which has been translated.

Translators, then, are historical authors, but only of the translations, not of the historical texts of the works they translate. Moreover, their originality is restricted to the choice and arrangements of the signs they use in place of the signs and arrangements used by the historical author of the historical text of the work they translate, and even there it is limited, for the choice of signs and their arrangements is dictated to a great extent by the meaning that is to be conveyed. Indeed, translators try to communicate meanings and works to persons who cannot understand the texts of historical authors. To that extent, they are in many ways interpreters, and translations are interpretations.[37] Translators are authors to some extent, but they cannot be considered on equal footing with the historical authors of the texts they translate.[38]

B.   Function of the Composite Author

There are important similarities between the function of the historical author and that of the composite author. The similarities lie in that both have as their aim the production of the historical text. Thus, the object at which their efforts are directed is the same. However, with this the similarities end, for in the case of the historical author, the aim is to produce something new and different from what was already available; that is why we spoke of creation when we spoke about the text produced by the historical author. But the aim of the composite author is not to create a new text in the sense of producing a text which is different from every text that has existed until that point. Indeed, if the result of the activity of the composite author were a creation in this sense, then such activity would be considered a failure and the composite author would not be a composite author in virtue of that activity, but a historical author of a new text. The aim of the composite author is to recreate the historical text, that is, to recover what had been lost or forgotten. In that sense, there is an element of relative novelty: The composite author presents something new to an audience that did not have it before. But this is not absolute novelty, for the lost or forgotten historical text is supposed to precede the text produced by the composite author.

There may also be an element of novelty in the text produced by the composite author if the composite author fails to re-create the historical text and creates a different text instead. It is for these reasons that I called the text produced by the composite author the *contemporary text*, rather than the *historical text*, for there may be, and often are, substantial differences between the two.

C.   Function of the Pseudo-Historical Author

The pseudo-historical author is the persona an audience believes, or is intended to believe, is the historical author of a text. As such, it is generally mythical, although it may approximate in various ways the historical author.

As a more or less accurate view of the historical author, the pseudo-historical author cannot be considered to have created anything in fact, even though he is presented precisely as the creator of the historical text. The function of the pseudo-historical author is primarily epistemological. The pseudo-historical author is supposed to help us understand—even if it may do just the opposite in some cases—a text. Knowledge about the identity of an author is supposed to help us figure out what the text means. The pseudo-historical author does not create anything and is not the cause of a text; the pseudo-historical author functions rather as one of the causes of the understanding an audience derives from a text; for it regulates and influences the understanding an audience derives from a text.

There is one exception to this conclusion, however. When the pseudo-historical author is a dramatis persona in the text, its function is more than epistemic, for it is one of the factors that determines textual meaning and thus textual identity. Consider the case of Chaucer in *The Canterbury Tales*, where he plays the role of author and pilgrim, creating, reporting, and affecting the tales. In situations such as this, the pseudo-historical author functions both epistemically and ontologically.

D.   Function of the Interpretative Author

The interpretative author may be understood in two ways: as an audience that develops an understanding of a text or as a person who adds something to a text to enable an audience to understand it. In neither case does the interpretative author have a causal relation of creativity to the historical text, and hence there is little in common between this author and the historical author. On the other hand, the interpretative author does have some things in common with both the composite author and the pseudo-historical author. There are similarities between his function and that of the composite author insofar as the interpreter seeks to understand the historical text and in so doing re-create its meaning in his or her own mind and in the mind of a contemporary audience. To that extent the interpretative author is involved in a task that is historical and mirrors the reconstructive task of the composite author.[39] The differences between the two lie first in that the composite author is concerned with the text as a whole—the entities that constitute it and the meaning—whereas the interpretative author is concerned with only the meaning. Second, the interpretative author, understood in the second sense mentioned earlier, adds to the historical text whatever he deems necessary to produce a contemporary understanding of it, whereas the composite author tries to avoid any such additions, being concerned primarily with the re-creation of the historical text as it was when first produced. Finally, it is frequently legitimate for the interpretative author to go beyond the meaning that the historical author of the text and his contemporaneous audience associated with the historical text, whereas it is never legitimate for the composite author to do so.[40]

There are also similarities and differences between the functions of the pseudo-historical author and the interpretative author. The main similarity is that the function of both (with the exception of the case in which the pseudo-historical author is a dramatis persona) is epistemological: they affect understanding. As such they have no causal relationship to the historical text. The differences between the two are first of all ontological. The pseudo-historical author is a projection of an audience that tries to understand a text, but the interpretative author is an actual person (or persons) who sets out to understand a text or to make it understandable for an audience. Second, the pseudo-historical author is the product of the activity of the interpretative author and not vice versa. Finally, the interpretative author, understood in the second way specified earlier, is the creator of an interpretation, whereas the pseudo-historical author creates nothing.

Having discussed the function of the author, we must now turn to the much debated issue of whether there is a need for an author at all. Can there there can be texts without authors?

III.   Need for an Author

The question of whether texts have authors is one that has been explicitly raised only recently. Indeed, from a commonsense point of view it would seem that if there is a text there must be or must have been an author that produced it,[41] although the existence of an author is not sufficient to make something a text. We refer to art objects, tools, and other artifacts as well as to thoughts, ideas, and actions as having authors, but these objects are not necessarily texts. If they turn out to be texts it is not solely in virtue of the fact that they have authors but owing to other factors as well. The view that having an author is not what determines that something be a text, however, is not the one under fire in contemporary circles. Rather, the view that has recently been attacked holds that authors are necessary for texts, that is, that there can be no texts without authors. The attackers fall into two groups. The most radical position argues that texts never have authors.[42] A less radical point of view maintains that, although some texts have authors, not all texts have them.[43]

Various factors have fueled the recent interest in the view that texts, or at least some texts, do not have authors. One such factor is the often noticed point that not only texts but also their meanings are independent of the authors that compose them. Texts have a "life," to use a standard metaphor, and an existence of their own after they are created that has very little to do with those who create them. Their creators may in fact die while the texts remain and continue to exert direct influence on audiences. Most old texts, as opposed to recently produced texts, fall into this category. Also along these lines, it is noted that often we understand the meaning of a text without knowing anything about its author. This is most clearly the case with simple, ordinary texts, such as the "No smoking" sign posted in the classroom where I teach. There are scores of anonymous texts whose meaning is not seriously questioned in spite of our ignorance of who produced them. The text of the epic poem *El Cid*, for example, is one of them. Its language, structure, and nature make it a relatively easy text to understand, even though no one knows who put it together. Finally, there are cases where persons other than the author of a text understand the text better than the author. This is often the case with very complicated texts, for example, where commentators who have devoted their lives to studying these texts are sometimes thought to know more about them and their meanings than the authors who produced them. There can be better Aristotelians than Aristotle, if you like.

These considerations fuel the speculation that authors are not necessary for texts. They also lead to another important point that results in the same conclusion; namely, that the meaning of a text has more to do with its audience than with its author. Indeed, some go so far as to say that the meaning of a text has nothing to do with the author but is solely up to the audience; the latter, rather than the author who composed the text, determines the meaning.[44]

More specific reasons can be given for the positions that only certain texts have authors or that no texts have authors. For example, one may wish to argue that it is certainly odd to speak of signs such as the words or letters of natural languages as having authors. And, indeed, it is odd to talk in this way, but the reason is not that the words and letters used in natural languages do not have authors, rather that their authors are frequently anonymous—we do not know who they are—or these words and letters are the result of collective rather than individual efforts. We generally associate authorship with known persons and with individuals rather than groups. The case of the symbols used in artificial languages should help us see the point, for I doubt anyone would object to calling whoever produced an artificial language its author. If the person in question is not an author, what is he? A maker? A producer? An inventor? A discoverer? None of these terms seem to apply as well.

Similar sorts of reasonings probably are behind the view that notices and simple texts do not have authors. It is difficult to pinpoint the first person who combined the words 'no' and 'smoking' into the text 'No smoking' to convey the request that someone not smoke tobacco. Before tobacco was introduced in Europe, such combination may not have been in use and, if in use, it could not possibly have been used to mean what we mean by it today. Yet, someone must have been the first person (or persons) to have done this, which means that the text has an author in the general sense indicated.

It is not the length of a text, however, that may preclude it from having an author, for some very short texts, such as the Japanese poems known as *haiku,* are universally accepted as having authors. Earlier I referred to relative simplicity as another reason that may be given for certain texts lacking authors. But again a haiku can be quite simple. So it does not look as if the length or degree of complexity have anything to do with whether a text has an author or not. Is there something, then, that is required of texts that have authors?

Another possibility is that only those texts capable of multiple interpretations have authors.[45] Now, this will not do as it stands, for any text can be the subject of multiple interpretations; even the most simple texts can be understood differently, whether correctly or incorrectly, by different people and in different contexts. The interpretations in question must be, if not correct, at least allowable. A text has an author, then, only if the text is of such a sort that it is legitimate for an audience to understand it in different ways.

Unfortunately, this view has at least one undesirable consequence: It excludes from the category of texts with authors scientific treatises that allow only one legitimate interpretation. I am thinking of such texts as Euclid's *Elements* and Newton's *Principia*. Those who composed these texts wanted to convey a very clear and specific message about the subject matter and not a variety of views about it. And the same can be said concerning shorter texts used in ordinary speech. When I ask my daughter "to open a window to let fresh air into a stuffy room" I mean exactly that I want her to open a window to let fresh air into a stuffy room and for someone else to understand what I say differently is to misunderstand it.

It cannot be, then, that only texts with a substantial range of legitimate interpretations can have authors. So, we are back at square one. It is true that it is quite different in many ways to be the author of the text of *Don Quixote* and the author of "No smoking." But the differences are a matter of degree. Fundamentally, those who produced both texts were engaged in the same kind of activity, the creation of something new. For that reason both texts can have authors.

The confusion associated with the question of whether texts require authors has to do in part with the complexity of the question and in part with what is meant by 'author.' Therefore, to bring some clarity to its discussion, we must examine it in the context of the various authors distinguished earlier.

A.   Need for the Historical Author

Two questions having to do with the historical author should be distinguished to prevent confusion. The first asks whether it is possible for texts to exist without causes; the second asks whether it is possible for texts to exist although they do not have subjects who intend to convey some specific meaning through them among their causes. The answer to the first question seems quite straightforward. It makes no more sense to hold that texts can exist without causes than that there is rain without something that produces it. No matter what entities are used to make up texts, whether artificial or natural, those entities and the texts they make up must have causes. Unless, like Hume, we are willing to challenge the whole notion of cause and to accept that there are entities with no causes, we must accept that texts too cannot exist without causes that bring them about.

The answer to the second question, by contrast, is not as easily determined. Some may wish to argue that, indeed, some texts are produced without the causal agency of subjects who intend to convey some specific meaning through them. Various examples may be cited to support this argument, but I shall refer to only two.[46] One is the case of "found" texts, to which reference has already been made. Consider the case of someone who is walking on the beach and finds a group of pebbles arranged in the same way in which an English speaker would put them if he wished to form the text 'No smoking.' Granted, I have not heard of anyone finding such an arrangement of pebbles and, indeed, it seems difficult even to imagine that the arrangement would occur naturally, without the intentional operation of a subject. But it is certainly logically possible for this to happen. A combination of high winds, tides, and so on could in principle produce the arrangement in question. And if that is the case, so goes the argument, then we have an instance of a text in whose production subjects have not played a role.[47]

At the outset it appears as if there were only two ways of answering this objection. One is to deny that the arrangement of pebbles on the beach is a text; the other is to find an author for the arrangement. But both of these alternatives run into difficulties. The first alternative has to account for the fact that a subject walking on the beach got meaning out of the arrangement. The second has to contend with the problem that no subject produced the arrangement. Must we then acknowledge that authors are not always necessary for texts?

I would like to propose a different way out of this dilemma, based on the distinction between the entities that constitute a text (ECTs) and a text itself.[48] The entities that constitute a text are whatever is used to convey meaning, considered apart from both the meaning and the fact that the entities convey this meaning. Examples of these entities are the pebbles on a beach about which we have been speaking, or any other physical or mental entities that constitute texts. The text, by contrast, is those entities taken as conveyors of certain meanings. Now, since we have two sorts of things, the entities that constitute the text and the text itself, the causes that account for them need not be the same. In our example, the causes that produce the particular pebbles and their arrangement on the beach need not be the same as the causes that produce the text (that is, the pebbles and their arrangement understood as having a certain meaning). The meaning "No smoking" and its connection with the arranged pebbles was not produced by the wind and the tide. The cause of that meaning and its tie to the arranged pebbles is the result of whoever first connected the shapes and arrangement instantiated by the pebbles to the meaning. But then, we may ask, is the person walking on the beach the author of the text on the beach, for she seems to be the first to think of the pebbles and their arrangement as having meaning? Again we must distinguish. For, although she is the first who identified the individual pebbles and their arrangement found on the beach as having meaning, she may not have been the first to have connected the particular sort of arrangement the pebbles display to this particular meaning. If she understood the arrangement of the pebbles to mean "No smoking" because she already knew that this certain arrangement meant "No smoking," then she is not the author of the text. She is not the author of the text insofar as she did not first make the connection in question. She is rather a user, for she uses what is already available.

This case is quite different from cases where a subject takes a natural object and uses it as a text by stipulatively connecting it to a meaning. In such a case, the subject who makes the connection is obviously the author, and thus this sort of case poses no difficulty for the view I have been defending here. This sort of situation is similar to the case of "found art," where, for example, a piece of driftwood is picked up by someone at the beach. The piece of driftwood is an aesthetic object that, for this reason, attracts the attention of a subject who then uses it as an art object by displaying it on the mantelpiece. The artist in this case is the subject who picked up the piece of driftwood and displays it, even though it was nature which produced the object that has become art.[49]

In short, we need not deny that the arrangement of pebbles on the beach constitutes a text, nor must we identify the passerby as the author of the text to hold that texts must have authors. For a text is not just the entities of which it is constituted, but rather those entities intended as conveyors of a certain meaning. In the example of the pebbles, the intention to convey a certain meaning with the particular arrangement exemplified by the pebbles belongs to whomever thinks of it first. The passerby need not be the author unless she is in fact the one who first establishes the connection between a particular arrangement of entities and a meaning. But an author there must be, for the connection in question is a matter of convention, not of nature, and conventions require subjects to adopt them.[50]

In the case of the pebbles it is not too difficult to envision the passerby as the author of the text. This is so because seeing a text composed of pebbles on a beach involves a "creative" mental selection of what objects, features of objects, and arrangements available on the beach are significant and thus constitute the text. The proof of that process of mental selection is that not everyone may see the text. This is very similar to what happens when someone looks at a cloud and sees a camel or when a person looking at stars sees patterns in them, such as a big dipper. Selection and arrangement do not require physical alteration—remember, some texts are mental. But the passerby is not so easily identifiable as author in other cases.

A second example that may be used to impugn the need for causal agents is the proverbial example of the monkey who, given sufficient time, will eventually type a copy of Shakespeare's *Hamlet* by randomly hitting the keys of a typewriter. This may be taken as a counterexample to the proposed view because the monkey in question knows nothing about the meaning of the text it produces, does not have any knowledge of the signs of which it is composed or the semantic or syntactical significance of their arrangement, and has no intention to convey meaning. And yet, there it is: the magnificent text of *Hamlet*, typed by the monkey.

The very idea that a monkey would be able to produce the text of *Hamlet* is farfetched, and we all know that the probabilities in question are infinitesimal. But this observation will certainly not do away with the counterexample.[51]

Three alternative strategies suggest themselves at the outset to deal with it. The first is to deny that what the monkey has produced is in fact a text;[52] the second is to argue that the monkey is the author of the text;[53] and the third is to hold that whoever first got hold of the monkey's manuscript and understood it as *Hamlet* is the author.[54] But none of these alternatives appears to be prima facie satisfactory. The first does not appear to work because the object the monkey produced can be read and understood by anyone who knows English in the way one would read and understand any copy of the text of *Hamlet* produced by a person. The second alternative does not seem satisfactory because the monkey knows nothing about the meaning of what it has typed and, therefore, has no intention of communicating that or any other meaning. And the third does not appear acceptable because the author of *Hamlet* is not the person who found the monkey's typescript but Shakespeare.

Following what was said concerning the case of "found texts," one could try to develop a solution by distinguishing between the entities produced by the monkey and the text of *Hamlet*. The entities produced by the monkey consist of certain marks on a paper, whereas the text is made up of those marks insofar as they are intended to convey meaning. In this respect, the example is very similar to the one of the pebbles on the beach and can be analyzed in the same way. The monkey is the agent that produces the marks (the counterpart of the wind and the tides), the author of the text is Shakespeare, who first connected those marks to the work or meaning that we know as *Hamlet*, and the person who finds the monkey's typescript is merely a user of the text (the counterpart of the walker on the beach).

Some difficulties, however, undermine this solution. For example, it might be argued that the typescript produced by the monkey has meaning, regardless of whether anybody finds it or anyone has authored the text. Suppose, say, that the monkey produced the text of *Hamlet* before Shakespeare existed (or suppose that Shakespeare never existed) and suppose further that no one ever finds the text. Under these circumstances can we say that we have a text, and if we do, who is the author? In this situation we cannot hold that Shakespeare is the author of the text or that the author is the finder, for Shakespeare does not exist and the typescript has not been found by anyone. Yet, we might like to hold all the same that the typescript has meaning. For the typescript is composed of signs belonging to English and arranged in ways that are consistent with the syntactical rules of English grammar in such a way that they could be recognized as meaningful by anyone who knows English. Indeed, if one were to find the typescript after all, one could read it, understand it, and even could pass as the author of *Hamlet* by peddling the manuscript as one's own.[55] Thus we are justified in asking, then, Who is the author in this situation?

One might try to answer this question by saying that the reason why the case of the monkey's typescript raises these questions is that it is composed of letters and words—artifacts created by subjects to convey meaning—that have established meanings; because of this the typescript appears to have meaning even though it has no author.[56] The monkey is using established linguistic signs to produce the typescript, and if these signs make sense at all they do so because they are arranged in accordance with the grammatical rules of the English language. Thus, the connection between the typescript and meaning that results in a text is latent in the accepted meanings of the signs and their arrangement. There is, then, no single subject who can be called the *author* of the text in this example, but rather the subjects who developed the language and its rules function as latent authors of the text. There is a subject component in the causal complex that is responsible for the monkey's *Hamlet*, and this component is represented by the language in which the text is composed, which is in turn a result of the fact that the monkey types on a machine made by subjects to produce linguistic signs. This is quite evident in the case of a short text like 'Fire!' accidentally typed by a monkey, for the author of the text (the counterpart of the text of *Hamlet*) is not the monkey, but whoever connected the shape of the composite 'Fire!' with the meaning that text has in English.

One might also add that, if a monkey strikes the keys of a typewriter, it most likely does this because it has watched humans do so. And this therefore involves a subject or subjects in an indirect way as well. Imitation, however, is not a necessary condition of the textuality of what the monkey produces, because the monkey could hit the keys whether it had seen anyone do so or not and the monkey has no intention to convey meaning in doing so.

The case of the monkey's typescript, then, does not appear to be exactly like that of the pebbles on the beach, for in the case of the pebbles it is possible to hold that the passerby is the author of the text at least in the unusual case in which she is the first person to attach meaning to the shapes formed by the pebbles. Nor does the case of the monkey's typescript seem exactly like that involved in the identification of cloud formations with animals and the like, which we do occassionally. In this case one could argue that the passerby is the author, because she is the one that connects the cloud, say, with a camel or the arrangement of certain stars with a big dipper. But the monkey's typescript is composed of well-established linguistic signs, namely, letters and words, that are not so on the basis of a similarity observed by someone, but on the basis of accepted conventions. The reader of the monkey's typescript cannot be considered to be "creative" in the way the passerby at the beach or the cloud watcher can.

In spite of all that has been said, however, we do not seem to have solved the problem posed by the text of *Hamlet* produced by a monkey, for the cases of the text of *Hamlet* and the text 'Fire!' are different insofar as 'Fire!' is a well-known and frequently used text in English, but the text of *Hamlet* (as produced by the monkey) is an original, new product. Society or whoever invented the text 'Fire!' may take authorial credit for it, but no one seems to deserve authorial credit for the text of *Hamlet*. The monkey cannot take credit for it because it knows nothing about the meaning and has no intention to convey it. Society cannot take the credit because it has not created the particular text of *Hamlet* about which we are speaking, although it has created a language whose possible arrangements include one such as that of the text of *Hamlet*. Moreover, if we were to give authorial credit to society in this case, why could we not give authorial credit to it in the case in which Shakespeare is in fact the person who composed the text? Finally, the finder of the monkey's typescript cannot take authorial credit because he or she did not create the typescript, the meaning, or the connection between the typescript and the meaning. We seem, then, not to have advanced toward a solution of this case. The typescript of *Hamlet* produced by the monkey is either not a text or, if it is a text, has no historical author.

Let us explore the second alternative first; namely, that the text has no historical author. One could argue that this is possible because a complex set of causes can come together and by chance produce what under normal circumstances only an author can produce. Thus, in the last analysis it would seem to be true that in at least one type of case there can be texts without historical authors; that is, there can be texts without someone who intentionally selects and arranges the signs of which the historical text is composed to convey a specific meaning to an audience in a certain context. But this is an anomaly, an exception, and does not mean that the existence of the text cannot be causally explained even though such a causal explanation includes an element of chance. Moreover, this view must be distinguished from the views described earlier in which texts were considered not to have authors at all, at least not always. For the understanding of what it means to have an author in those views and the one presented here is different.

This alternative may be clarified further by referring back to the discussion of meaning in Chapter 1. There we saw that textual meaning is related to certain entities that, when considered by a subject, can yield understanding of the meaning in the subject. Moreover, because texts must have meaning, it appears that subject understanding is required for textuality. The problem with the cases of the monkey's typescript and "found texts" is that they are understandable to audiences that were not instrumental in producing them and yet they were not understood by the agents or causes that produced them.

Now, in the case of signs and texts that were produced by agents before they were accidentally reproduced by causes unaware of their meaning, it is obvious that their authors are those who first consciously produced them. There is no problem here. Moreover, there is no problem concerning signs that are first regarded as signs by someone other than the causes that produced the entities of which they are constituted. In this case, that someone is the author. The problem arises with texts that are produced by unconscious causes, make sense, and have never been produced before by conscious agents. This would be the case of the text of *Hamlet* produced by a monkey before Shakespeare produced it. One way to try to dispel any lingering doubts is to argue that in this case there are conscious agents who developed the signs and rules whereby those signs could be arranged. Thus, although no single, overall conscious agent is responsible for the text, there are conscious agents whose intentions make possible the connection between the work *Hamlet* and its text. Indeed, the meaning of texts and therefore the texts themselves are the result of a multiplicity of factors, even when an author can be identified as their producer.[57] So it makes sense to argue that these factors, considered together, make up for the absence of what is required under normal circumstances.

Finally, it could be added that it is precisely the complex nature of texts and the fact that their meaning is in part the result of the meaning of the signs of which they are composed that makes this explanation plausible. If the components of an entity are meaningful and fall into semantically significant arrangements, the entity is bound to be a text even when no subject is responsible for that entity.

Still, the truth of the matter is not only that this alternative violates the definition of texts adopted in the Introduction but that it seems to go contrary to some of our most basic intuitions about textuality. The idea that there can be texts without authors who intend to convey some specific meaning through them seems absurd. But, then, can the alternative view, that the monkey's typescript is not a text, be defended? I believe it can because I think that its implausibility stems from an assumption that has gone unquestioned in the discussion so far. The assumption is that the typescript has meaning. But can we really question this assumption? After all, any reader who knows English and reads the monkey's typescript seems to understand it. Moreover, the typescript is composed of words belonging to the English language that appear in arrangements in accordance with the grammatical rules of the language. So, how can anyone possibly argue that the typescript is not a text because it does not have meaning?

If one examines the example in more detail, however, it becomes clear that the situation is not that simple. The reason is that the meaning of the signs of which the typescript is composed is not clear because signs, like texts, are historical entities, the products of conventional uses whose meanings change from time to time. Thus, the meaning of the monkey's typescript in the sixteenth century might be different from its meaning in the eighteenth or the twentieth centuries. Because the monkey is a historically neutral entity (not having an understanding of what it has typed) and the typescript has not been produced in a social context (there is no audience for it), we cannot possibly say that the meaning of the typescript is this rather than that.[58]

Consider another example. Suppose the monkey typed 'Fire!' instead of the typescript of *Hamlet*. In this case we have a situation where the meaning of

'Fire!' is undetermined, for there are several possible meanings that could be attached to it, which are incompatible. Does it, mean, for example, that some-one should pull the trigger of a firearm? Or does it mean that a certain building is on fire? Or is it merely a report of someone who is learning the use of the English word 'fire'? The point is that context is essential for meaning and a typescript that lacks context must lack meaning. Note that the point I am mak-ing is not epistemic, although epistemology confirms it. We have no way of knowing the meaning of what appears to be a text outside its historical context; texts outside history are silent. The point I am making is ontological, for it con-cerns the fact that, for entities to acquire meaning and become signs and for signs to compose texts, they must be picked and endowed with meaning in cer-tain arrangements at some point in history. Otherwise they are no more than the entities they are. Texts outside history are not texts.

Nor is this view affected by the fact that a particular text may have a range of meanings or be open ended in meaning. The determination of the limits of meaning is established ultimately by the cultural function of a text and that cultural function depends on historical circumstances. Thus, such function and historical circumstances are necessary to establish the range of meaning even in cases in which such a range is open ended. What the monkey's typescript lacks precisely is a determinant of the range. So it cannot be argued that the case of the monkey's typescript is the same as the case of a text that has been deter-mined by cultural function to have an open-ended range of meaning.

Our conclusion, then, is that texts do need historical authors, for texts without authors are texts without history and texts without history are texts without meaning; that is, they are not texts. Thus, in spite of what appear to be counterexamples, historical authorship is a necessary condition of textuality.

These considerations open up another possibility for typescripts such as the one produced by the monkey. It is that, after all, the one who finds the type-script for the first time may function as its author. For what that person does is to fix the meaning of the signs of which the typescript seems to be composed in accordance with the usages and conventions of the time. Of course, the orig-inality of this author would be rather limited and would be in many ways similar to that of the interpretative author, but nonetheless there would be an authorial thrust to such activity.

B.   Need for the Pseudo-Historical Author

The pseudo-historical author is a mental construct that is believed by an audience—or constructed by someone (sometimes the historical author) to lead an audience to believe it—to be the historical author. The answer to the ques-tion whether there can be texts without pseudo-historical authors is easily de-termined if we compare this question with the questions raised in the previous section concerning the historical author. The reason it is easily determined is that it can be based on empirical evidence. In our everyday experience we are acquainted with scores of texts that have no pseudo-historical authors. For example, I doubt very much whether anyone has an idea about the author of the "No smoking" sign posted in the classroom where I teach on Thursdays. Indeed, signs understood in the sense of notices posted are mostly regarded as not having authors. That does not mean that anyone believes that they are uncaused. Obviously, someone painted the words on the wall, someone ordered them painted, and someone must have been the first person who put the words together to convey the command not to smoke. But no one bothers to think about the persons who did these things. The reason is that the meanings of those signs are so clear and contextually transparent, and the signs in question generally have so little originality and value in themselves, that it is unimportant either for understanding or in terms of proprietary interests who their author is. This is not always so, however, even with relatively simple signs. We are interested in identifying a person who painted a swastica on a tombstone of a Jewish cementery, for that involves a violation of the law and reveals something about the mind and beliefs of the person who did it.[59] But in general signs whose meaning is clear and whose import is simple do not elicit a pseudo-historical author. The pseudo-historical author is a construct of an interpreter who wishes to know more about a text or wishes to pass judgment upon its author.

Texts of literary, philosophical, religious, or scientific works, for example, elicit pseudo-historical authors. The reason is that they are subjects of interpretations or present characteristics of originality and value that lead to the development of proprietary interests in them. Even if a text is semantically transparent, it can elicit a pseudo-historical author as a result of its originality, for example. We want to know and have images of the authors of well-known clichés even if their meaning is quite clear.

The identification of pseudo-historical authors with historical authors seems to be the main reason why some philosophers hold the position that texts do not require authors and that some texts do not have authors. For what they really mean is that some texts do not have pseudo-historical authors and do not need them for carrying out their function.[60]

The view that no texts have authors is a reaction to the obvious fact that some texts do not have pseudo-historical authors and that there is no absolutely real demarcating criteria between those that do and those that do not. Those philosophers who adopt this view solve the problem of authorship by holding that only works, which they understand as texts that have been subjected to interpretation, have authors. Texts that have not been subjected to interpretation have no authors (i.e., pseudo-historical authors) but only "writers" (i.e., historical authors).[61]

My objections to this position go not so much against what it maintains concerning the pseudo-historical author but against what it holds about works and texts. I already presented my objections to these aspects of the view else-where, so I need not repeat them here.[62] The main merit of the view is that it recognizes the pseudo-historical author as a mental construct, the product of an interpretation of a text.

C.   Need for the Composite Author

Are composite authors necessary for texts? Do all texts have composite authors? The answer to both questions is negative. The composite author is the author of only those contemporary texts that are not the historical text, for the author of the historical text is the historical author. The composite author is composed of the historical author, the scribes that made copies from the token historical text, and the editors who tried to reconstruct the historical text. If it turns out that the token historical text survives, the contemporary text is the his-torical text and its author is not the composite author, but the historical author. Similarly, if the historical text was lost before any copies of it were made, there can be no contemporary text and correspondingly no composite author. There are composite authors only of contemporary texts that are not historical texts. This means that not every text has to have a composite author.

Having said that, however, we should add that most old texts survive in contemporary versions and, even if the original token survives, copies are made of it which differ from that token in various ways. Under such conditions, it turns out that we generally know historical texts through contemporary texts, and this entails the existence of composite authors who put them together.

D.   Need for an Interpretative Author

Can there be a text without an interpretative author? Although the notion of interpretative author is complex, the answer to this question is the same. On the one hand, if the interpretative author is understood as an audience that has an understanding of the text which differs from that of the historical author, then many texts have no interpretative authors. Some may not have them simply be-cause no one else but the historical author is acquainted with them. Others may not have them because all of the audiences acquainted with the texts understand them in the ways in which the historical authors understood them.

On the other hand, if the interpretative author is understood as someone who produces an interpretation of a text to facilitate the understanding of the text by an audience, then again not all texts need to have or actually have in-terpretative authors. Many texts are semantically transparent and need no interpretation in order to be understood by an audience. Audiences contempo-raneous with the historical author and the text he produced often need no inter-pretation produced by someone else to understand the text. Only when the text is extraordinarily complex or the audience is contextually separated from the text are interpretations needed. Of course, if the audience of a text is composed of persons not familiar with the language used in the text, an interpretation in the form of a translation is necessary even in cases when the text in question is simple and clear.

We can see, then, that the question of whether all or any texts have authors depends very much on the identity of the author and the way the question is understood. Once these matters are clarified, it becomes evident that all texts have causes. We also know that all texts have historical authors but only some have composite authors and interpretative authors. They have interpretative authors when these are understood either as authors who differ in their understanding of the historical texts from the understandings the historical authors had of them or who produce interpretations of historical texts for the sake of audiences.

The notion of author I have proposed is very general, so there can be not only authors of works and complex texts but also of simple texts and even of signs. Thus, for example, it is possible for someone to be the author of individual signs in an artificial language, as long as the signs in question are new in some way. Likewise, there are authors of short texts that function as signs when signs are understood as notices, such as the 'No smoking' sign posted in my classroom and of short texts that are not signs in this sense, as when I say, "I visited Egypt four years ago." In this chapter in particular I have been speaking of the author in reference to texts, but the understanding implicit in what has been said allows for the extension of this notion to signs and works.

The views of some recent philosophers, however, would seem to go contrary to this conception of authorship. For some, only complex texts have authors and for others only works do so. In this sense, to be an author implies more than just being the creator of a text; it involves whatever is meant by saying that one has created a work or a particularly complex text.

One of the reasons behind the desire of some contemporary philosophers to say that only certain texts have authors is that they hold literary texts as paradigmatic of textuality, where indeed the legitimate range of interpretations is usually broad. I suspect that they do this because somehow they believe that in literature one finds the epitome of textual creativity. And they may be right to some extent in this belief, insofar as literature imposes fewer constraints on its practitioners than, say, philosophy or science. But they are wrong in maintaining that texts that allow for a lesser range of legitimate interpretations and display less originality can have no authors. They have authors indeed, even though those authors may be less creative than the authors of other texts.

IV.   Repressive Character of the Author

Another important reason why some recent philosophers have argued against the need or desirability to posit authors of texts is that they see the function of authors as fundamentally repressive.[63] Although views on this matter differ widely, the repression in question is interpreted as a kind of limitation on the parameters within which a text may be understood and as an imposition of a certain understanding of a text on an audience. The figure of the author closes the range of possible understandings of a text. This point has been made in many ways, but it can be easily illustrated by saying that, if a text is identified as having been composed by a particular author, our knowledge and opinion of the author, his views and authority, will impose boundaries on the ways the text may be understood, so that other ways of understanding it may be regarded as spurious or illegitimate. This not only limits the freedom of the audience, sub-jugating and dominating it in various ways, but also may prevent a deeper and broader understanding of the text, for the text is seen, then, only as an expres-sion of an agent that reveals to us something about that agent.[64] Thus, for ex-ample, the so-called *Theology of Aristotle* was believed in the Middle Ages to be a work by Aristotle, and this biased scholastics toward a certain under-standing of the text of that work, not only producing historically incorrect in-terpretations of it but also curtailing the freedom of those who sought to understand it. Now that we know the work does not belong to Aristotle, we have been able to appreciate its strong Neo-Platonic flavor.

The author accused of exercising repression is what I called earlier the pseudo-historical author; it is this author that functions epistemically, influ-encing the way an audience may understand a text. It makes no sense to speak of the historical author as repressive, because this author is simply the person who produced the historical text, and everything we know about him is part of the pseudo-historical author. The historical author has no epistemic signifi-cance; he exists epistemically only through the pseudo-historical author. The historical author is a metaphysical entity, but epistemically he is the author-I-know-not-who.

Likewise, it does not make sense to speak of the composite author as re-pressive, for this author too has no epistemic significance. The only way in which one could speak of the composite author as repressive is insofar as in producing the contemporary text—which may or may not differ from the his-torical text—he shapes the object of understanding. A certain edition of a text, for example, will allow only a certain range of understandings, which may or may not coincide with the range allowed by a different edition.

Finally, the interpretative author may effect closure if taken as the pro-ducer of an interpretation for the sake of an audience. Insofar as an interpreta-tion yields a certain understanding or range of understandings of a text, it influences those who come into contact with it and thus stands in the way of other and different understandings. In many ways the work of scholars, partic-ularly "authoritative" ones, imposes or can impose as many, or even more, lim-its on the understanding of texts as those imposed by pseudo-historical authors. In what follows, however, I will discuss primarily the repressive character of the pseudo-historical author, for it is this author that more clearly can function repressively, and it is this author that is identified in the literature as repressive, although generally without recognition of its true pseudo-historical nature.

One need not advocate the extreme view that texts have no historical authors to avoid the repression associated with authorship. A more reasonable approach, easily documented in contemporary literature is that a text should be understood apart from what we know about the historical author, that is, independent of the pseudo-historical author, even though, indeed, one accepts that there is a historical author of the text. The text is supposed to speak to the audience for itself, independent of any relationship that it may have with the pseudo-historical author; that is, with what we know about the historical author. For, once a text is seen as belonging to an author, the understanding of the audience is limited in certain ways and channeled in certain directions.

This point of view makes quite a bit of sense in the context of a descriptivist view of proper names. Descriptivist views of proper names hold that proper names have meaning in addition to reference and thus are no different from definite descriptions.[65] Consider the case of Socrates, for example. According to descriptivists, 'Socrates' *refers* to Socrates but *means*, say, "the teacher of Plato." Moreover, they argue that what determines the reference of a proper name is precisely its meaning. So that 'Socrates' refers to Socrates precisely because it means "the teacher of Plato." If 'Socrates' meant "the most famous disciple of Plato," then it would refer instead to Aristotle. We need not get involved in the intricacies of the descriptivist theory to see that such a theory lends support to the view that the use of the name of an author in connection with a text imposes on the audience of the text certain limitations and leads in certain definite interpretative directions.

One obvious way to argue against the view that the use of the name of the author in connection with a text is repressive, is to adopt a referential theory of proper names. The referential view holds that proper names have reference but no meaning or, to put it as some who support this view do, that their meaning is their reference.[66] The meaning of 'Socrates' is simply Socrates and not the sorts of descriptions that descriptivists claim. This is, so referentialists hold, the primary feature of proper names and the one that distinguishes them from common names. Naturally, if the use of a name does not carry with it any kind of descriptive baggage, it becomes very difficult to argue that the attribution of a text to an author somehow limits the audience's understanding of it or directs such an understanding along certain ways.

If either of these theories were accepted, the task of deciding on the repressive character of the author would be easier. The recent literature on proper names, however, has made clear that neither of these theories is unassailable. This has given rise to other views. Among these, the most popular is the so-called causal theory of proper names.[67] The main tenets of this theory are three:

(1) proper names have reference but no meaning; (2) the reference of proper names is initially fixed through descriptions, but the names are not subsequently or necessarily tied to those or any other descriptions; and (3) after the reference of the proper name has been fixed in an initial act (called by proponents of this view *baptism*), reference is fixed through a causal chain of communication in which speakers who learn the name must intend to use it to refer to the bearer of the name intended by the person from whom they learned it, all the way back to the original baptism.

Elsewhere I have argued that none of these three theories is acceptable in the form in which it is usually presented.[68] My objection to them is that they tend to emphasize only one aspect of the problem involved in the meaning and reference of proper names, neglecting the others. Because I have already dealt with these matters at some length, it is not necessary for me to dwell on them here. It should suffice to point out that the view I propose, which I call the *threefold view,* holds that three questions must be answered in this matter: (1) What is the function of proper names? (2) How are proper names established? (3) How do language users learn to use proper names effectively? The answer to the first is that the function of proper names is to refer. The answer to the second is that proper names are established through a kind of baptism. And the answer to the third is that language users learn to use proper names through descriptions.

When we apply this view to the question of repression concerning the use of the name of an author in connection with a text, we see that, indeed, as with the descriptivist position, there is room for limitation and thus repression. For, although the function of proper names is not to describe but to refer, we learn to use them through descriptions, and memories of those descriptions may color our understanding of texts. This means that I cannot develop an effective argument against those who hold the use of the name of an author in connection with a text to be repressive, based on the theory of proper names I find most acceptable. I must, then, either accept that such use is repressive or adopt a different strategy. Because I am not convinced that we must give in to the theory of repression so easily, I propose to take the second course of action.

My strategy consists in arguing that the theory of the repressive character of the author relies on a faulty assumption, and once this assumption is eliminated the necessity with which those who favor this theory see the author as repressive disappears. The assumption in question is that to limit the range of understanding of texts is somehow necessarily bad because it curtails the creativity of the audience in its effort to understand a text. This assumption is true only if the aim of the audience is exclusively creative, but that is not the aim of the audience in most, let alone all, cases. Although creativity is desirable and must be encouraged, it is certainly not a good thing in every situation. There are good and bad ways to be creative, depending on the goals being pursued. For example, a surgeon who is operating on someone, should by all means be encouraged to be creative *insofar as* the novel procedures introduced are conducive to the well-being and prompt recovery of the patient. A new way to perform the operation that, say, diminishes bleeding, should certainly be encouraged. But I do not think anyone would want to encourage the surgeon to be novel and creative in a way that would produce excessive bleeding, thus harming the patient. Unbridled creativity is not necessarily a good thing for surgeons. Indeed, most surgical training is geared to teach surgeons tested procedures to which they should adhere in the practice of their craft. The introduction of experimental procedures is no doubt to be encouraged also, otherwise surgeons would still be operating as they did long ago and no progress in surgery would have been made, but such experimental procedures are to be encouraged only within well-defined boundaries, where goals are clearly stated and pursued.

If we apply what has been said concerning surgeons and operations to audiences and their understanding of texts, it becomes clear that the imposition of limitations on the interpretation of texts is not necessarily nefarious. Whether creativity in understanding is or is not a bad thing will depend on the goal or goals that such an understanding is to achieve. If the goal of such an understanding is to grasp what the author had in mind when he produced the text or what the audience contemporaneous with the author understood when it understood the text and so on, then it is clear that any limitation that will facilitate the achievement of those goals will be good, whereas those that do not will be bad. If, for example, my aim is to understand how Plato's contemporaries understood the text of the *Timaeus*, it would help to limit the parameters of its meaning by a consideration of the cultural context within which the dialogue was produced. To attempt to understand the dialogue apart from its cultural location would make no historical sense.

Of course, if the goal of my reading of the text of the *Timaeus* is not to understand what Plato meant and was understood by his contemporaries, but rather to test my creativity, to see what I can do with a text, then any limitations imposed by a knowledge about the author would hamper that aim and thus be nefarious. The imposition of limitations on the understanding of texts is not necessarily bad and, consequently, neither are the limitations that the consideration of its author may impose.

This conclusion, however, does not entail that the consideration of the author is always beneficial. In some cases the consideration of the author may indeed be pernicious in the sense that it promotes understandings and uses of a text that are not conducive to the understanding that is sought. An interesting case of this situation occurred in the Middle Ages. The author of *Fons vitae* was a Jew by the name of Ibn Gabirol. Yet in the Middle Ages he was thought to be a Christian, called Avicebron. Naturally, the result of this confusion was not only that the use of the *Fons vitae* was not objectionable to Christian theologians—indeed it became quite popular at the time—but the work was understood in Christian terms. The misunderstanding concerning the author of the text made possible its survival, but it also distanced the scholastic understandings of the text from whatever Ibn Gabirol intended or his contemporaneous audience grasped through the text.

I have argued that the function of the use of an author's name and what we know about the historical author, namely, what I call the pseudo-historical author, in connection with a text is neither necessarily repressive nor necessarily beneficial and thus, by implication, that it can be repressive or beneficial, depending on the goals being pursued and the circumstances involved. Those goals and circumstances also determine what aspects of the pseudo-historical author prove repressive or beneficial. For example, if the aim is to understand the philosophical point of view expressed by a text, it would seem both pertinent and beneficial to consider other philosophical texts believed to have been produced by the pseudo-historical author. On the other hand, it might be of no use, and perhaps even pernicious, to consider the personal psychological idiosyncrasies of the author.[69]

There is, therefore, a good deal of sense in the notion that authorship is repressive, but the current balance of opinion has swung too far in that direction. There are both beneficial and nefarious effects of authorship and both have to be taken into account in a sensible theory of texts and their relations to authors and audiences. Needless to say, the nefarious or beneficial effects of authorship depend to a great extent on the accuracy with which the pseudo-historical author known by the audience reflects the historical author as well as on the purposes for which a text is used. Accuracy concerning the pseudo-historical author entails knowledge of the historical author as a subject, and therefore we need to turn next to the author's subjectivity.

V.   Subjectivity of the Author

Most of the recent controversy surrounding the authors of texts has centered on the notion of subjectivity and what that implies for the understanding and interpretation of texts. It is generally accepted that authors are subjects, something which I do not wish to dispute. What is not always clear—hence the controversy—is, first, what subjectivity is and the role it plays in the production of a text and, second, to which of the authors of a text it applies. I shall begin by discussing subjectivity and then turn to the authors to which it may apply.

Much of the contemporary discussion of this notion is opaque partly as a result of the poetic language frequently used in connection with it and partly because an attempt is seldom made at distinguishing various types of subjectivity. I shall try to clarify matters both by avoiding the use of metaphorical language and by distinguishing up front among various types of subjectivity that may be applied to the author of a text.

Subjectivity in general has to do with what is underneath, a fact revealed by the etymology of the term 'subject,' from which 'subjectivity' is derived. 'Subject' comes from *subjectum*, which in Latin refers to what is lying under. In spite of this very general understanding of the term, the notion of subject varies from discipline to discipline. In grammar, the subject is opposed to the predicate and consists of a part of a sentence that is syntactically determined. In logic, also, the subject is opposed to the predicate, but its determination is not based on syntax, rather it has to do with logical form. Thus, what is a grammatical subject may not always be a logical one and vice versa. In ethics, the subject may be understood in at least two ways. In one way, it is the initiator of action, and in another, it is the receiver of action. In metaphysics, the subject has been interpreted in widely different ways, but it is frequently opposed to features (properties, accidents, qualities, characteristics) and is said to be that in which those features inhere or to which they adhere.

Some of these understandings of subject are relevant for the understanding of 'author.' The ethical notion of subject as initiator of action applies to the author, who indeed produces the text. Authors are also subjects in the metaphysical sense of having features that are related to the texts they produce. Finally, the logical and grammatical notions of subject also apply to authors, since the term 'author' can become the grammatical subject of a sentence and the notion of subject can function as logical subject. None of these understandings of what it is to be a subject, however, has attracted as much attention in philosophical discussions concerned with authors as the epistemic notion of subject. The reason for this should be obvious: Texts are used for communication, and communication has to do with knowledge.

The single most important feature of a subject considered epistemically is that it displays consciousness. Much has been written about the ontology of consciousness, that is, about whether it is a relation, a state, a quality, and so on. All that, although philosophically interesting, has little to do with the issue that concerns us here, so I shall ignore it. For our purposes it is sufficient to understand consciousness as a kind of awareness. Some philosophers have identified consciousness with self-consciousness, so that to be conscious is always to be conscious of oneself. This understanding of consciousness, however, is too restrictive, for we can be conscious of things other than ourselves without in fact being conscious of ourselves. I can, for example, be aware of the paper on which I am writing without being aware of myself.

Consciousness is not a passive activity in which a subject acts simply as the receptor of whatever he or she is conscious of. Indeed, many philosophers have noted that there are both active and passive aspects in consciousness.

Aristotle clearly indicated that the workings of the mind involve both active and passive elements, and some medieval authors, following him, noted that even in an act of awareness (simple apprehension) a part of the mind actively abstracts from the data it receives to grasp it passively—and all this before engaging in any kind of judgment.[70] The point at stake is that even grasping the presence of an object involves a process of fitting that object into some kind of categorial structure of concepts. Indeed, this extends to the most basic perceptions. One perceives pain or pleasure, red or blue, and so on, which entails a categorization of the perception in some way. Thus, even if a subject, considered epistemically, is not involved in any outwardly noticeable activity, it is engaged in an active role of categorization, fitting the perception into the conceptual and experiential framework it possesses.

This means that a subject brings to a text a conceptual and experiential framework that has much influence on how the subject relates to the text itself. The subjectivity of an author, then, is precisely the framework of concepts and experiences that make a subject what he or she is and how that subject views the world.[71]

What I have in mind here is not the sort of general categorial scheme that functions as a grid of experience for Kant. If Kant is right, that scheme is something that also must affect the production of a text, but it does so in a general way, which is common to all subjects. Nor do I mean the common cultural and social categories that a subject shares with other subjects who belong to the same culture or social group. For, again, these are common factors to many subjects and, therefore, display a certain objectivity and public character that true subjectivity lacks. What I have in mind concerning subjectivity is rather the peculiar elements that each individual subject brings to consciousness and thus influence the unique way in which he or she views the world. This kind of personal framework makes each subject interpret the same picture in different ways and thus understand his or her surroundings differently.[72]

Having presented a brief characterization of subjectivity, we must now determine to which of the authors discussed earlier subjectivity applies and how it does so in relation to texts. There is no difficulty with the application of subjectivity to both the historical author and the composite author, for both of these are persons or groups of persons who bring to the production (in the case of the historical author) and to the reconstruction (in the case of the composite author) a complex conceptual and experiential framework that influences how they construct or reconstruct the text. The text in this context must be seen as the locus of the confluence of various factors: the objects or features of objects selected as signs by the author, the meanings the author wishes to convey, the author's views concerning the audience of the text, the author's awareness of the contextual factors relevant to the text, and the whole conceptual and experiential framework that constitutes the uniqueness of the subject, his or her subjectivity. The consciousness of the author functions as a caldron where the text is produced, and in that consciousness many of the disparate elements that determine the meaning of a text are to be found.

It should be obvious, then, that the subjectivity of both the historical and the composite authors are determining factors in the shapes that the historical and contemporary texts finally take. As such, those subjectivities have a direct influence on the texts in question.

By contrast, the subjectivity of the interpretative author has no direct bearing on the text; its direct influence is exercised over the understanding of the text derived by the interpretative author himself or by the audience for which he produces an interpretation. It follows from the conception of the interpretative author I have presented that the interpretative author has a direct influence on the understanding of a text by an audience, regardless of whether he is conceived as an audience that understands the text or as the creator of an interpretation intended to make an audience understand the text. In either case, the complex framework of concepts and experiences of the interpreter will have a bearing on the understanding of the text by the audience. In the first case this is so because that subjectivity directly affects how the interpreter himself understands the text and in the second, because that subjectivity directly affects the interpretation produced by the interpreter, which in turn directly affects the understanding derived by the audience. Of course, in the latter sense the influence on the audience's understanding is indirect, through the influence of the interpretation.

The case with the pseudo-historical author is different, however. The pseudo-historical author does not seem to have any subjectivity at all, a fact that precludes his subjectivity from influencing the understanding of the text by the audience. For the pseudo-historical author is not a person but a mental construct entertained by the interpretative author. How can my view of Aristotle, for instance, be said to have any subjectivity? The answer to this question is that, strictly speaking, the pseudo-historical author has no subjectivity, and therefore, his subjectivity could not affect the understanding of a text. The only way in which a pseudo-historical author affects the understanding of a text is through the interpretative author. If any subjectivity is involved in this process, it is the subjectivity of the interpretative author and not that of the pseudo-historical author.

There is nothing mystical about the subjectivity of the author. The subjectivity of an author is no more than the epistemically relevant features of authors and of the contexts within which they produce texts as they see them. Yet, although not mysterious, this subjectivity is tremendously important and influential when it comes to the significance of a text, for it is in this context that the text makes the sense intended to be conveyed by its historical author. Moreover, it is a largely intangible element whose role in the creation of a text and in its interpretation is most difficult to ascertain. It is not mysterious, because there is nothing incomprehensible or irrational about it that defies explanation, but it is most often beyond our capacity to reach it when it belongs to anyone other than ourselves. Indeed, even when it does belong to us, it is difficult to unravel because of our immersion in it and the difficulties involved in objectifying it. If in order to grasp it the subjectivity of the author must be objectified, it is perhaps impossible to grasp it without changing it—thus making it virtually inaccessible. Some psychologists, like Freud, see even deeper and inaccessible unconscious aspects in human subjectivity. If their views are correct, then the subjectivity of authors is largely beyond our reach.

VI.   Conclusion

By way of conclusion, let me recount briefly the main points made in this chapter. I began by posing a series of questions concerning authors and their relations to texts. The first and perhaps most pressing of these has to do with the identity of the author, for upon close examination it turns out that when we speak of authors we may mean widely different things. Texts themselves are multiple, so it is only to be expected that there be also many authors. I identify four. The historical author is the person who produces the historical text, and, although most often this author is a single person, in many cases this is not so. I argue, moreover, that authorial identity must be distinguished from personal identity. It is quite possible—indeed frequent—that the same person may have produced two different texts, but the conditions under which the first text was produced are such that under those same conditions the same person could not have produced the second text. Thus, the identity of the authors who produce a text may be different even though the identity of the persons is the same.

What we know about the historical author is usually quite limited, so we must distinguish between him and the pseudo-historical author. The latter is either a composite of what we know or think we know about a historical author, or the persona the historical author wishes us to believe composed the historical text. Most of us have different information and perspectives, so there are many pseudo-historical authors in the first sense noted, as many as the different conceptions audiences have of him. The pseudo-historical author never exists in reality outside the mind of some person or persons, but he exercises epistemic influence over the audience.

The composite author is the author of the contemporary text. It is composed of all those who in one way or another, as editors, scribes, and so on, helped put together the version of the historical text we have. Depending on the state and history of the historical text, this group of authors is tremendously important.

Finally, the interpretative author is the author of the ideal text. He is the person or persons who set out to reconstruct the historical text using various criteria.

Perhaps the most important question concerning authors has to do with their function, and therefore I devote a good portion of the chapter to this topic. The view I defend is that authors are the creators of texts and must be distinguished from their users. The creator of a text is someone who puts together an individual instance of a universal text that has not been instantiated before. Creation has to do with novelty in the production of something separate and other from the producer. It does not involve, in this case, the production of something out of nothing, but only the production of something new and separate. The novelty in question, in the case of a universal text can be in the signs of which the text is composed, in their arrangement, or in the meaning of the text. In the case of an individual text, the differences may have to do with those specified for universal texts or with the conditions of individuality and continuous existence. It is not, however, the creation of any instance of a universal text that makes someone an author, but the creation of the first historical instance of a universal text.

Strictly speaking, the conditions of authorship are those we have specified. However, because there is always the possibility that more than one author may simultaneously create first instances of a universal text, and it is also possible that one may have created an instance of a universal text of which other instances had been produced before, without knowledge of such instances, it would seem that in some cases there may be more than one author of a text. That is, it is possible that there be more than one author when this is understood distributively rather than collectively. Yet, although we may be willing to accept multiple authorship in cases of simultaneous creation, in cases of nonsimultaneous creation we regard the creator of the first temporally produced text as the author. This indicates the historical and contextual nature of authorship. Authorship always occurs at a certain time and within particular circumstances.

After the question of authorial function comes the question of whether authors are necessary for texts. We found that this apparently straightforward question could be unpacked into two other questions, one concerned with the existence of texts without causes that bring them about and the other concerning the need for someone who selects and arranges the signs of which a text is composed with the intention of conveying some specific meaning to an audience in certain circumstances. The answer to the first question was that texts, like anything else, cannot exist without causes that bring them about. In answering the second question also, we found out that texts cannot exist without authors, for what appear to be texts without authors lack meaning and thus turn out not to be texts.

Next I took up the alleged repressive character of authors. By this is meant that knowledge of the author of a text, whether correct or incorrect, tends to impose limitations on the way one may understand the text and thus limits the interpretative freedom of the audience. The conclusion of the discussion was that knowledge of the author of a text can be repressive but that it can also be helpful, depending on the end pursued by the audience. If what the audience seeks is to discover what authors understood when they understood the texts in question, then accurate knowledge about the authors cannot be other than helpful. On the other hand, if the aim of the audience is to give free reign to its interpretative fancy, then such information would turn out to be counterproductive.

Finally, I discussed the question of the author's subjectivity and its relevance for the understanding of texts. I understand subjectivity as the unique framework of concepts and experiences that influences how a subject views the world. The author's subjectivity, then, consists of the epistemically relevant features of authors and the contexts within which they produce texts in various ways. There is nothing mysterious about subjectivity understood thus, even though it may not be possible for those other than the subject or even the subject himself or herself in certain circumstances, to know it.

Texts are produced by authors to convey meaning to audiences. Therefore, having discussed authorship, we must now turn to the audience.

4

AUDIENCE

The audience is the real or imaginary group of persons who are in fact acquainted, could be acquainted, or are meant to be acquainted with a given text. Etymologically, the term 'audience' refers to a group of listeners. This meaning of the term goes back to a time when the primary form of acquaintance with the work of an author was through the spoken word. From the invention of the printing press until the time when the use of the radio became widespread, however, written texts were the primary way of learning about an author's work. And, although contemporary media have changed that to a certain extent, in science and the humanities it is still true that the audience for an author's work consists largely of readers. For my present purposes, the distinction between readers and listeners is immaterial and, hence, I often refer to an audience as a group of readers, although what I say about it applies, mutatis mutandis, to listeners as well.

The notion of audience raises all sorts of interesting philosophical issues. Perhaps the most obvious of these is whether texts must have audiences at all. Some authors claim that they do not, because they themselves have no audience in mind when they compose a text. Yet, if texts are intended to convey meaning, it would appear that they must at least be intended for audiences. How is this conflict to be resolved? Adding to the puzzle is the question of the identity of the audience. Is the audience whoever is intended by the author to understand the text? Is the audience whoever actually comes into contact with the text? Or is the audience whoever potentially could come into contact with the text? Apart from this, because audiences are composed of individual persons, we must ask how these individual persons are related and whether their understanding of texts is to be taken collectively or distributively.[1]

Moreover, the understanding of texts varies from person to person, implying differences between the way in which the author understands the text and the ways others understand it. Does this imply that audiences always distort the meaning of texts? Is there an adversarial relationship between audiences and authors? Can audiences intentionally misunderstand texts, or is their misunderstanding always unintentional? And if it is intentional, as it appears to be in some cases, does that not create a problem, for an intentional misunderstanding seems to imply a correct understanding? Finally, the way particular audiences relate to texts depends to a great extent on the fact that audiences are, or are composed of, subjects, and subjects bring with them their subjectivity. But how is the subjectivity of audiences to be understood, and what role does it play in an audience's understanding of texts? Does subjectivity always determine understanding, and if so, does it lead inexorably to misunderstanding?

Some of the issues raised by the consideration of audiences have to do with audiences themselves considered apart from any relation they may have to texts, but others arise precisely when one tries to provide an account of the relation between audiences and texts. My concern in this book is with texts, so the latter sorts of issues are more pertinent. However, some of these latter issues cannot be discussed, or discussed well, without reference to the solution of the former issues. I shall, therefore, address issues of both sorts. Five issues in particular seem pertinent and in some ways correspond to some of the issues raised concerning authors in the preceding chapter: the identity of the audience, the function of the audience, the need for an audience, the audience's subjectivity, and the subversive and repressive character of the audience.

I.   Identity of the Audience

In the preceding remarks I have been speaking of the audience of a text as if the audience's identity were clear. And, indeed, in many ways we all have some idea of what an audience is. A bit of reflection reveals, however, differences among various types of audiences that prove significant for the understanding of the relation between a text and its audience. I shall begin then, by attempting to clarify the identity of the audience. First, I shall take up the different types of audiences that a text may have and, second, I shall discuss the number of persons that may compose them.

A.   Types of Audience

There are at least five different types of audiences for a text. I have named them as follows: author as audience, intended audience, contemporaneous audience, intermediary audience, and contemporary audience.

1.   *Author as Audience*

From the moment an author has put something down in writing, has said something, or even has thought about the parts of the text he is composing that are already established, even if only provisionally, and goes back to what he has written, said, or thought, he becomes an audience.[2] If the text is written, it acquires a status more independent from the author than if it is spoken or thought. But even a spoken text or a thought text could be examined by an author as an audience examines it when it is recorded on a tape or in the author's memory.

In all cases, the author who approaches the text he has composed may function as audience insofar as he goes to the text with the aim of understanding it. Indeed, the whole process of composing a text involves the author in a continuous switching back and forth between the roles of author and audience, whether as writer and reader, speaker and listener, or thinker and rememberer. To see the effect of what he says and how he says it, he needs to look at it as an observer rather than a composer.[3]

In many ways, the effectiveness of authors depends on their dexterity at this switching of roles and understanding the needs of an audience. Good writers, for example, say only what needs to be said to convey a certain meaning; they use what the audience already knows to determine what to write; they are economical and effective. Bad writers, on the other hand, repeat material the audience already knows and fail to say what is necessary for understanding—they are thus boring or unclear. The ability of the author, then, to become the audience and see his own work as an audience would, is vital to making his writing effective. There is nothing paradoxical or odd in considering the author as the audience, although he cannot be the audience precisely insofar as he plays the role of author. Only insofar as an acquaintance and identification with the needs of the audience help him in his role of author properly speaking can the author be the audience.

Even where the author does not compose a text with an audience in mind, as is the case of the pratitioners of the *nouveau roman*, for example, the process of composition, revision, and correction force upon him the role of audience. The difference is that in such cases the author does not seek to impersonate someone other than himself whom he, consciously or unconsciously, identifies as the audience of the work. Yet, the critical stance that leads him to make changes in the text indicates that he has distanced himself from the text and adopted the role of audience.

But what of the case of an author who produces a text in a stream of consciousness, mechanically, without ever going back to it? Or consider the case of an author like Sartre, who is reputed to have written *Critique of Dialectical Reason* without going back to what he had written, because he did not care to revise, to keep what he had said consistent, and so on? Can it still be argued that the author functions as audience in these cases? The answer is affirmative, for even in these unusual cases the production of a text involves additions of signs to previous signs and thus changes of overall arrangement in previous sign arrangements, implying an understanding of those previous signs and sign arrangements. This assumes, of course, that what is being produced is a text. If what is being produced are disconnected signs and there is no resulting text, then we might be tempted to conclude that the author does not function as audience. But even in this circumstance, although not an audience of a text, in most cases the author would still function as audience of signs or parts of signs.

The reason is that most signs are composites of sounds or symbols and thus their completion involves some awareness and memory in the process of production of their components.

Consider someone who is producing a sentence such as the following: "Having arrived at this point in my deliberations, I need to reflect further on the problem in order to find new ways of solving it that will not only satisfy my craving for clarity and adequacy but also. . . ." And let us suppose that the person who got as far as the 'also' that marks the end of the sentence as we have it is the author of the text. It stands to reason that, to complete the sentence, the author will have to have present in his mind in some sense the first part of the sentence, understanding what it means and thus act as an audience with respect to it. How could he otherwise complete the sentence? Indeed, because in most cases texts are composed of natural languages whose use prescribes the use of certain signs in determinate arrangements, it is necessary for users of those languages to be aware of the signs and the arrangements they have produced in order to add to them further signs and produce different overall arrangements. And this procedure entails a role of audience even for those who are engaged in the production of texts and are, therefore, authors. The point, then, is that to be an author entails also playing the role of audience. The reverse is not true, however, for the active role audiences have to play in the understanding of texts does not generally entail authorship, unless we are speaking of audiences as interpreters.[4]

An author may function as audience in processes other than that of composition. After a text has been completed, an author often goes back to it, interpreting and judging it, thus assuming the role of audience in still another sense. The classic case in contemporary philosophy is Wittgenstein, who seems to have been concerned in his later career with attacking some of the theses he had defended in his earlier writings.[5] A more common example is that of an author who, after writing a book, spends some of his time clarifying or defending what he said in it.

Knowledge of the historical author of a text can be both helpful and harmful to those who seek an accurate understanding of a historical text. It can be harmful insofar as a distorted picture of that author, that is, a very inaccurate pseudo-historical author or an accurate but partial pseudo-historical author, can be misleading. But in some cases it can also be helpful. Naturally, because the author also may function as audience, knowledge of the author as audience may be likewise helpful or harmful to other audiences who seek to understand a text.

2.   *Intended Audience*

The intended audience is the person or group of persons for whom the author composes the text.[6] The author may sometimes ostensibly dedicate a work to someone. In that case he probably intends for that person to read it, if we are dealing with a written text, and either profit by it or do something for the author. Many famous books, and not a few infamous ones, were dedicated to powerful figures from whom the authors sought fortune, protection, and other favors. And many others were intended for the edification of those to whom they were dedicated.

Apart from persons to whom a work may be explicitly dedicated, authors often have in mind specific groups of persons as audience. Philosophers usually write for other philosophers, scientists for scientists, and so on and frequently even for small groups within those classes. Only literary authors generally aim for a wider audience, but even then there are audience restrictions that have to do with education, culture, and language, among others.

It is not necessarily the case that the intended audience of a text be the person or persons to whom the text is addressed. Authors often say and write things for persons other than the ones to whom they speak and for whom they ostensibly write them.[7] When the president of the United States, for example, speaks to a group of farmers in Iowa and says something threatening about subsidized farming in Europe, his intended audience probably includes the political leaders of the nations who subsidize farming in Europe and is not restricted to, or perhaps even intended to be, necessarily the farmers to whom he is speaking.

What distinguishes the intended audience from the three that still remain to be discussed is that the intended audience need not become acquainted with the text in question or even exist at all. The intended audience may never come into contact with the text and may in fact be no more than a figment of the author's imagination. There may be no persons of the sort intended as audience by the author, and if there are, there is no assurance they will ever encounter the text. Incidentally, it should not be taken for granted that the intended audience is always contemporary with the author. Many authors feel that their contemporaries cannot understand them and thus write for future generations. A case in point is Rousseau.

An understanding of the intended audience helps other audiences in the understanding of a text, for it presents them with the person or group of persons that the author thought would be most affected by the text. In that sense, the intended audience indirectly reveals some of the author's intentions and how the text should be approached. If, for example, we know that a text is intended for professional philosophers who work within a certain philosophical tradition and share certain assumptions about method, we will be in a better position to understand and evaluate the text than if we do not. For then it would be easier for us to supply those methodological assumptions that the author took for granted the audience would supply.

3. *Contemporaneous Audience*

The contemporaneous audience is composed of all those persons who are contemporaneous with the historical author and have become or could become acquainted with the text. They share with the author much that other, later audiences do not share with him. Living during the same time period, even if in a different country and culture, would seem to entail some basic and common elements, although this may not always be the case. Qua audience, an illiterate tribesman will have very little in common with a Nobel laureate in literature even if they are contemporaries, and it is probably true that, conceptually, a contemporary Aristotelian will have more in common with Aristotle than with a self-proclaimed postmodernist.

By the *contemporaneous audience,* then, I do not mean to refer to persons who are culturally and educationally far removed from the historical author. I mean members of his and similar social groups who have the basic educational and cultural tools to be in principle capable of understanding the text in question and who are roughly contemporaneous with the author.[8] Under these conditions, this audience is better prepared to understand the text than subsequent audiences.

The contemporaneous audience may be the intended audience in cases in which the author of a text identifies his cultural, educational, and temporal contemporaries with the audience of the text. But it need not be so. The intended audience may be only one of the members of the contemporaneous audience or only a subgroup of that audience. Or it may turn out that the author intends as audience a future person or group of persons, as noted earlier.

Knowledge of the contemporaneous audience of a text can be very helpful to those who seek to understand the text, provided such knowledge is accurate. It is reasonable to suppose that the common cultural and social context shared by the author and the contemporaneous audience determines to a great extent the rules and procedures for the composition and understanding of texts under which both the author and the audience operate. The language used by the author, for example, is also in most cases the language of the contemporaneous audience. We can learn much about Plato's dialogues if we know something about Athens at the time he wrote them and the kind of Greek spoken and written at the time, as well as about the cultural and social mores of the period. If the knowledge one has of the contemporaneous audience of a text is not accurate, however, then it may mislead rather than help in the determination of a text's meaning.

4. *Intermediary Audience*

The intermediary audience consists of the group of persons who have or may have become acquainted with the text, but who are neither contemporaneous with the author nor contemporaries of those who are trying to understand the text. They are, therefore, separated from the author not only by individual idiosyncrasies but also by time. Living at a different time and under different conditions, the context within which they would approach the text is different from that of the historical author's contemporaneous audience and it is also different from the context in which the interpreter's contemporaries will read it. How different the context is will vary not only with the temporal separation between the intermediary audience and the moment at which the historical text was produced, but also with the degree to which the ideological assumptions and climate of the age have changed. Temporal distance is not directly proportional to conceptual distance. Some temporally very distant ages may be closer together conceptually than other ages that are temporally closer.

Knowledge of this audience is helpful to interpreters only where intermediary audiences have produced interpretations of the historical text and such interpretations survive. In these cases, knowledge of the intermediary audience may help in the understanding of the interpretations of the historical text they produced and thus indirectly help in the understanding of the historical text. This is possible, of course, because they are contextually closer to interpreters than the author and the contemporaneous audience. If the intermediary audiences did not produce interpretations or such interpretations have not survived, then there is nothing that knowledge of them can contribute to later understandings of the text. The role of intermediary audiences is very important in the process of transmission and understanding of texts from past ages far removed from the time when an interpreter is seeking to understand those texts.

5.   *Contemporary Audience*

The contemporary audience is composed of the group of persons who have or may become acquainted with the text and are not the author, his contemporaries, or the intermediary audience. In some cases, it will consist simply in the generation of persons that comes after the contemporaneous generation. If that is the case, then there will not be an intermediary audience between the contemporaneous and the contemporary audiences. In all other cases, however, there will be at least one generation of persons that may be acquainted with the text between the contemporaneous audience and the contemporary audience, allowing for an intermediary audience.

The difficulty for the contemporary audience to understand a historical text is not only one of temporal, cultural, or conceptual distance between the text and itself, but also the fact that it may have at its disposal interpretations of the text provided by both the contemporaneous and the intermediary audiences and sometimes even by the author himself. Furthermore, the number of interpretations tends to increase as time passes. These interpretations can be both helpful and unhelpful to the contemporary audience in developing understandings of the text. They can help insofar as they establish bridges between the contemporary audience and the historical text, but they can also be obstacles insofar as they may be mistaken and may lead the contemporary audience into directions which take it farther from rather than nearer to the meaning of the historical text.

Before I turn to the composition of the audience, it should be made clear that the distinctions among the various audiences identified here are not to be considered hard; there is some degree of overlap. For example, the contemporaneous audience may be composed of persons of different ages, some of whom one may argue could also become part of the intermediary audience, or even the contemporary audience. This possibility underscores the artificial character of these categories and, therefore, the possibility of grouping audiences in other ways or adding other categories to the ones I have presented. For example, in addition to the categories suggested, one could add that of historical audience, which would comprise the categories of author as audience and of contemporaneous audience.[9] Still others, which I do not use, are also possible. The artificial character of these categories, however, does not undermine the points I have made or the hermeneutical and heuristic usefulness of the categories.

We have discussed the various types of audiences that a text may have in terms of the identity of those who constitute them. Now we turn to the composition of the audience.

B.   Composition of the Audience

So far I have been speaking about the audience as if it always were plural, except for the case of the author (who could also be plural but about whom I have generally been speaking in singular terms). Yet the plurality of most audiences discussed could be understood in two ways: distributively, as a plurality composed of single persons who become or may become acquainted with a text in their individual privacy; or collectively, as a group understanding of texts. The latter suggests that a plurality of individual persons can come together as a whole and act collectively as audience. These considerations raise interesting questions concerning the relation between audiences and texts.

A text is like a piece of a puzzle that makes sense only as an element of a larger whole, and the audience supplies an important part of that larger whole. However, that the audience can be single or plural may entail that what is supplied by the one might be different from what is supplied by the other and, therefore, the understanding of a text by an individual person may be different from its understanding by a group. In one way this does not seem alarming. We may agree that the understanding I have of the text of the American Declaration of Independence is different in some ways from the collective understanding the American people have of it, but we may not regard this as alarming because the differences in question are not significant. On the other hand, this fact may become alarming if those differences are such that there is no hope of bringing them together in some way. After all, it is no good to me to understand a text differently than society at large understands it. If I understand a 'No Parking' sign as meaning "no parking for everyone else but myself" I will most likely get a parking ticket and will have to pay a fine.[10]

The undesirable inference that the individual person and the group have different understandings of texts is predicated on the assumption that the individual person and the group are somehow totally unconnected or at least that their connection is irrelevant or too tenuous to affect their respective understandings of texts. And there is no question that there are grounds on which to defend this assumption. After all, the understanding of an individual person appears to take place in her own mind, separate and unconnected from that of others. Understanding seems to be a private affair that can be described as acts of an individual person's mind. Thus, the understanding I have of the text of the American Declaration of Independence is mine and mine alone, known only to me in the privacy of my consciousness. By contrast, what a group understands appears to be something public, shared by all members of the group. Hence, what the text of the American Declaration of Independence means for Americans considered as a group, so the argument goes, is something public and different from what it means to me.

One way in which one might try to object to this conclusion is to argue that the fact that an understanding is public is not sufficient to make it different from a so-called private understanding. The public understanding of '$2 + 2 = 4$' is that two plus two equal four, and that is also my private understanding of it.

But this reply does not appear effective, for it might be retorted that the difference in context represented by the individual person in contrast with the group will ensure that understanding will be different. Most texts are elliptical and the context in which they are found affects their meaning as much as the signs of which they are composed and the arrangement of those signs. But the context involved in the case where an individual person understands a text is radically different from the context that the group brings to bear on the understanding of a text. The individual person has a very particular set of assumptions, beliefs, and so on that are the result of that person's past and experience. And this contrasts with the assumptions and beliefs commonly shared by the group. Because the understanding of texts depends in significant ways on the context of assumptions and beliefs within which they are placed, it stands to reason that the understanding of a text by an individual person will differ from the understanding of the same text by a group.

Those who do not wish to accept this conclusion have only two courses of action. The first (I) is to argue that there are no significant differences between an individual person and a group; the second (II) is to argue that, although there are significant differences between them, their relations are such that they make possible a community of understanding.

Let me begin with I. This view can take two forms. One (1) reduces the group to the individual persons that compose it; the other (2) reduces the individual persons to the group to which the persons belong. The first reduction (1) can be accomplished by pointing out that the group is nothing other than the persons that compose it. There is no common mind to a group over and above the minds of the persons that compose the group. Thus, whatever understanding of a text a group has is nothing other than the distributive understandings of a text the members of the group have. The difference between the understanding by an individual person and the understanding by a group of persons is simply the difference between one understanding and several understandings.

The problem with this sort of reasoning is, first, that it does not accomplish what it sets out to do. By reducing the group to the individuals of which it is composed, it does not eliminate differences of understanding among individual members of the group. Second, it fails to distinguish between understanding and the object of understanding. If understanding is an act of the mind and the object of understanding in the case of texts is their meaning, it is possible to have numerically different understandings of the same meaning.[11] And for this it is not necessary to reduce groups to individuals.

The other reductionist approach (2) tries to reduce individual persons to the group to which they belong in order to show that persons and groups can have the same understanding. This may be done by noting that what is relevant in terms of context for the understanding of texts are assumptions and beliefs, and the assumptions and beliefs of individual persons are socially derived, that is, they are the same as the common assumptions and beliefs of the group to which the persons in question belong. Thus, for understanding texts, groups and their individual members are the same, because they share common assumptions and beliefs.

The obvious mistake of this position is not that it holds our concepts have a social origin. In that it may be right, provided origin is understood correctly, although I am not prepared to defend this view here. The mistake is rather that this position rules out the possibility of having those concepts combine in the mind of individual persons in different ways from those in which they appear in the society at large or in other members of the society. Indeed, for this view to be correct, all members of the group would have to think alike and the mere possibility of a different way of thinking would have to be ruled out. But none of this accords with our experience, for we do think differently from the way other members of the groups to which we belong think, as the existence of the various arguments we have been discussing here clearly indicates. Moreover, individual persons often also disagree with views generally held by society at large.

The reduction of individual persons to the group or of the group to the individual persons that compose it is, then, undesirable. The position I would like to defend (II) holds a middle ground between these two extreme views. It accepts that there are differences between individual persons and groups that are significant when it comes to the understanding of texts, but at the same time it holds that there are important relations between these persons and groups that are also significant for such an understanding. Those relations make possible common understandings of texts.

On the one hand, I am prepared to accept that an individual person engages in acts of understanding that are separate and private and, therefore, cannot be shared by other persons or by a group. The group in fact has no acts of understanding such as those of the individual person. What is usually referred to as the "understanding of a text by a group" is some agreed upon text which is added to the original text. This is what, together with the text, I call an *interpretation*. Moreover, it is also true that an individual person has experiences that are unique and result often in views and beliefs that are idiosyncratic. These experiences are retained in the individual person's memory (or subconscious if one is willing to accept such a notion). The group, on the other hand, has no memory of the sort individuals have, where common experiences could be stored. Society's memory are archives and libraries, that is, collections of texts and records and therefore generally different from a person's memory (or subconscious), which is not primarily textual. For example, the memory I have of my college graduation consists of a series of images and experiences that do not function as signs for anything else. By contrast, the collective memory of that event consists primarily of a series of texts—newspaper articles, records, and so on—kept in various archives and libraries, although there may also be some photographs, paintings, and even films.

All this seems largely uncontroversial, but no less evident is the fact that a person's beliefs depend to a great extent on a conceptual framework inherited from society. Nor is it less evident that society depends on its members for the concepts and views it develops. The interdependence between person and group occurs at various levels. Human beings differ genetically from each other, and individual survival is also connected to other members of the group. But these and other similar relationships are not significant when it comes to the understanding of texts. For the latter what is important is that persons are socially dependent for many of the signs they use and the rules they employ to arrange them, as well as for the meanings they convey through them. In turn society depends on individual persons for the preservation of the meanings that signs are supposed to express, for the entities that make up texts are not by themselves capable of producing understanding nor do they contain or imply meanings. The individual person, therefore, is not a semantic island isolated from the mainland of social meaning nor is the group semantically separate from the individual persons that compose it. The relations between the group and its members make possible a community of understanding. This can be illustrated by the way a group arrives at an understanding of a text.

Let us take a philosophy class as a group, composed of say ten students and a faculty member, that is trying to understand Anselm's notorious argument for the existence of God. The class begins after all its members have read the text of Chapters 1–4 of the *Proslogion*. Consequently we can assume that each member of the class has an understanding, which may or may not be different from the understandings of other members of the class, of Anselm's argument. Once the class assembles and discussion begins, it becomes clear that the understandings of the text by different members of the class do not always agree. One person argues that faith is a necessary condition for the argument to work, and she bases her views on some statements at the end of Chapter 1 of the *Proslogion*. Another person argues that faith is not a necessary condition for the argument to work based on Anselm's statements at the end of Chapter 4, but grants that the argument is preceded by a statement of faith. Still another student points out that there seem to be two arguments rather than one, one given in Chapter 2 and the other in Chapter 3. And so on. What we have, then, is several understandings of the text that differ sometimes in minor and sometimes in major ways. Yet, we must not forget that even those that differ in major ways have much in common. Indeed, it is because they have much in common that disagreement is possible, for disagreement implies communication and communication entails common ground. This common ground, of course, has to do with signs and their meaning and arrangement, as well as with a context of presuppositions and beliefs that makes communication possible.

But let us further assume that, on the basis of the discussion, the class as a whole—that is, every one of its members—comes to accept the same understanding of, if not the whole text, at least some part of it. For example, let us assume that everyone in class understands how Anselm's negative and comparative formulation is significantly different and stronger than Descartes's affirmative and superlative formulation of what God is.[12] And let us assume further that this common understanding is the result of the give and take that has taken place in class. What does this common or group understanding amount to? If by *understanding* we mean an act whereby something is understood, then the common or group understanding boils down to the numerically different understandings, that is, the numerically different acts, of each member of the class; in this sense there is no one understanding, ontologically speaking, that is other than the individual acts of understanding of each person. On the other hand, if by understanding is meant the meaning that is understood, that is, the meaning understood through the individual acts of understanding, then the understanding is common to all members of the group. Finally, it is also clear that the causes of both the individual and common understandings are the group's interaction. True, it is possible that understanding could have come about in a student's mind outside class and independent of the class discussion. But in our example it was as a result of that discussion that it happened. The point, then, is that a group does have an important causal effect on individual understandings, for it confronts the individual person with views that he or she may not consider. This in turn is the result of the different conceptual contexts within which each person functions. The group makes accessible to its members contexts with which they may not be acquainted, thus expanding the semantic possibilities of a text for them.

Now let us go back to the various audiences discussed earlier and ask which of these audiences is paradigmatic of the audience of a text? It is clear that it is not the author when he acts as audience, for this is, indeed, a view for which I had to argue and which is not intuitively obvious by any means. Nor is it the contemporary audience or the intermediary audience, for those audiences vary and appear to be removed both from the text and its author in ways that prevent them from being considered paradigmatic of the audience of a text. Two remain, then, the intended audience and the contemporaneous audience. Both of these seem to have strong claims. The first because it is the audience the author had in mind, assuming he had one in mind. The second, because it is the audience that, whether or not the author had in mind an audience, most likely fits the role of audience more appropriately and is better prepared to understand the text. Both of these have strong claims, then, and I believe are generally regarded as paradigmatic.

Another point that should be noted before we move on to the next section is that the audiences of a text may also function as authors. The most obvious case is that of an audience that misunderstands a text or interprets it in idiosyncratic ways. The misunderstanding of a text by an audience involves endowing the ECTs of the historical text with a meaning different from the meaning they had in the historical text and hence the production of an interpretation that results in a new text. This is one of the roles of the interpretative author or audience as author. The second role, that of adding to a text to help others understand it, also implies an authorial role, but the resulting text is a different one. The former authorial function can apply to any of the audiences discussed previously, for they all could misunderstand the text or understand it idiosyncratically and thus function authorially. The point is not that the same person or persons may function sometimes as audience and sometimes as author. That, of course, is always possible. The point is that the same person or persons may function as audience and, in virtue of that function, when the exercise of that function results in misunderstanding or idiosyncratic understanding, may function as well as author. All this needs to be taken into account for the understanding of how audiences function in relation to texts.

II.   Function of the Audience

The general function of an audience is to understand a text; indeed, what characterizes an audience, qua audience, is that it is meant to understand a text. The author, by contrast, when acting as author, is related to a text as its creator and, therefore, has as his aim to select and arrange the signs of which the text is composed in some way that will convey a specific meaning and thus produce understanding. Of course, the ultimate goal of an author in creating a text may be more than just to produce understanding. The author may be trying to cause some behavior or emotion in the audience. Or the author may just be trying to vent a feeling. In such cases, the primary function of a text may not be to produce understanding on the part of an audience. For example, the intended effect of an order to open a door is an action on the part of the person to whom the order is given. If that person is considered to be the audience of the text, then it would seem that the function of audiences is not necessarily to understand but rather the function will depend very much on what the author of a text intends to accomplish with the text.

To this one might answer that even in these cases some understanding on the part of the audience is a prerequisite for the effective accomplishment of the author's goal.[13] Understanding in some sense is necessary for the ulterior goal to be achieved even if that goal is not understanding. Moreover, because this understanding is meant to take place on the part of the audience, the function of the audience must include understanding after all.

This answer, however, is not altogether satisfactory for my purposes, because it would still undermine the view I wish to defend; namely, that the primary function of an audience of a text is to understand the text. Indeed, if we were to rest with this answer we would have to grant that there is no primary function of audiences qua audiences, for texts have many functions other than to produce understanding and therefore affect audiences in many different ways.

A different and more effective answer involves making a distinction between the person or persons for whom a text is intended and the various roles that the person or persons in question are intended to play.[14] Putting this distinction to use, we could claim that only when such persons function in a role in which they are primarily intended to understand a text do they function as audiences. When they play other roles, they cannot be considered to be audiences properly speaking; under these circumstances whatever role they are intended to play determines who they are. Thus, an audience's function is, indeed, to understand a text even if the aim of the text is to produce some other effect in the person or persons for whom it is intended.

Let me give an example. When person P_1 says to person P_2, "Clean the house in this way," P_1 intends P_2 to function as a servant who carries out P_1's orders. In that capacity, P_2 is not an audience. However, P_1's action of using a text to order P_2 to carry out certain tasks implies also that P_1 intends P_2 to understand what P_1 says. In this latter capacity P_2 is an audience. Thus, P_2 is both a servant and an audience, and there is no conflict between the two, although P_2 is not a servant insofar as he is an audience or an audience insofar as he is a servant, and he can be a servant without being an audience and vice versa.

That the function of an audience is to understand does not mean that the audience must be considered passive, as some historiographers used to think.[15] On the contrary, the audience approaches the text actively, but its relation to the text and the aim it has, qua audience, are different from those that characterize authors.[16] The primary thrust of authors is to create a new text, whereas that of audiences is to understand a text already created. Both are engaged in connecting meaning to entities, but authors are freer than audiences insofar as they determine, with whatever materials they have at their disposal, the character of the texts they compose. Audiences are less free because they are presented with a fait accompli; their challenge is not to produce texts but to understand already existing texts. Perhaps the differences between the function of authors and audiences will become clearer if we look at what is involved in the understanding of a text by an audience.

The active character of the roles audiences play in understanding texts is evident at several levels.[17] First, it is present at the level of acquaintance with the text. If the text is physical, this acquaintance will take the form of perception; if the text is mental, then it will consist in some kind of nonphysical awareness. Most texts with which we are acquainted are physical, so we will, for the sake of simplicity, deal only with them. Apart from acquaintance with or perception of a text, the audience must, second, understand the meaning of the signs of which the text is composed. This involves connecting each sign to some meaning. Third, the audience must recognize the significance of the arrangement in which the signs appear. This does not mean that the audience must be aware of the rules according to which the signs that compose the text are arranged in the sense that the person or persons who compose the audience could explicitly formulate these rules. Knowledge of English grammar in this sense, for example, is not required for the understanding of English texts—this is particularly evident in the case of oral texts. What is required is only the skill to derive semantic significance from syntactical arrangements. Finally, the audience must also fill in the lacunae present in the text. Most texts are elliptical—they contain gaps to be filled with materials supplied by the audience according to context. Texts are like maps, where only prominent landmarks are recorded; if taken by themselves, they provide at best a general outline of the conceptual terrain they chart.[18] Some of these gaps are intentional, and they may have rhetorical force; others are simply there because the author unconsciously takes for granted what is supposed to fill them up. In both cases an accurate understanding of a text requires that the audience supply appropriate materials to fill these gaps.

With respect to the lacunae, moreover, it is not always the case that there is one and only one way to fill them. Take the case of lacunae that are intentionally left by the author.[19] In some cases they are meant to be filled in only one way. This is the situation in the case of certain gaps in most medieval manuscripts, for example. Owing to the relative scarcity and high price of materials to be used for writing surfaces, medieval authors frequently left out the conclusion of syllogisms. They record the first two premises and had them followed by an *et cetera* and no conclusion. It is the job of the reader to fill in the blank, as it were. At the time these texts were written this task was probably easy, because the members of the audience for which the texts were meant were aware of the rules for filling in the blanks, appropriate terminology, and so on. But, as anyone who has tried to do this today knows, it is by no means easy for a contemporary reader, even though the authors of the texts intended those blanks to be filled in only one way.

There is no reason, however, why authors should not intend to have the lacunae in their texts filled in different ways, some of which they may have thought as possibilities and others that did not occur to them in particular, although they may have anticipated the possibility of their existence. There is no reason, for example, why an author may not leave unwritten the last chapter of a novel, letting the audience supply the ending according to its imagination. Indeed, there are examples of this sort of procedure in contemporary literature. And much humor is based precisely on textual ambiguity owing to incompleteness.

What has been said concerning intentional lacunae would seem prima facie to apply also to unintentional lacunae. After all, one could argue that, if there is a gap, there may be one or more ways to fill it. But this may not be as it seems. Unintentional lacunae are due to the author's assumption that the text says something when in fact it says it only because the author is unintentionally supplying (frequently through context) some element missing in the text. In such cases, it would seem more sensible to surmise that the author is using only one context rather than several. Indeed, use of several contexts for the same gap would seem to presuppose consciousness of them and thus of the gap, which is precisely what the author does not have in this case. Therefore, it does not seem likely that unintended lacunae can be filled in more than one way by the audience while respecting the historical integrity of the text. One obvious exception to this rule occurs when there are several equivalent ways to fill the gap, for in such a case it does not matter much which one is chosen. But this is not the complete story, although it is all I need to say at this point about lacunae and audience understanding in this context.[20]

From what has been said it follows that the role of the audience in understanding texts is active insofar as it has to connect meaning with signs and their arrangement and fill in intended and unintended gaps. Lest a lingering temptation remain to view these tasks passively, I would like to bring in another consideration that I hope will be sufficient to illustrate the active role that audiences play in understanding texts. This is the view for which I have argued at length elsewhere, that the understanding of at least some texts requires value judgments about the views those texts present.[21] I argued for this position by noting that when we try to understand the past, we must engage in both reconstruction and evaluation. Reconstruction involves filling in what is unstated as well as the context; evaluation involves making value judgments of various sorts, including judgments concerning truth. And this applies to texts as well. To understand a text in its historical dimension we must supply a context and make value judgments regarding what the text means based on what makes sense and what does not, what is true or not, and what is historically possible or not. All this indicates that the audience is engaged in a process which can hardly be described as passive.

To this must be added, finally, that at least three of the audiences identified earlier in this chapter have a causal role in the production of a text. In one case this role is direct, for when the author functions as audience during the process of the creation of a text, his understanding of the part of the text he has created affects what he will do subsequently in a direct way. The author and the audience are one person, so they share the knowledge that determines the ultimate shape of the text. In all other cases, however, the role of the audience is indirect, for the audience does not really participate efficiently in the production of the text; only the author does that. The audience exercises an indirect causal influence on the text through the author. This may involve consciousness in the case of the intended audience, where an author explicitly considers an audience for whom he is producing a text and designs the text accordingly. But it need not be conscious in the case of the contemporaneous audience, when an author does not explicitly consider an audience but his actions imply the existence of the audience. In this case, the presence and influence of the audience cannot be denied because the author uses particular sets of signs belonging to natural languages and he must follow rules concordant with the uses of texts by particular groups of people.[22] Philosophers most often write for philosophers in a language they think can be understood even if they are not consciously writing for philosophers, and so do sociologists, physicists, and so on. Thus, the influence of the audience on a text begins even before the audience is acquainted with it.

Not every audience, however, acts as partial cause of a text. Because the influence of an audience is carried out through an author, only the audience as a person who is also an author or the audience as conceived by the author, whether consciously or unconsciously, has this role; only the author as audience or the intended and contemporaneous audiences can be involved in this process.

In short, the role of the audience in the understanding of texts is active, but this does not entail that the role of the audience is to be confused with the role of the author. The sort of activity in which the audience, qua audience, engages is different from the sort of activity the author, qua author, performs. That the audience is not passive does not mean that its activity must be equated with that of authors, as some think.[23] If the role of audiences were not distinguishable from that of authors, there would be only authors; and the purpose of texts, the conveyance of meaning, would be frustrated. The pendulum of contemporary opinion seems to have swung too far in favor of an active role for the audience. An audience is active in the understanding of a text, but does not create it. The text is already an existing reality—even if incomplete and subject to diverse understandings—before the audience encounters it, and the audience's role is not to change it but to grasp its meaning and significance, even if in some cases the meaning and significance are open ended. In that sense, the role of an audience is like that of the historian who wishes to account for the past. Audiences are directed toward the past, whereas the role of authors is fundamentally antihistorical. The function of authors is directed toward the future.[24]

Before we leave this section, we must raise the question as to whether the distinctions among the various audiences discussed in Section I affect the conclusions we have reached concerning the function of audiences. We have seen that it does, at least in the causal role audiences may indirectly play in the creation of texts, because only the author as audience and the intended and contemporaneous audiences play such a role. However, when it comes to the primary function of audiences, that is, the understanding of texts, the type of audience seems to make no difference. Although the author as audience and the intended, contemporaneous, intermediary, and contemporary audiences may opperate at different times and under different circumstances, their primary goal is still to understand the text. They may, as we have seen with the causal function exercised by the author as audience and the intended and contemporaneous audiences, have other secondary functions as well. Indeed, knowledge of the author and of the intended, contemporaneous, and intermediary audiences on the part of the contemporary audience may help the contemporary audience to understand a text better, but that does not change the primary function of those audiences. In short, what has been said concerning various types of audience does not affect the conclusions reached in this section concerning the primary function of an audience.

III.   Need for an Audience

The view that texts are meant for audiences and thus that an audience, either actual or imagined, is a necessary condition of texts is one of those assumptions that, even if seldom explicitly stated, is generally implicitly accepted in the pertinent literature.[25] Recently, this view has come under fire, however, from some authors who claim that their business is not with an audience at all. Practitioners of the *nouveau roman*, such as Alain Robbe-Grillet, believe that for a writer the aim is to write, and whether what the writer writes is read or not is actually unimportant.[26] (Robbe-Grillet's third novel, *Jealousy*, sold only 300 copies in the first year even though he was already famous at the time.) According to this perspective, an audience is neither necessary nor important for the author; hence its consideration could not be necessary or important for the existence or understanding of a text.

This point of view appears sensible at first. Indeed, if some authors claim in good faith that when they produce texts they do not intend to convey any kind of meaning to anyone, how can anyone argue that their aim is in fact to do so? To argue that way would imply either that we think they are lying or that we think they do not know what they intend. The first alternative does not make sense unless we can produce a reason why they would wish to lie. If we cannot, then we must assume they speak in good faith.

Further, adherents to this point of view can easily point to examples in which texts are used for purposes other than to convey meaning to audiences. They might cite, for instance, the case of expressions that are meant to vent emotion, as when someone utters a profanity while in a state of rage. Likewise they may note that the writing of a poem may have a therapeutic purpose rather than a communicative one. Some persons experience a sense of release and contentment after they have written a poem, even if the poem is not meant for anyone and is kept private or is destroyed after it is written. Finally, one might argue an author who produces a text in a stream of consciousness, in a mechanical, nonreflective way, could hardly be said to be working on something meant to be understood by someone else.

In spite of the impressive case that may be built to support the view that audiences are not necessary for texts, some observations can be used to undermine this position. The first of these is that texts are linguistic in nature, and language is public rather than private. It is neither necessary nor pertinent to recount the many arguments that have been used in support of this view in this century. Let it suffice to say that the notion of a private language is seldom defended nowadays, and I share the view that such a notion is untenable.[27] Hence, if language is public and texts are composed of language, they must themselves be public. An obvious question that comes up at this point is why someone whose aim is not to communicate with others would use a medium that is nonprivate. Does this make any sense? It would seem that the production of texts, just as the use of language, carries with it the intent to communicate—regardless of the particular intention of the author. Whether or not an audience actually receives that communication, or whether the author had an idea of a particular audience or any audience in mind, does not matter, for the procedure that authors undertake, the signs that they use to compose a text, the rules that they follow in arranging them, and so on entail not only an audience but a particular audience. For example, an author's use of English words in a text surely entails that the audience of the text is composed of persons who know English, and an author's use of a symbolic language of logic, implies the text is intended for those who are used to such symbolism. Finally, as already noted earlier, authors function as audiences even when they do not consciously go back to the texts they are producing to complete them. The role of author depends on the role of audience and thus it is not possible to engage in the production of a text without adopting in some sense the role of audience.

But what of the examples just given? Do they not show that an audience is superfluous? The answer to this question is negative, for the examples show only that texts have multiple functions, not that texts are not meant for audiences. The utterance of a profanity may have the function of expressing anger—we might say that expressing anger is one of the illocutionary acts performed when the locutionary act is performed. But the function of the profanity might also be to scare or shock someone in addition to venting emotion, and in that case we must assume that some communication is intended. The use of a language in the composition of a poem intended primarily as release likewise indicates a public dimension to the poem in addition to the author's aim of release. Perhaps the author is afraid of what the poem reveals about himself, and that is why he keeps it private or even destroys it, but the act of producing entails a public aim of communication. The same could be said with respect to the practitioners of the *nouveau roman* and stream-of-consciousness texts: Qua texts, composed of language, they imply a public dimension that in turn implies an audience. In addition, all of them have authors and the role of author presupposes the role of audience. Even where no other audience is intended, the author fills that role in the composition of the text.

Let me finish by pointing out that claims to the effect that audiences are unnecessary for texts are often based on a conception of audience that excludes both the contemporaneous audience and the author from being part of the audience of a text. Such claims usually take for granted that the audience of a text is the intended audience; that is, the audience consciously and explicitly intended by an author to understand the text he is producing. And, indeed, if the audience is conceived exclusively thus, it is quite clear that not every text has an audience, for many authors do not intend any person or group of persons to understand the text they produce. That does not mean, however, that the text has no contemporaneous audience, for if the text is composed in a natural language, this implies that it is understandable by those who understand and use this language. Indeed, the very composition of a text in a language implies a nonprivate character and thus an actual or at least possible audience. Finally, the narrow identification of an audience with the intended audience leaves out the audience that is absolutely indispensible to a text; namely, the author. For even the practitioners of the *nouveau roman* and authors who compose texts in a stream-of-consciousness mode function as audiences while doing so. Hence, there is always an audience for a text, even when the author has no particular audience in mind at the time of composition.

IV.   Character of the Audience

Much discussion in contemporary circles has been about the repressive character of authors, a topic discussed in Chapter 3. What has generally been ignored until relatively recently, particularly in literary circles, is the subversive and repressive character of audiences.[28] Let me begin with the subversive character.

A.   Subversive Character

I have chosen the word 'subversive' to convey the particular feature of audiences that I wish to discuss because the term has a very negative connotation and also because literally it means "to turn upside down." Now, that audiences can and do frequently understand texts very differently from the way their authors understand them is a fact of our experience.[29] Consider the following example.

A student in one of my seminars, where this issue was being discussed, cited an excellent example of this phenomenon. His roommate wrote a short story for an English course that was supposed to be read to the entire class. In the story, he meant to put forth the argument that widespread homosexuality could cause the termination of the human race because heterosexual behavior is necessary for the preservation of the species. Being a rather conservative type, and somewhat naive, he took this argument very seriously but was worried about the impact the story would have in the class, for he knew that several openly homosexual students were enrolled in it. Yet, he had no cause for concern. His classmates loved the story, for they took it as a spoof on the sort of homophobia common in certain circles of our society.

This is a good example of how an audience can arrive at an understanding of a text that is contrary to the understanding intended by its author. The reasons why the author and the audience had different understandings of the text are easy to identify. In each case, they were working under different assumptions. The class could not conceive that anyone would take the story at face value and thus proceeded to understand it ironically (which by the way, is in perfect accord with the sort of aim pursued by much literature). The author, by contrast, did not see the text ironically, but rather understood it nonironically because it made sense to him in that way.

That audiences can understand texts in ways that can be described as nothing less than subversive, that is, in ways opposite to the way the authors of the texts understood them, raises two important issues: (1) whether audiences can understand texts differently, and even contrarily, to the way their authors understood them and yet not misunderstand them; and (2) whether it is legitimate for audiences to understand a text in ways which the author did not have in mind or which are contrary to what the author had in mind. Should the aim of audiences be no more than the understanding of texts in the ways in which their authors understood them? Or is it legitimate for audiences to get out of texts more than authors put in them, or even something contrary to what authors put in them? Indeed, we may go even further and ask whether audiences can understand texts better than their authors? These are important questions for which answers need to be provided and I have done so elsewhere.[30] The issue that concerns us here is whether audiences that misunderstand texts are to be considered subversive and the sense in which that subversive character should be understood. Can we describe the act of misunderstanding a text as subversive?

The answer to this question depends largely on what is meant by subversive. To clarify the issue let us consider three different cases in which textual misunderstanding may occur. The first is a case in which misunderstanding of a text occurs even though the audience wants to understand the text and is doing everything that can reasonably be done to do so. This is frequent enough and is due to a variety of factors that are quite evident in everyday experience and need not concern us at this moment. The second case is one in which misunderstanding of a text occurs with the full compliance of the audience's will. In other words, the audience wants to misunderstand a text and does so. This again is quite frequent in our experience. In a heated argument, one of the contestants may misunderstand something his opponent says precisely because he wants to corner the opponent and wishes to use any ammunition he can to achieve his purpose. In this situation, I assume that the audience (i.e., one of the contestants) misunderstands because it wants to, but it does so without understanding what the author of the text means. There is, moreover, a third possibility; namely, that the misunderstanding occurs even though the audience understands what the author means but, ignoring it, goes on to act as if what the author meant were what the audience wishes him to mean. The first kind of misunderstanding may be called *unintended,* the second, *intended but unconscious*; and the third, *intended and conscious.*

The first of these kinds of misunderstandings, the unintended, seems immune from criticism. Our experience testifies to the fact that misunderstandings are frequently unintended—indeed, often they are regretted by the party who misunderstood. The second and third kinds of misunderstanding, however, are not beyond criticism. Consider the third—intended and conscious misunderstanding. One may object to this by pointing out that this kind of misunderstanding implies a correct understanding of the text and thus can hardly be a misunderstanding. Strictly speaking, this seems to be right. Misunderstanding in this sense presupposes understanding and thus cannot be regarded as a misunderstanding. It does not seem possible to claim that I willfully think that Peter meant that Mary should smoke in this room and consider that a misunderstanding of what Peter said, when I understand what Peter said as meaning that Mary should not smoke in this room. However, there may be no difficulty in this case after all, provided we keep in mind that in this case we have two different acts, the original act of understanding and a subsequent act of misunderstanding in which the audience engages because it wants to, say, convey that misunderstanding to someone else so that the author be misunderstood, and so on. Thus, we really do not have the same thing being both an understanding and a misunderstanding. Rather, we have two acts, one of understanding and one of misunderstanding, which not only are ontologically separate but also yield different causal analyses.

The problem of the second, the misunderstanding that is intended but unconscious, is that it postulates a willfull misunderstanding without having an understanding. How can I think that Peter meant that Mary should smoke in this room, and consider that a willful misunderstanding of what Peter said, when I understand what Peter said only as meaning that Mary should smoke in this room? It would appear that willful misunderstanding requires understanding and thus that it always has to be conscious.

I do not believe, however, that experience bears this conclusion. In many cases we know that, when we adopt a certain understanding of a text, we are misunderstanding it precisely because we see that it could not be understood as we choose to understand it, even though we do not really know what it means. Indeed, in some cases we know that the author could not have meant what we say he means because it would obviously be unhelpful to his argument, or because he denies such a view elsewhere, but nonetheless we attribute such meaning to the text, thus willfuly misunderstanding it.

Having clarified three different cases of misunderstanding, we may now go back to the word 'subversive' and see how it is that audiences may be subversive. By calling an audience subversive one may mean three different things: (1) that an audience has misunderstood a text, but has done so unintentionally; (2) that an audience has misunderstood a text intentionally, but without knowing the meaning the text has; and (3) that the audience has misunderstood a text intentionally, knowing the meaning of the text. Of these three, it seems to me that only the last two senses truly warrant the use of the term 'subversive.' Audiences are subversive when they intentionally divorce the text from its meaning, but they are not subversive if their misunderstanding is not intentional. When audiences act subversively, they are not acting as audiences but as authors, even though they may style themselves to be audiences. In such cases their function turns out to be interpretative in one of the senses described in Chapter 3, where the audience was understood to be searching for an ideal text of its own devising. Under these conditions, an audience is indeed subversive insofar as it pretends to be what it is not and at the same time distorts the meaning of the text.

So far we have been speaking of the audience of a text as if it were one. However, we saw earlier that there are four different audiences of a text: the author considered as audience, and the contemporaneous, intermediary, and contemporary audiences. It is quite obvious that what has been said concerning subversiveness easily applies to all these but the first. There is no difficulty in conceiving a contemporaneous audience, for example, as being subversive in its understanding of a text. We frequently see this in political debates, where texts are taken out of context and thus purposefully misunderstood. And the same can be said about the contemporary and intermediary audiences. It is frequent to find philosophers whose attitude toward historical texts is such that their understandings of those texts are filled with historical inaccuracies. Sometimes this is the result of a purposeful attitude resulting from ideological or apologetic considerations; sometimes they are unintended consequences resulting from poor methodological procedures based on mistaken historiographical principles; and other times they are the result of the philosopher's frame of reference, which tends to color his or her perspective.[31] The only audience to which subversion seems difficult to apply is the author when he is considered as audience, but even here there are situations where one might want to argue that subversiveness is possible.

Consider a situation in which an author has composed a text expressing a point of view that later on the author realizes is dangerous insofar as it may imperil his well-being because those on whom he depends for that well-being disagree or condemn the point of view. And suppose that, when the author is called to task by those persons concerning the views the text expresses, he indicates that it was not at all the view he intended to convey through the text but some other view that is in perfect accordance with the view of his questioners. Could it not be argued that, in a case such as this, the author is subverting the text and thus understanding it in a way that purposefully distorts its meaning? Moreover, he is doing so not because he may have forgotten what he originally meant and thus unintentionally, but rather because he intends to change the text's meaning to save his skin? I am not speaking of retractions, such as those of Augustine and Galileo, but of attempts on the part of authors intentionally to distort the meaning of texts they have composed.

It does not make a great deal of sense to argue that authors can become subversive audiences while the process of production is going on, but there is nothing odd about accepting that they can become so at periods after the process of production has taken place. This can happen as a result of factors that make it in their best interest to misunderstand texts they have produced.[32]

B.   Repressive Character

Apart from the subversive character, one may also raise the question as to whether audiences exercise repression in ways similar to the ways authors may act repressively. An extended discussion of the repressive character of authors was presented in Chapter 3, so there is no need to say much about repression itself here; what was said there suffices for our purposes. It is enough to remind ourselves that repression is understood here as involving the imposition of limitations on others and thus the exercise of power and dominion over them.

An author could be understood to exercise power and dominion over the audiences of the text he creates insofar as he limits the range of understandings of the text open to those audiences. Moreover, we saw that it was not the historical author, but the pseudo-historical, the composite, and the interpretative authors that could function repressively. Now we mean to ask, first, whether it makes sense to say that audiences also may be repressive by exercising undue power and dominion and, second, about the identity of the persons who are the object of repression.

To a certain extent the answer to these questions has already been given insofar as it was granted earlier that the interpretative and composite authors are also audiences. As audiences, they understand texts and that understanding, when communicated to other audiences, imposes constraints on those other audiences. Audiences exercise power and dominion over other audiences whenever their understanding of a text guides and limits the understanding of those audiences. The contemporaneous audience may indeed exercise power over the intermediary and the contemporary, and the intermediary over the contemporary. Obviously, because there is an order of temporal priority among these, the exercise of power is uni-directional and points toward the contemporary audience.

This is not all, however, for audiences can also exercise power over the author, including the historical author, even when those audiences do not actually exist. This occurs through the author's views about the audience. An author may feel constraints not only on what he can say but also in the way he says it because of the audiences he thinks may have access to the text he produces. Philosophers in particular have frequently been conscious of these constraints and have dealt with them in various ways. Averroes, for example, advises his philosophical readers—his intended audience—that they should be careful with what they say because only those bright enough, educated enough, and with sufficient leisure to think philosophical issues through can be trusted with philosophical information. For those who, either because of their deficient nature, insufficient training, or lack of time, cannot understand what philosophers say are liable to misunderstand it and cause suffering to philosophers.[33] This is a testimonial to the power audiences have over authors.

But, we may ask, is the power of audiences over other audiences, and even over authors, to be understood always as repressive? The answer to this question is negative because the repression depends on the objective in question and the circumstances involved. That I have to write in English because my audience reads English imposes on me certain constraints, because at times it seems to me that I could do better in my native tongue. But the constraints are not repressive insofar as there are no serious and deleterious consequences to my adherence to the demands of my audience—there may be some insofar as my English-speaking audience may feel that the text I produce is not clear enough or lacks the luster that a native speaker of English could give it. On the other hand, if, like Averroes, I could not criticize the president of the university where I teach because were I to do so I would lose my job, we have obviously a case of pernicious limitation and thus repression.

Something similar may apply to the power exercised by audiences on other audiences. It would be a case of repression for an audience to exercise power over another if such power prevented the second audience from understanding a text correctly. Suppose that a teacher is explaining a certain equation, and student A understands it in one way and student B is guided by A's understanding, when in fact A has misunderstood the equation. This may be taken to be repressive, perhaps, but it would certainly not be repressive for A to influence B provided A is right and B's object is to understand the equation correctly. Of course, I am assuming that no external constraints are involved. If some were, the influence of A would be repressive even if the outcome were desirable, but it is questionable that in such cases A would be acting as an audience.

The audience, then, just like the author, may act repressively but need not do so. Repression is not in the nature of the audience, just as it is not either in the nature of the author.

V.   Subjectivity of the Audience

On the matter of the subjectivity of the audience, not much can be added to what was said in Chapter 3 concerning the subjectivity of the author. Audiences, like authors, are subjects, and how that affects texts is in many ways similar in both cases.

As in the case of the author, the epistemic dimensions of subjectivity are most important when discussing the relation of an audience to a text. Moreover, that subjectivity is likewise to be interpreted as a framework composed of the concepts and experiences of the audience. In the case of a group audience, this framework is the group's accumulation of pertinent individual views and concepts; where the audience is composed of only one person, it is the pertinent concepts and experiences of that person.

The subjectivity of the audience functions as a context within which a text is encountered and on the basis of which it is understood, for in that subjectivity the connection between the entities that constitute the text and the meaning of the text is made. Moreover, within that subjectivity, in the concepts and experiences that compose it, the audience finds both the rules and elements that allow the subject to fill in the lacunae in the text. Finally, in the context of that subjectivity, the acts of understanding of the audience take place and thus the meaning of the text is grasped.

Qua subjectivities, the subjectivity of the author and that of the audience are no different. Their differences stem from two other sources. The first is that the author and the audience are individually distinct subjects (except in the case of the author considered as an audience discussed earlier). This numerical distinction opens up the possibility, indeed the certainty in our world of experience, of a diversity of conceptual frameworks and experiences that modify in important ways the relationship between each of the subjects and the text.

The second source of difference has to do, as should be expected, with the different roles of author and audience. The author functions as the creator of the text, whereas the audience is expected to understand it. The subjectivity of the author, then, has a direct causal relation to the text and what it will be. By contrast, the subjectivity of the audience, except where the audience in question is the author, has a direct causal role only in the understanding the audience derives from the text. Its causal role on the text itself is only indirect, insofar as the author consciously or unconsciously considers the audience in the composition of the text and shapes the text in such a way that it will have the effect he desires on the intended audience. The subjectivity of the author, then, directly affects what the text is. The subjectivity of the audience affects the text only indirectly, but it directly conditions the understanding the audience has of the text.[34]

In the discussion of authors, a distinction was drawn between two parts of the subjectivity of authors: nonindividual experiences and cultural elements authors bring with them to the composition of texts, on the one hand, and the purely individual elements unique to them, on the other. Now, if the subjectivity of the audience is to be understood in a similar way, then we must conclude that such subjectivity includes the set of conceptions, beliefs, and experiences unique to the audience. But this creates a problem. For, if this is so and the understanding of texts is rooted in that subjectivity, then it follows that each audience may understand texts differently and also differently from the way their authors understood them.

The situation, however, is not as serious as it looks, for two reasons. The first is that the subjectivity of audiences includes common elements of culture that function as bonds and bridges, as in fact language does. The second is that, even though the experiences and beliefs of different persons may vary widely, they are experiences and beliefs of human persons and thus are rooted in a common foundation. Subjectivity does not imply complete difference and consequently alienation. It is possible to grant uniqueness to some elements of the subjectivity of authors and audiences and yet accept that they can understand texts in the same way. The common elements make common understanding possible; the elements of difference make possible the creativity displayed by authors and explain the different understandings and misunderstandings of texts by audiences.

VI. Conclusion

Let me close this chapter by stressing the main points made in it. First in order of importance is that, contrary to a position recently adopted by some philosophers and literary critics, audiences are necessary conditions of textuality. There are no texts if there are no actual or potential audiences for those texts. Indeed, because I have argued that authors function as audiences during the creative process, my view is that there is always an audience for a text, even if in some cases that audience is restricted to the author of the text.

A second point that needs to be stressed is that the function of an audience of a text is to understand the text. This function, contrary to formerly widespread views, is not wholly passive but involves both passive and active elements. The audience does not just receive understanding; the understanding of texts takes active participation and work and involves filling lacunae, tying artifacts to meanings, reconstruction, and evaluation.

This active character of the audience leads to the possibility that the audience may be subverting the intended meaning of texts. In this area, the view defended here is that audiences may misunderstand texts in three different ways: unintentionally, intentionally but without knowing the meaning of the text, and intentionally but knowing the meaning of the text. Only in the last two senses may an audience be said to act subversively, for in the first the change in the meaning of the text is unintentional.

With respect to the repressive character of audiences, we concluded that audiences can function repressively with respect both to other audiences and to authors. But such a function is not part of the nature of audiences, depending on the case in question, the objective pursued, and the circumstances surrounding it.

Audiences turn out to be of various sorts. In addition to the author of a text, who in composing the text functions in part as its audience, there are also intended, contemporaneous, intermediary, and contemporary audiences. Audiences, therefore, vary a great deal and with them vary the contexts in which texts are approached, leading to different understandings of these texts. Moreover, audiences can be composed of a single person or many persons, which again may lead to different understandings of texts. These different understandings are not the result of a mere difference in the number of persons or of the individual persons that compose the audience. Rather, they are the result of the subjectivity of the audience; namely, individual experiences and views in the case of single persons and common cultural traits and beliefs in the case of groups of persons. Moreover, because the audience affects texts indirectly, through the author's intentions based on his knowledge of the audience, this subjective aspect of the audience acquires extraordinary importance for the understanding of texts.

CONCLUSION

In the preceding pages I have presented a view of the ontological status and identity of texts and of the relationship of texts to authors and audiences. It completes the basic elements of the theory of textuality whose logical and epistemological foundations I presented in *A Theory of Textuality*.

The main tenets of the part of the theory I have explored here are that texts are ontologically complex and constituted by entities considered to have a mental relation to meaning. The entities in question can be individual or universal, physical or mental, and substances or the features of substances. But texts can be constituted only by substances considered as characterized by features or by the features of substances. Moreover, texts are always aggregates with meanings but, like their meanings, they can be individual or universal.

Individual texts have the existence and location proper to the individuals in question. In contrast, universal texts are neutral with respect to existence and location, and their historicity is the historicity of their instances.

The identity conditions of texts—whether we are speaking of achronic, synchronic, or diachronic identity—include the identity conditions of the entities of which they are constituted and their meaning. Accordingly, the identification and reidentification of texts require knowledge of those conditions in most cases.

The notion of author is not univocal. One can distinguish among several authors of a text and therefore several functions as well, although the historical author is generally regarded as paradigmatic. Historical authors are responsible for the elements of novelty in a text; they create texts and therefore are necessary to them.

The often discussed repressive character of an author is not always so and never applies to the historical author. When repression occurs, it is exercised by the view an audience has of the historical author; that is, by the pseudo-historical author.

The audience also is not univocal and neither are its functions. The audience contemporaneous with the historical author is paradigmatic, and its function is to understand the text. Texts are never without audiences for the author includes the function of audience. Audiences, like authors, can act repressively, and they can be subversive when they distort the meaning of texts.

These views are intended to reflect our most basic intuitions about texts, to eliminate some of the inconsistencies that characterize those intuitions, and to deepen our understanding of the philosophical issues posed by texts. They have no claim to completeness. Even a superficial glance at what has been accomplished will reveal important gaps that need filling. For example, I say very little, except in passing, about the ethical, political, and aesthetic issues that can be raised in connection with texts. I have not considered the issues of power, ideology, and economics that have been raised in some of the recent literature on texts. I have omitted discussion of notions such as document, version, draft, discourse, and the like, which are the special purvue of editors. I have largely ignored matters involved in the relation of texts to culture, society, and history, although I have paid some attention to these in *A Theory of Textuality*. Even in the areas I discuss, such as ontology, many questions have been left unanswered and others have not been raised at all. For example, I have ignored issues of ontology and taxonomy that arise from the peculiar character of certain texts such as dramatic texts, although I believe my theory contains the elements necessary to deal effectively with these issues. And I have paid insufficient attention to issues of particular interest to textual critics concerned with the identity of texts, although again I believe my theory contains the elements necessary to address those issues successfully. My only excuse for these omissions is that to fill the gaps in a satisfactory manner would have turned this book into a very large and unwieldy volume. In spite of these shortcomings, however, I hope the views I present constitute a good start for those who concern themselves with textuality.

The position I have presented, incomplete though it may be, lays the groundwork for an approach to texts that makes some headway at least in the clarification of the issues posed by textuality, the interrelation of those issues, and the articulation of a consistent theory that could be used as a point of departure for future discussions.

I make no claims to finality or ultimate truth. My hope is that those who have stayed with me have profited from their effort and have found in the discussion the kind of stimulation that will lead them to examine further the issues I raise and to develop their own views with respect to those and other related issues. The true life of the mind is active and so I trust the reading of this book will lead to activity and not rest. In that sense, I would rather have it produce active disagreement than contented acquiescense.

NOTES

Introduction

1. *A Theory of Textuality*, Part I.

2. There are ordinary senses of the term 'sign.' For example, 'sign' may mean a notice posted somewhere. But this is not the sense I have in mind here.

Chapter 1. Ontological Status

1. Aristotle himself never settled on ten—the number varies—but in the *Categories* he lists ten. See 1b25, p. 8.

2. Among other categories used to describe the ontological status of texts are action, event, process, possibility, and assemblages. See Section V and n. 37 in this chapter. See also Ricoeur, "The Model of the Text: Meaningful Action Considered as a Text." The most ambitious attempt to date to establish an ontology of texts by a textual critic appears in Shillingsburg's "Text as Matter, Concept, and Action."

3. It does not follow from this, however, that texts are relations, as some philosophers propose. See n. 30.

4. Gracia, *Individuality*, pp. 45 ff.

5. Not everyone agrees with this statement. See Margolis, "The Ontological Peculiarity of Works of Art," p. 47. For Peirce, see *Collected Papers*, vol. 4, par. 537.

6. Cf. Castañeda, "Individuation and Non-Identity," p. 132b; and Bunge, "¿Qué es un individuo?" p. 123.

7. Most scholastics after the twelfth century believed so. See, for example, Suárez, *Disputationes metaphysicae,* Vol. 5, 1, 4, and 5, 7; in Gracia's translation, pp. 32 and 139 ff.

8. Aristotle, *Categories* 2a11, p. 9.

9. Cf. Ayer, "Individuals," pp. 1 ff., and my discussion in *Individuality*, pp. 58–60.

10. For the much discussed problem of the ontological status of art objects, see Zemach, "Nesting," pp. 296 ff.; Gracia, *Individuality*, pp. 102–3; Wolterstorff, "Toward

an Ontology of Art Works," pp. 115 ff.; Margolis, "The Ontological Peculiarity of Works of Art," pp. 45–50; and Ingarden, who devotes the entire *The Literary Work of Art* to this issue. Wolterstorff's view is that works of art are "kinds" (i.e., universals). Margolis's view is that they are tokens of a type that exist embodied in physical objects. And Ingarden speaks of ideal concepts. As I have pointed out in the place noted, the ontological status of a work of art depends very much on what one understands by 'work of art,' and something similar applies to texts. The utterance of an oral text appears to be related to the text in ways similar to the ways in which the performance of a musical piece is related to the piece.

11.   As Tanselle has pointed out in *A Rationale of Textual Criticism*, p. 51, no two printed books are exactly alike, even when they use the same type of script. But I am discounting differences that in practice do not make us challenge the identity of a text. Indeed, I am assuming that differences in script (uncial vs. Gothic, for example) do not alter the identity of the text. More on this in Chapter 2.

12.   Some textual critics follow an entirely different strategy; they appear to identify the type or universal with the work and the tokens or individuals with the texts. See, for example, McLaverty, in "The Mode of Existence of Literary Works of Art," pp. 83–86. And Shillingsburg seems to identify the universal with the work and its instances with what he calls *material texts*. See "Text as Matter, Concept, and Action," pp. 75 and 81. Neither of these proposals works in my scheme.

13.   There may be questions as to whether the meanings of 3 and 4 are the same, but even if they were not, this would not weaken my argument irreparably, for the questions would be about the example and not about the point the example is supposed to illustrate.

14.   Gracia, *Individuality*, pp. 141–78.

15.   Ibid., pp. 170–78.

16.   Another way of looking at texts is to see them as sensible and nonsensible rather than physical and mental. This way of classifying them goes back to the traditional classification of signs in that way. But obviously this is a relational way of looking at texts and signs that does not tell us much about texts, or signs, themselves. The Conimbricenses thought of signs as both sensible and nonsensible. See *De signo*, q. 1, a. 1, p. 6. But this view is not universally shared. For Augustine, for example, all signs are sensible. See *De doctrina christiana*, 2, 5, p. 35.

17.   That texts are physical in this sense does not entail that everything about them is physical, for texts are ECTs with meaning. For an author who rejects the claim that texts can be physical, see Jones, *Philosophy and the Novel*, p. 181. Among those who argue for the physicality of texts are Howard-Hill, in "Variety in Editing and Reading," p. 55, and Proctor and Abbott, in *Introduction to Bibliographical and Textual Studies*, p. 3. The controversy over the physical vs. the nonphysical character of texts most often takes place in the context of editorial policy. Traditional editorial policy has looked upon texts as stable physical objects, the products of authorial intention. But this view

has been challenged by those who claim that texts are not products but processes, and unstable rather than stable. See Shillingsburg, "The Autonomous Author, the Sociology of Texts, and Polemics of Textual Criticism." For other views on this issue, see Eggert, "Textual Product or Textual Process"; McLaverty, "Issues of Identity and Utterance"; and Grigely, "The Textual Event."

18.   The classification of physical texts according to the senses through which they may be perceived, coupled with the kind of ordinary language we use to talk about the objects we sense and sensations, produces considerable ambiguity. Strictly speaking, it is one thing to speak about a physical entity that may be perceived in a certain way and another to speak about the sensation itself. It is one thing to speak of the entity that is the cause of a smell and another to speak of the smell itself. But often this distinction is not made, as is evident from the way we speak about sound. So the question arises as to whether the ECTs of an olfactory text, for example, are the entities that produce certain smells or are the smells themselves (the sensations) of the olfactory text. This raises the kind of issues that drove early modern philosophers to distraction. I do not wish to get into this controversy here, but I do want to alert the reader to the ambiguity that characterizes the discussion and is a direct result of a much deeper ambiguity in the way we speak about the objects we sense.

19.   It used to be the case that oral texts were taken as paradigmatic of textuality in many quarters, but deconstructionists have challenged this position, identifying textuality with writing (*écriture*) rather than speech (*parole*). This shift has important implications, as Abrams points out in "The Deconstructive Angel," pp. 428 ff., leading to some of the views I explore in Chapter 4 of *A Theory of Textuality*. The problematic nature of the relation and order of priority between written and oral texts has been recognized at least as far back as Plato. See *Phaedrus* 274–78, pp. 519–24.

20.   Augustine, *De libero arbitrio* 2, pp. 287–88.

21.   For some recent hermeneuticists and textual critics, only written texts qualify as texts. The reason, they argue, is that only written texts have the permanence that goes beyond the circumstances of their composition and that is necessary for textuality. But this is not right, for oral texts can be taped and thus can have as much permanence as written texts. Ricoeur restricts textuality to written texts in *Hermeneutics and the Human Sciences* (1989), p. 108. Grigely, however, has argued for oral texts in "The Textual Event," pp. 187 ff.

22.   Other differences have been suggested as well. Searle suggests a degree of permanence in "Reiterating the Differences," p. 200. Ricoeur has suggested that in oral texts the meaning of the text coincides with the speaker's intention but in written texts this is not the case, in *Interpretation Theory*, p. 29.

23.   The *Phaedrus* notes that writing is an image of speech (276b) and Aristotle thought that written words are always signs of spoken words (*On Interpretation*, ch. 1, 16a3, p. 40). This view was subsequently adopted by many scholastics, such as Suárez and the Conimbricenses.

24. As Searle has noted, the dependence of writing on spoken language is a historically contingent fact, for artificial languages reverse this dependence without contradiction. "Reiterating the Differences," p. 207. See also Shusterman, "The Anomalous Nature of Literature."

25. For Peirce, this applies only to tokens, for tokens are directly signs for types and indirectly signs for whatever else they signify. Dipert, "Types and Tokens," p. 588.

26. I have been speaking as if the same text could have more than one meaning. In fact I oppose this façon de parler both in Chapter 2 of this book and in Chapter 4 of *A Theory of Textuality*. A text has only one meaning, but that meaning can be broad, varied, and even open ended, depending on the cultural function of the text.

27. This does not entail that perception is a criterion of physicality—indeed, presumably matter is physical and yet it is not perceivable. I am merely indicating a difference between one kind of physical text and mental texts.

28. The literature on this topic is staggering, but a place to start is Feigl's *The "Mental" and the "Physical."*

29. I am omitting discussion of an issue frequently discussed by philosophers and others: the relative value and reality of texts qua bearers of meaning. In the Platonic tradition, exemplified by Augustine and others (see *De magistro* IX, 25), meanings are regarded as more valuable and real than the signs used to convey them. For some recent authors, like Derrida, the order is reversed (see "Signature Event Context"). See also Greetham, "[Textual] Criticism and Deconstruction," p. 4.

30. The relation of ECTs to meaning coupled with the assumption that meaning is always something present in a subject is probably the reason why Gadamer, for example, speaks of texts as if they were relations. *Truth and Method*, pp. 262 and 267. Wachterhauser attributes to Gadamer the assumption that texts are relations in "Interpreting Texts," p. 441.

31. See n. 8.

32. For some of the background to these distinctions, see Porphyry's *Isagoge*.

33. Another reason that could be given is that the very notion of substance includes the notion of features and therefore that it makes no sense to speak of substances considered apart from their features. I do not have the space to discuss the merits of this reason, but for someone who has argued in favor of the notion of characterized substances, see Long, "Particulars and Their Qualities."

34. See Nehamas, "Writer, Text, Author, Work," p. 277, and "What an Author Is," p. 688. Nehamas vacillates, however, between characterizing texts as actions and as the products of actions (see the first article, p. 278). See also Bakhtin, *Speech Genres and Other Late Essays*, p. 105.

35. For Austin, see *How To Do Things with Words*.

36.   This is perhaps what McLaverty is getting at in "Issues of Identity and Utterance," p. 140.

37.   Other positions have been developed by textual critics. Shillingsburg thinks of texts as processes in "The Autonomous Author, the Sociology of Texts, and Polemics of Textual Criticism"; Grigely conceives them as events in "The Textual Event"; Hay argues for a view of them as possibilities in "Does Text Exist?"; and McGann defends the view of a text as a polytext or a never-complete assamblage. Unfortunately I lack the space to do justice to these positions. Suffice it to say, first, that these views conceive texts as unstable because of the fluctuation of what I have called ECTs, their meaning, or both. Second, some of these positions can be accommodated within my framework because the authors do not always address the same ontological issue I have raised. Third, some of the categories used by these authors, such as process and event, can be reduced to the categories of substance and feature I have used.

38.   For an altogether different approach to this question, see Hay, "Does Text Exist?" She conceives a text as nothing actual but rather as a necessary possibility in relation to a pre-text, a post-text, and a written work. The notion of pre-text was first posited by Bellemin-Noël in *Le texte et l'avant-texte*. A similar approach is that of McGann, for whom a text is "a series of acts of production," a never-ending assemplage or polytext; *Critique of Modern Textual Criticism*, p. 52. Among textual critics the first to raise the question of the existence and location of texts were Bateson, in *Essays in Critical Dissent*, p. 10, and Welleck and Warren, in *Theory of Literature*. McLaverty takes up the issue in "The Mode of Existence of Literary Works of Art," but is concerned primarily with the difference betwen textual and nontextual works. The question he asks is: "If the *Mona Lisa* is in the Louvre, where are *Hamlet* and *Lycidas*?" This is an interesting question for which I have no time here. Suffice it to say that the written text of *Hamlet* is a different text from the oral text of *Hamlet*. The written text in this case plays the role a score plays for a symphony. See my *A Theory of Textuality*, ch. 3.

39.   Cf. Putnam, *Reason, Truth and History*, p. 19.

40.   Most authors who conceive texts as physical hold this view. See the references in n. 17.

41.   For these authors a text is an ideal thing. See Tanselle, *A Rationale of Textual Criticism*, pp. 64–65. Compare this to Shillingsburg's notion of a work as an ideal entity, in "Text as Matter, Concept, and Action," p. 49. I have discussed the notion of an ideal text in *A Theory of Textuality*, ch. 3.

42.   The confusion between individuals and universals is rampant in the literature on texts and art objects. It leads Gadamer, for example, to some of his enigmatic statements about the existence of games and works of art. See *Truth and Method*, pp. 110 and 95. Searle accuses Derrida of similar confusions in "Reiterating the Differences."

43.   Gracia, *Individuality*, pp. 104–12.

44.   Or with the view that texts do not exist. Among those who deny existence, whether factual or mental, to texts, is De Man, in "The Rhetoric of Blindness," p. 107. The view that denies existence to universals takes many forms. See my *Individuality*, pp. 70–85.

45.   *Individuality*, p. 74.

46.   I take it that it is something like this Wollheim had in mind in "On an Alleged Inconsistency in Collingwood's Aesthetic," p. 259.

47.   Gracia, "Cutting the Gordian Knot of Ontology."

48.   Gracia, *Individuality*, pp. 134–40.

Chapter 2. Identity

1.   Not everyone agrees. Many recent textual critics hold that new texts are not the same. For example, Grigely argues that no text is iterable or repeatable, for each iteration or repetition is a new text owing to the new circumstances that surround the iteration. See "The Textual Event," pp 171–86. I do not intend to show that Grigely is wrong but rather that there is a sense in which we can speak of texts as being the same and as being different.

2.   There are others as well, of course. For example, there is a view that considers authorial intention as determinant of textual identity, but this view presupposes the notion of an intended text, which I rejected in Chapter 3 of *A Theory of Textuality*. The notion of intended text is frequently used in the literature. See Tanselle, *A Rationale of Textual Criticism*, pp. 70 ff.

3.   This is one way to understand Derrida's view (for a second way, refer to the third view, which follows). The possibility of different and even contradictory meanings does not bother Derrida—*la différance* is for him of the essence of language; "Signature Event Context," particularly pp. 183–84, and 192–93. Meiland has also accused Hirsch of holding this view. See "Interpretation as Cognitive Discipline," pp. 32–33. Shillingsburg also appears to subscribe to a version of this view in *Scholarly Editing in the Computer Age,* p. 49. See also Goodman, *Languages of Art*, pp. 116 and 207.

4.   This position has been attributed to Gadamer by Wachterhauser in "Interpreting Texts," pp. 442 and 453–55, where he criticizes it. It appears to be defended by Fish, in *Is There a Text in This Class?* p. vii.

5.   This is a less radical version of the first view described. It may also be a way of understanding Derrida's position. See the reference in n. 2, and Grigely, "The Textual Event," p. 170.

6.   See, for example, McGann, *The Textual Condition*, p. 4.

7.   See Austin, *How To Do Things with Words*, pp. 98 ff.

8. McLaverty has defended the view of a text as an utterance, but he understands an utterance as *the product* of certain acts such as putting forth, issuing, expressing, publishing, and so on. He also brings in authorial intention, not intention of meaning (as do Hirsch and others), but of utterance. A text is the intended product of certain authorial acts such as publishing. See "Issues of Identity and Utterance," particularly pp. 140 and 144. Bakhtin also describes a text as an utterance in *Speech Genres and Other Late Essays*, p. 105.

9. For an exception, see Currie's "Work and Text."

10. Several of the articles in Cohen's *Devils and Angels* take up this issue. Particularly relevant is McLaverty's "Issues of Identity and Utterance."

11. There is no general agreement on the best way to understand similarity and sameness (identity). For a recent but different understanding of these notions, see Brennan, *Conditions of Identity*, p. 6.

12. Cf. Gracia, *Introduction to the Problem of Individuation in the Early Middle Ages*, p. 26.

13 Cf. Chisholm, "Identity through Time," pp. 25 ff. Diachronic sameness is not the same notion as duration. Duration involves for X to be the same at t_n and t_{n+1} (diachronic sameness) and to have been the same throughout the time elapsed between t_n and t_{n+1}. The conditions for X's duration between t_n and t_{n+1} involve more than the conditions of diachronic sameness. I discuss these conditions later, in the context of the diachronic sameness of individual texts.

14 Cf. Gracia, *Individuality*, pp. 38–41, and "Numerical Continuity in Material Substances."

15. I have discussed this matter in Chapter 1 of *A Theory of Textuality*.

16. Quine's view that no two sentences from two different languages can have the same meaning does not undermine the view that a necessary condition of textual identity is meaning identity, although it does preclude the possibility that two sentences from two different languages could be textually the same. See "Indeterminacy of Translation Again," pp. 9–10.

17. This opinion is frequently put into practice and sometimes explicitly voiced. For an instance of the latter, see Ingarden, *The Literary Work of Art*, p. 11.

18. See *A Theory of Textuality*, ch. 4. This is my solution to the issue raised by textual critics concerning what is essential and accidental in texts, and applies not only to meaning, but also to features of the texts' ECTs, spellings, and so forth. See Shillingsburg, "An Inquiry into the Social Status of Texts and Modes of Textual Criticism"; Tanselle, "Textual Study and Literary Judgment"; and Thorpe, *Principles of Textual Criticism*, ch. 5.

19. The most recent version of this view considers a text as an utterance or use of "a word sequence" and thus makes the author, as the one who engages in the speech

act, a condition of textual identity. See, for example, Tolhurst and Wheeler, "On Textual Individuation," p. 188. Note the use of the term 'individuation' in a context where, in accordance with my nomenclature, what is at stake is the identity of a universal.

20.   Borges, "Pierre Menard, Author of the Quixote," p. 43.

21.   The issue of authorial identity has been much discussed in reference to forgeries in art, and the issues raised in that context directly affect the answer to our question in the case of artistic texts. However, because not all texts are artistic, a general discussion of textuality need not dwell on the specific issues that affect them. For a discussion of these issues, see Dutton, "Artistic Crimes"; Koestler, "The Aesthetics of Snobbery"; and Lessing, "What Is Wrong with a Forgery?"

22.   For speech acts, see the reference to Austin in n. 7.

23.   The meaning cannot be identified with the illocutionary or any other of the speech acts distinguished by Austin, although the performance of these acts necessitates that the locution have meaning and reference. Austin, *How To Do Things with Words*, p. 94.

24.   Wachterhauser has briefly discussed the possibility of a transcendental ego as the key to textual identity in "Interpretating Texts," p. 454.

25.   Cf. Tolhurst, "On What a Text Is and How It Means," pp. 4 ff.

26.   See Katz, *Propositional Structure and Illocutionary Force*, p. 14. At the opposite extreme is Derrida, "Signature Event Context."

27.   See *A Theory of Textuality*, ch. 1.

28.   This does not entail that the author and audience must be historically identifiable. Signs are part of language and as such generally have the same features vis-à-vis authors and audiences that languages have. See Chapter 2 of *A Theory of Textuality*.

29.   There are cases in which a sign belongs to two different languages but has the same physical appearance, meaning, and grammatical function (e.g., the noun 'taco' is used both in Spanish and English for a taco). In these cases the context is determinative, for it will identify the language to which the sign belongs and thus allow for different identity. For the sake of simplification I am ignoring regional uses of 'taco.'

30.   There are also cases of written signs that look the same but are different and are pronounced differently. This is the case of 'read' in the present tense and 'read' in the past tense.

31.   See *A Theory of Textuality*, ch 3.

32.   Goodman and Elgin make syntactical function the necessary and sufficient condition of textual identity in "Interpretation and Identity," pp. 54 ff. By the syntax of a language they mean "the permissible configuration of letters, spaces, and punctuation marks" (p. 58).

33. To speak only of spelling rather than appearance, as is frequently done, does not do justice to the complexity of the issue. For spelling as a condition of identity, see Wilsmore, "The Literary Work Is Not Its Text," p. 312. Goodman goes further than this; he identifies works with texts, making sameness of spelling a necessary and sufficient condition of the identity of works. See *Languages of Art*, p. 115.

34. Of course, capitals may function semantically. For example, the use of capitals on the Internet is understood to mean that the text is being shouted.

35. Thus, 'labor' and 'labour' are the same sign in spite of the different spelling. In this case the explanation is that 'o' and 'ou' signify the same thing. Qua ECTs, 'labor' and 'labour' are different, but qua signs they are the same. For a dissenting opinion, see the text of Goodman to which reference was made in n. 32.

36. Cf. Wittgenstein, *Tractatus Logico-Philosophicus* 3.318 ff., pp. 52 ff. These sentential contexts need not be sentences in which the sign is used; they can be sentences of the metasystem in which the sign is mentioned.

37. The example and the problem are discussed by Goodman and Elgin in "Interpretation and Identity," p. 58.

38. See *A Theory of Textuality*, ch. 4.

39. Most of the objections would be based on the fact that 'Aristotle' is a proper name, whereas 'the Philosopher' could be construed as a definite description. But then it is questionable whether 'the Philosopher' is really a definite description. See Kripke, *Naming and Necessity*, p. 26; Searle, *Speech Acts*, p. 173; and Gracia, *Individuality*, pp. 227–29.

40. The difference between feature-aggregate and substance/feature-aggregate texts does not make a substantial difference for achronic sameness so I am leaving out the discussion of these cases.

41. In cases where the entity that has the features is not a substance in the Aristotelian sense but rather another feature, this view would hold that the substance also provides the conditions of identity.

42. See *Individuality*, ch. 4.

43. See my *A Theory of Textuality*, ch. 1.

44. My criticism is found in *Individuality*, pp. 88–89. For a defense of the view, see Allaire, "Bare Particulars."

45. Gracia, *Individuality*, pp. 21–24.

46. Ibid., pp. 179–96.

47. See *A Theory of Textuality*, ch. 1.

48. Ibid., chs. 4 and 5.

Chapter 3. Author

1. Authors are not necessarily restricted to texts. We frequently think of authors in connection with other things, including deeds. Hobbes, for example, thought of authors in the context of any action. *Leviathan* 1, 16, p. 125.

2. Historical questions also may be raised concerning the origin and history of the notion of an author. Indeed, Barthes, among others, has claimed that the figure of the author is a modern creation. But I will dispense with this sort of historical question here. For Barthes's views, see "The Death of the Author," pp. 142–43.

3. Some of these have been addressed in *A Theory of Textuality*, chs. 4–6.

4. The historical author has parallels to what Nehamas and others call *writer*. The notion of "writer," however, is too restrictive, for there are authors of both oral and mental texts, for example. See Nehamas, "What an Author Is," pp 685–86, and "Writer, Text, Work, Author," pp. 272 ff.; also Currie, "Work and Text," p. 333. Morgan uses the expression "historical agent" to refer to the historical author in "Authorship and the History of Philosophy," pp. 331 and 354–55.

5. For a guide to the literature on personal identity, see A. O. Rorty, *The Identity of Persons*.

6. By 'could not' I do not mean logically impossible but only factually so.

7. Unamuno makes a similar point in "On the Reading and Interpretation of *Don Quixote*," p. 977. For a different view, see Cruttwell, "Makers and Persons," p. 489.

8. The notion of pseudo–historical author understood thus has some parallels to Foucault's and Nehamas's "author." See Foucault's "What Is an Author?" pp. 121 ff., and Nehamas's "What an Author Is," p. 689, and "Writer, Text, Work, Author." Morgan, in "Authorship and the History of Philosophy," seems further to divide what I have called the pseudo-historical author into the surrogate author and the actual author. The surrogate author is the author constructed by an interpreter when subjecting a text to analysis; the actual author is also constructed by the interpreter, but is rather an ideal of what the author is and has no determinate content (see pp. 342 and 355). Cf. Walton's notion of "apparent artist" in "Style and the Products and Processes of Art," pp. 88 ff.

9. In this sense, the pseudo-historical author is a fiction created by the historical author. In art, such authors have been called *fictional creators*. See Walton, "Style and the Products and Processes of Art," p. 82. Dickie speaks of the dramatic speaker of a work in *Aesthetics*, p. 116.

10. Gracia, *Philosophy and Its History*, pp. 44–45. Maintaining the distinction does not entail a realistic position with respect to history, for the ultimate status of the events of which the historian provides an account may still be understood in different ways. The contradiction arises from holding that an account of events is the same thing as the events of which it is an account. For the controversy between realists and anti-

realists, see the articles by Goldstein, Krausz, Levine, and Makkreel in *The Monist* 74, 2 (1991).

11. For this reason it is a mistake to think about the pseudo-historical author as a merely partial or incomplete historical author, as Schmitz has suggested in "The Actual Nature of Philosophy Disclosed in Its History."

12. Foucault speaks of a "second self" in this connection in "What Is an Author?" pp. 129–30.

13. Cf. Miller, "Ariachne's Broken Woof," p. 59.

14. See, for example, Booth, *The Rhetoric of Fiction*, p. 71. For a criticism of this view, see Nehamas, "Writer, Text, Work, Author," pp. 273–74.

15. The notion of intended text is used frequently in textual criticism. See Tanselle's *A Rationale of Textual Criticism*.

16. Consider the poor state in which Whitehead left *Process and Reality*. See the Editors' Preface to the Corrected Edition, by Griffin and Sherburne, pp. v–x.

17. For a discussion of various types of editions and editorial traditions, see Mc-Gann, *The Textual Condition*, pp. 48–68. For a discussion of how theoretical stances influence editing, see Greetham, "The Manifestation and Accommodation of Theory in Textual Editing."

18. This has led some to say that editing always involves "disfiguration." Cf. Greetham, "[Textual] Criticism and Deconstruction," p. 19.

19. Many critics undermine the importance of the editor; but Shillingsburg is a welcome exception. See *Scholarly Editing*, p. 93, and "The Autonomous Author, the Sociology of Texts, and Polemics of Textual Criticism." Tanselle notes that in some cases the editor becomes in effect "a collaborator of the author"; "Textual Study and Literary Judgment," p. 114.

20. See *A Theory of Textuality*, chs. 4 and 5. McGann has noted that "readers and editors may be seen . . . as authors and writers" (*The Textual Condition*, p. 95). See also Shillingsburg, "The Autonomous Author, the Sociology of Texts, and Polemics of Textual Criticism," pp. 39–41, and "Text as Matter, Concept, and Action," pp. 72 ff.

21. See *A Theory of Textuality*, ch. 5.

22. Lewis and Short, *A Latin Dictionary*, p. 198.

23. See the references to Nehamas and others in the section devoted to the pseudo-historical author.

24. See, for example, Tomas, *Creativity in the Arts*.

25. Two qualifications need to be added. First, it should be obvious that my argument rests on the viability of a subject-object, mind–content-of-mind distinction.

Second, the understanding of *ad extra* I have provided is different from the understanding of *ad extra* used in Christian theology. In Christian theology the world cannot be a feature of God's mind, *malgré* Berkeley. But a mental text is precisely that, a feature of whoever thinks it.

26.   Understood in this way, not all creation *ex nihilo* entails novelty. It is possible for a divinity, for example, to create a duplicate of an entity out of nothing whatever. In this sense, one might want to distinguish newness from novelty, for the duplicate would be new, because it did not exist before, but it would not be novel, because it is a copy of something else. For purposes of our discussion, however, I will ignore the distinction between novelty and newness.

27.   The view that creativity involves the production of something new is widespread. See Tomas, *Creativity in the Arts*, pp 98. ff. But some have proposed a distinction between creating and making.

28.   Cf. Wolterstorff, "Toward an Ontology of Art Works," pp. 137 ff.

29.   See *A Theory of Textuality*, ch. 3.

30.   Cf. Glickman, "Creativity in the Arts," p. 140; and Margolis, "The Ontological Peculiarity of Works of Art," p. 45.

31.   For a different solution to this problem, see Margolis, ibid., pp. 46 ff.

32.   Cf. Nehamas, "What an Author Is," p. 686.

33.   Barthes introduces a distinction between author and scriptor in "The Death of the Author," p. 145, and Nehamas and others also speak of the "writer" in contrast to the "author." See n. 4.

34.   Cf. Goodman and Elgin, "Interpretation and Identity," p. 64, and Wolterstorff, "Toward an Ontology of Art Works," p. 137. In the case of short texts the notion of simultaneous production does not pose serious problems, but in the case of long ones it does. It is not clear, for example, what is required for simultaniety in the production of a text as long as *Don Quixote,* which was not written at once and which the author corrected at various times. This difficulty, however, should not cloud the issue we are addressing.

35.   Goodman and Elgin refer to these as "jointly authored" and "multiply authored" texts. "Interpretation and Identity," p. 64.

36.   For a different view about this issue in the context of art, see Koestler, "The Aesthetic of Snobbery." See also my "Falsificación y valor artístico."

37.   See *A Theory of Textuality*, ch. 5.

38.   It is possible to imagine cases, however, in which the translator is more original than the historical author of the text he or she translates. This can occur, for example, when the originality of the historical author is limited, say to few of the type signs used in the text. In such a case it may turn out that the translator is more original if the

type signs he uses display more novelty. Consider, for example, FitzGerald's translation of Omar Khayyam's *Rubaiyat*.

39.   This view is not completely opposed to the view proposed by both Foucault and Nehamas. According to them, the role of the interpreter is to create new meanings for a text that are different from the meaning understood by the historical author. In Chapter 4 of *A Theory of Textuality*, I argue that it is legitimate for audiences to understand a text in ways that are different from the ways in which the historical author and his contemporaneous audience understood it in cases where the function of the text allows it. Moreover, I also hold that the meaning of a text is not limited by the meaning the historical author and his contemporaneous audience understood, again, in cases where the function of the text allows it. And I maintain that in some cases it is the function of audiences to create new meanings for texts; that is, where the function of the texts in question is precisely determined by the culture and society of which they are part. But I reject the view that the function of audiences is always to create new meanings, for that would defeat the very purpose of texts.

40.   See *A Theory of Textuality*, ch. 5.

41.   Cf. Plato, *Phaedrus* 276e. In spite of recent attacks, this view is still defended today. See, for example, Hirsch, "Three Dimensions of Hermeneutics," pp. 259–60, and Juhl, "The Appeal to the Text," pp. 277–87.

42.   According to one version of this position, the author is not the person who created the text but "a function" developed by post-Renaissance literary critics. See Foucault, "What Is an Author?" p. 121. This does not imply, however, that there is no person who puts together the entities that constitute the text, but that person is not the author of the text. Cain makes this point in "Authors and Authority in Interpretation," p. 619. But there are more extreme versions of this view. Barthes, for example, holds that "one never knows if he [i.e., the author] is responsible for what he writes (if there is a subject behind his language); for the very being of writing (the meaning of the labor that constitutes it) is to keep the question *Who is speaking?* from ever being answered." *S/Z*, p. 140. He makes a similar point in "The Death of the Author."

43.   Nehamas, "What an Author Is," p. 685, and "Writer, Text, Work, Author," p. 275.

44.   Thus, the meaning is said to be "constructed" rather than "discovered" by the audience. See Stern, "Factual Constraints on Interpreting," p. 205. I discuss this view in Chapter 5 of *A Theory of Textuality*.

45.   Nehamas, "What an Author Is," p. 686, and "Writer, Text, Work, Author," pp. 281 ff. Note that by 'interpretation' is meant understanding in this context.

46.   Other examples are the case of persons who talk in their sleep, are in a trance, mumble something, or are under hypnosis. Can the sounds these persons utter be considered texts even though there seems to be no intent to convey meaning? The question of sleep, Freudian slips, trances, hypnosis, and the like can be explained in terms of subconscious intentions, but the case in which one makes sounds that are taken as

meaning something, even though the utterer does not intend them to do so, cannot be explained in the same way. Another example is that of computer-generated texts. See Dickie, *Aesthetics*, p. 112. Dickie uses this example to argue against intentionalists who wish to identify the meaning of a text with the author's intention. For a different line of argument against intentionalism, see McGann, *The Textual Condition*, ch. 2, pp. 48 ff. More on this in Chapter 4 of *A Theory of Textuality*.

47.   Similar examples have been used in the literature. See Knapp and Michaels, "Against Theory," pp. 727 ff.

48.   See *A Theory of Textuality*, ch. 1.

49.   Some aestheticians introduce distinctions between different senses of art work or art object, giving primary status to such things as paintings and the like and only a secondary, derivative status to things classifiable as found art. See Dickie, *Art and the Aesthetic*, pp. 25 ff. These distinctions do not affect the point I am making.

50.   See Juhl, "The Appeal to the Text," p. 282, and Searle, *Speech Acts*, pp. 16 ff.

51.   A less farfetched case with which most of us are in fact familiar is the utterance of sounds by a parrot. A parrot presumably does not understand what it says, but what it says appears to have meaning. Some scholastics argued that, because the parrot had no understanding of what it says, what it says has no meaning and thus cannot be considered to be signs. Others rejected this view and found the sounds uttered by the parrot to be significant. The first view was defended by Pedro Hurtado de Mendoza, *Logica* 8, 2, 23; the second was defended by Thomas Compton Carleton, *Logica* 42, 3, 10.

52.   Juhl, "The Appeal to the Text," p. 284. See also Knapp and Michaels, "Against Theory," p. 728.

53.   Goodman and Elgin, "Interpretation and Identity," pp. 63–64.

54.   Those who, like Barthes and Fish, emphasize the audience in the construction of a text, must accept this view. See Barthes, "The Death of the Author," and Fish, "Interpreting the *Variorum*."

55.   This seems to be Dickie's position with respect to computer-generated texts. *Aesthetics*, p. 112.

56.   In the seventeenth century, the words that compose languages were frequently compared to money. Just as money acquires value from the will of the prince and not from those who use it, so words have meaning from those who made them. Cf. Dascal, "Language and Money." The metaphor originates in the scholastic discussions of signs going back to the Middle Ages and still persists today in authors like Davidson and Ricoeur. For its use by Ricoeur, see "Creativity in Language," p. 121.

57.   See *A Theory of Textuality*, ch. 4.

58.   See Grigely, "The Textual Event," p. 179, and Danto, *The Transfiguration of the Commonplace*, pp. 35–36.

59.   In this case we are probably talking about a sign rather than a text, but the point applies to both texts and signs.

60.   This, I believe, is behind the often quoted statement of Samuel Beckett, "What matter who's speaking, someone said, what matter who's speaking." See *Texts for Nothing*, p. 16.

61.   Cf. Nehamas, "What an Author Is," p. 688, and the references in n. 4.

62.   See *A Theory of Textuality*, ch. 2.

63.   See Foucault, "What Is an Author?" pp. 124 ff., and Nehamas's exposition of Foucault in "What an Author Is," p. 686. Nehamas in fact argues against the necessarily repressive character of authors in the same article, pp. 690–91, and in "Writer, Text, Work, Author," p. 287. But Barthes accepts and develops a similar view in "The Death of the Author."

64.   This point is made clear by Nehamas in his discussion of Foucault, "Writer, Text, Work, Author," p. 271. See also McGann, *The Textual Condition*, ch. 2.

65.   See Russell, *Human Knowledge*, p. 303; and Searle, *Intentionality* p. 232.

66.   See Mill, *A System of Logic*, p. 21; Russell, *Logic and Knowledge*, pp. 200–1; and Wittgenstein, *Tractatus* 3.203, p. 47.

67.   See Donnellan, "Proper Names and Identifying Descriptions" and "Reference and Definite Descriptions," pp. 46–48; and Kripke, *Naming and Necessity*, pp. 96 and 59, n. 22.

68.   Gracia, *Individuality*, pp. 216–26.

69.   I discuss this issue in the context of philosophical texts in *Philosophy and Its History*, pp. 229–31.

70.   Aquinas, *Summa theologiae* I, 85, 5, vol. 1, pp. 563–64.

71.   The notions of "frame" and "framework" have attracted attention from those working on artificial intelligence. See Petöfi, "A Frame for Frames"; Schank, *Conceptual Information Processing*, p. 367; and Winston, *Artificial Intelligence*, pp. 235–36 and 265–70.

72.   This does not entail, as Rorty seems to think, that subjective is associated always with the "emotional" or "fantastical," for not everything originating in a subject is of this sort. For Rorty, see *Philosophy and the Mirror of Nature*, p. 339.

Chapter 4. Audience

1.   As with authors, there is no prima facie reason why we should not include nonhumans in the category of audiences. I refer to members of audiences as persons for the sake of simplicity and economy.

2.   McGann notes that "authors and writers may be seen . . . as readers and editors." *The Textual Condition*, p. 95. Note, however, that strictly speaking it is not the

author who plays the role of audience, but the person playing the role of historical author who abandons this role and adopts the role of audience. For our present purposes, however, this precision makes little difference and does cause some awkwardness. In this context I shall refer to the person who plays the role of historical author as the historical author.

3. The need for a real distinction between "speaker" and "listener" is often denied by philosophers. See, for example, Thomas Compton Carleton, *Logica* 42, 4.

4. Refer back to Chapter 3, where I discuss the interpretative author.

5. There are other cases in which the author in question is conscious of the situation. For example, Allaire talks about the author of a paper he wrote years before and about the paper itself as if he were not the author of it. See "Berkeley's Idealism Revisited," p. 197.

6. Eco has proposed the view that it is the text, rather than the author, that determines its audience. *The Limits of Interpretation*, p. 55.

7. Tolhurst, "On What a Text Is and How It Means," p. 12.

8. Fish refers to this audience as the "intended reader." Apart from the fact that this narrows the audience to readers, it also does not take into account that the author may have intended someone in particular for the text. *Is There a Text in This Class?*, p. 160.

9. Gracia, *A Theory of Textuality*, ch. 4.

10. To simplify matters I am assuming at the outset that when a group is said to understand P, 100 percent of the members of the group understand P. In ordinary experience this is not always so. 'A group understands P' often means that a majority of the members do, just as 'Americans favor tax cuts' often means that a majority of them do.

11. Gracia, *A Theory of Textuality*, ch. 4.

12. Cf. Gracia, "'A Supremely Great Being.'"

13. Gracia, *A Theory of Textuality*, ch. 1.

14. This distinction is similar to the one drawn in Chapter 3 between person and author.

15. The concern for the freedom of the audience is what drives many postmodernists. See Barthes, *S/Z*, p. 10.

16. Walton has argued recently that too much emphasis is put on the differences between audience and author in the case of art objects and that their roles are closely analogous; "Style and the Products and Processes of Art," pp. 77 ff. I sympathize with this point of view, as will become clear immediately, but nonetheless there are differences between these roles in the case of texts that cannot be ignored; the features that apply to art objects cannot be extended to texts in this instance.

17.   Even prior to the levels mentioned here, the active role of the audience is evident in the selection of a text or parts of a text for observation and understanding. Panofsky, "The History of Art as a Humanistic Discipline," p. 8. Tanselle has emphasized and illustrated the active role of audiences in Chapter 2 of *A Rationale of Textual Criticism*.

18.   Ingarden speaks of them as "schematized structures," sort of skeletons in which the flesh is supplied by audiences. See Ingarden, *The Literary Work of Art*, pp. 264 ff.; and Eco, *The Limits of Interpretation*, p. 47. But the fillings that the audience has to provide are not of the sort that Fish suggests. For Fish, the fillings are open and thus can never be incorrect or misguided, for the audience "makes" the text. See Fish, "Interpreting the *Variorum*," p. 482. For a discussion and criticism of this view, see Abrams, "How To Do Things with Texts," pp. 576 ff.

19.   For textual gaps in general, see Iser, *Prospecting*, pp. 9 ff., and "The Reading Process," pp. 31–41; also Mowitt, *Text*, p. 8.

20.   I say something more in *A Theory of Textuality*, ch. 4.

21.   Gracia, *Philosophy and Its History*, pp. 72–88.

22.   Phelan, "Validity Redux," p. 105. The role of the audience is also indirect when an author consults with it, or observes its reaction, and as a result makes changes in a text.

23.   For Fish, the audience creates the text. See "Interpreting the *Variorum*," p. 482.

24.   Gracia, *A Theory of Textuality*, ch. 4.

25.   Barthes makes it explicit when, in his desire to do away with the author, he makes the audience (i.e., the reader, for him) responsible for the unity of a text. "The Death of the Author," p. 148.

26.   As Eco points out, "in a structuralist framework, to take into account the role of the addressee looked like a disturbing intrusion" (*The Limits of Interpretation*, p. 44). Black and Chomsky have argued against the need for an audience in "Meaning and Intention," p. 264, and *Problems of Knowledge and Freedom*, p. 19, respectively, but Davidson disagrees in *Inquiries into Truth and Interpretation*, p. 272. On this issue, see also Ricoeur, *Hermeneutics and the Human Sciences*, p. 108, and Rosenblatt, *The Reader, the Text, the Poem*, ch. 4, pp. 48–70.

27.   For the notion of a private language and the arguments for and against its possibility, see Saunders and Henze, *The Private Language Problem*. Even deconstructionists like Derrida reject the notion of a private language; see "Signature Event Context," p. 180.

28.   There are reasons for this neglect. For example, according to Barthes, the audience (i.e., the reader for him) could function neither subversively nor repressively. It could not do the first because texts have no historical or authorial meaning, or even

reality, apart from the audience; it could not do the second, because audiences are "without history, biography, [or] psychology . . . " ("The Death of the Author," p. 148). Some textual critics, however, have noted the point. Greetham speaks of "suppression" and "disfiguration" in the context of editorial readings. "[Textual] Criticism and Deconstruction," pp. 15–20 in particular. He garners support from Harold Bloom, Archibald Hill, and Paul de Man. Shillingsburg discusses readers and the subversion of texts in "Text as Matter, Concept, and Action," p. 36.

29.   Goodman and Elgin, "Interpretation and Identity," p. 55. See the discussion of this issue in Chapter 4 of *A Theory of Textuality*. This is perhaps what led Foucault to say that signs are not benevolent. "Nietzsche, Freud, Marx," p. 65. The abuse to which audiences may subject texts was noted as early as Plato. *Phaedrus* 275e, p. 521.

30.   Gracia, *A Theory of Textuality*, ch. 4.

31.   Gracia, *Philosophy and Its History*, pp. 223 ff.

32.   Still, in accordance with what was said in Chapter 3, one may want to argue that in such cases, although the person of the author is still the same, the historical author of the text has ceased to exist, for the person subjecting the text to misunderstanding could not create the historical text. And this applies also to the person subjecting the text to misunderstanding because he could not create the text as a result of memory loss, for example. But if the person is capable of composing the text, even though he does not wish to do so for whatever reasons, then matters are different.

33.   Averroes, *On the Harmony of Religion and Philosophy*, pp. 63 ff.

34.   The exception to this principle is the case of texts that, because of their cultural function, are receptive to creative understandings by audiences; see Chapter 4 of *A Theory of Textuality*.

SELECT BIBLIOGRAPHY

This bibliography primarily lists sources cited in the book, although some background materials have also been included in it. For a more comprehensive and complementary list of sources, see the Bibliography of *A Theory of Textuality*.

Abrams, M. H. "How To Do Things with Texts." *Partisan Review* 46 (1979): 566–88.

———. "The Deconstructive Angel." *Critical Inquiry* 3 (1977): 425–38.

Adler, Mortimer, and Van Doren, Charles. *How To Read a Book*, rev. ed. New York: Simon and Schuster, 1972.

Allaire, Edwin B. "Berkeley's Idealism Revisited." In Colin M. Turbayne, ed. *Berkeley: Critical and Interpretative Essays*, pp. 197–206. Minneapolis: University of Minnesota Press, 1982.

———. "Bare Particulars." *Philosophical Studies* 14 (1963): 1–7.

Aquinas, Thomas. *Summa theologiae*, ed. De Rubeis, Billuart, et al., 4 vols. Turin: Marietti, 1926–27.

Aristotle. *Basic Works*, ed. Richard McKeon. New York: Random House, 1941.

———. *Categories*. In Richard McKeon, ed., *The Basic Works of Aristotle*, pp. 3–37. New York: Random House, 1941.

———. *On Interpretation*. In Richard McKeon, ed. *The Basic Works of Aristotle*, pp. 38–61. New York: Random House, 1941.

Augustine. *De libero arbitrio*, ed. V. Capanaga, et al. In *Obras Completas de San Agustín*, vol. 3, pp. 213–437. Madrid: Biblioteca de Autores Cristianos, 1971.

———. *De doctrina christiana*, ed. W. M. Green. *Corpus scriptorum ecclesiasticorum latinorum*, vol. 80. Vienna: Tempsky, 1963.

Austin, J. L. *How To Do Things with Words*, ed. J. O. Urmson. Cambridge, MA: Harvard University Press, 1962.

Averroes. *On the Harmony of Religion and Philosophy*, trans. G. F. Hourani. London: Luzac and Co., 1961.

Ayer, A. J. "Individuals," *Philosophical Essays*, pp. 1–25. London: Macmillan and Co., 1954.

Bakhtin, Mikhail M. *Speech Genres and Other Late Essays*, trans. Vern W. McGee, ed. Caryl Emerson and Michael Holquist. Austin: University of Texas Press, 1986.

Barnes, Annette. *On Interpretation: A Critical Analysis*. Oxford: Basil Blackwell, 1988.

Barthes, Roland. "The Death of the Author." In *Image, Music, Text*, trans. Stephen Heath, pp. 142–48. New York: Hill and Wang, 1977.

———. *The Pleasure of the Text*, trans. R. Miller. New York: Hill and Wang, 1975.

———. *Théorie du texte*, in *Encyclopaedia Universalis*, vol. 15. Paris: Encyclopaedia Universalis, 1973.

———. *S/Z*. Paris: Editions du Seuil, 1970.

Bateson, F. W. *Essays in Critical Dissent*. Totowa, NJ: Rowan and Littlefield, 1972.

Beardsley, Monroe C. "Fiction as Representation." *Synthese* 46, 3 (1981): 291–311.

———. "Aesthetic Intentions and Fictive Illocutions." In P. Hernadi, ed., *What Is Literature?* pp. 161–77. Bloomington: Indiana University Press, 1978.

Beckett, Samuel. *Texts for Nothing*, trans. Samuel Beckett. London: Cader and Boyars, 1974.

Bellemin–Noël, Jean. *Le texte et l'avant-texte*. Paris: Larousse, 1972.

Black, M. "Meaning and Intention: An Examination of Grice's Views." *New Literary History* (1972–73): 257–79.

Booth, Wayne. *The Rhetoric of Fiction*. Chicago: University of Chicago Press, 1961.

Borges, Jorge Luis. "Pierre Menard, Author of the *Quixote*," trans. James E. Irby. In Donald A. Yates and James E. Irby, eds. *Labyrinths*, pp. 36–44. Norfolk, CN: New Directions, 1962.

Bowers, F. *Essays in Bibliography, Text, and Editing*. Charlottesville: University Press of Virginia, 1975.

———. *Bibliography and Textual Criticism*. Oxford: Clarendon Press, 1964.

———. *Textual and Literary Criticism*. Cambridge: Cambridge University Press, 1959.

Brennan, Andrew. *Conditions of Identity: A Study in Identity and Survival*. Oxford: Clarendon Press, 1988.

Bunge, Mario. "¿Qué es un individuo?" *Theoria* 1, no. 1 (1985): 121–28.

Cain, William E. "Authors and Authority in Interpretation." *Georgia Review* 34 (1980): 617–34.

Carleton, Thomas Compton. *De signo*. In *Philosophia universa* (*Logica, Disputatio* 42), pp. 156–63. Antwerp, 1649.

Castañeda, Héctor-Neri. "Individuation and Non-Identity." *American Philosophical Quarterly* 12 (1975): 131–40.

Charolles, M. "Coherence as a Principle in the Interpretation of Discourse." *Text* 3, no. 1 (1983): 71–97.

Chisholm, Roderick M. "Identity Through Time." In H. E. Kiefer and M. K. Munitz, eds., *Language, Belief, and Metaphysics*, pp. 163–82. Albany: SUNY Press, 1970.

Chomsky, Noam. *Problems of Knowledge and Freedom.* New York: Pantheon, 1971.

Cohen, Philip. *Texts and Textualities.* New York: Garland, forthcoming.

———, ed. *Devils and Angels: Textual Editing and Literary Theory.* Charlottesville and London: University Press of Virginia, 1991.

——— and Jackson, David. "Notes on Emerging Paradigms in Editorial Theory." In Philip Cohen, ed., *Devils and Angels: Textual Editing and Literary Theory*, pp. 103–23. Charlottesville and London: University Press of Virginia, 1991.

Conimbricenses. *De signo.* In *Commentarii Collegii Conimbricensis et Societatis Jesu. In Universam Dialecticam Aristotelis Stagiritae*, Secunda pars, pp. 4–67. Lugduni: Horatius Cardon, 1606.

Cruttwell, Patrick. "Makers and Persons." *Hudson Review* 12 (1959–60): 481–507.

Currie, Gregory. "Work and Text." *Mind* 100 (1991): 325–39.

———. *An Ontology of Art.* London: Macmillan, 1989.

———. "What Is Fiction?" *The Journal of Aesthetics and Art Criticism* 43, no. 4 (1985): 385–92.

Danto, Arthur C. *The Transfiguration of the Commonplace: A Philosophy of Art.* Cambridge, MA: Harvard University Press, 1981.

Dascal, Marcelo. "Language and Money: A Simile and Its Meaning in Seventeenth Century Philosophy of Language." *Studia Leibnitiana* 8, no. 2 (1976): 187–218.

Davidson, Donald. *Inquiries into Truth and Interpretation.* Oxford: Oxford University Press, 1984.

Davis, T., and Hamlyn, S. "What Do We Do When Two Texts Differ? *She Stoops to Conquer* and Textual Criticism." In *Evidence in Literary Scholarship: Essays in Memory of James Marshall Osborn*, ed. René Wellek and Alvaro Ribeiro, pp. 263–79. Oxford: Clarenden Press, 1979.

De Luca, Vincent. "A Wall of Words: The Sublime as Text." In *Unnam'd Forms: Blake and Textuality*, eds. N. Hilton and T. A. Vogler, pp. 218–41. Berkeley and Los Angeles: University of California Press, 1986.

De Man, Paul. "The Rhetoric of Blindness: Jacques Derrida's Reading of Rousseau." In *Blindness and Insight: Essays in the Rhetoric of Contemporary Criticism,* pp. 102–41. Minneapolis: University of Minnesota Press, 1983.

Derrida, Jacques. *The Resistance of Theory.* Minneapolis: University of Minnesota Press, 1986.

———. *Positions,* trans. Alan Bass. Chicago: University of Chicago Press, 1981.

———. "Signature Event Context." *Glyph* 1 (1977): 172–97.

Dickie, George. *Art and the Aesthetic: An Institutional Analysis.* Ithaca, NY: Cornell University Press, 1974.

———. *Aesthetics: An Introduction.* Indianapolis: Bobbs-Merrill, 1971.

Dipert, Randall R. "Types and Tokens: A Reply to Sharpe." *Mind* 89 (1980): 587–88.

Donnellan, K. "Reference and Definite Descriptions." *Philosophical Review* 75 (1966): 281–304. Reprinted in S. Schwartz, ed., *Naming, Necessity and Natural Kinds,* pp. 42–65. Ithaca, NY: Cornell University Press, 1977.

———. "Proper Names and Identifying Descriptions." *Synthese* 21 (1970): 335–58.

Ducrot, Oswald, and Todorov, Tzvetan. *Encyclopedic Dictionary of the Sciences of Language,* trans. C. Porter. Baltimore: Johns Hopkins University Press, 1979.

Dutton, D. "Artistic Crimes." In D. Dutton, ed., *The Forger's Art: Forgery and the Philosophy of Art,* pp. 172–87. Berkeley and Los Angeles: University of California Press, 1983.

Eco, Umberto. *The Limits of Interpretation.* Bloomington and Indianapolis: Indiana University Press, 1990.

Eggert, Paul. "Textual Product or Textual Process: Procedures and Assumptions of Critical Editing." In Philip Cohen, ed., *Devils and Angels: Textual Editing and Literary Criticism,* pp. 57–77. Charlottesville and London: University Press of Virginia, 1991.

Eisenberg, Paul. "Jorge J. E. Gracia's *Philosophy and Its History.*" Unpublished commentary delivered at the 1994 Eastern Division meetings of the American Philosophical Association. Spanish translation forthcoming in *Revista Latinoamericana de Filosofia.*

Faigley, Lester, and Meyer, Paul. "Rhetorical Theory and Reader's Classifications of Text Types." *Texts* 3, no. 4 (1983): 305–25.

Feigl, Herbert. *The "Mental" and the "Physical".* Minneapolis: University of Minnesota Press, 1967.

Fish, Stanley. *Is There a Text in This Class? The Authority of Interpretive Communities.* Cambridge, MA: Harvard University Press, 1980.

————. "Interpreting the *Variorum*." *Critical Inquiry* 2 (1976): 465–85.

Foucault, Michel. "Nietzsche, Freud, Marx." In G. L. Ormiston and A. D. Schrift, eds., *Transforming the Hermeneutic Context: From Nietzsche to Nancy*, pp. 59–68. Albany: SUNY Press, 1990. Original French text in *Nietzsche*, in Calhiers de Royaumont, Philosophie No. VI, VIIe colloque—4–8 juillet 1964, pp. 183–92. Paris: Les Editions de Minuit, 1967.

————. "What Is an Author?" trans. Donald F. Bouchard and Sherry Simon. In Donald F. Bouchard, ed., *Language, Counter-Memory, Practice: Selected Essays and Interviews*, pp. 113–38. Ithaca, NY: Cornell University Press, 1977.

Gabler, Hans Walter. "The Text as Process and the Problem of Intentionality." *Text: Transactions of the Society of Textual Scholarship* 3 (1987): 107–16.

————. "The Synchrony and Diachrony of Texts: Practice and Theory of the Critical Edition of James Joyce's *Ulysses*." *Text: Transactions of the Society of Textual Scholarship* 1 (1981): 305–26.

Gadamer, Hans-Georg. *Truth and Method*, 2nd ed., trans. Garrett Barden and Robert Cumming. New York: Crossroad, 1975.

Glickman, Jack. "Creativity in the Arts." In Lars Aagaard-Mogensen, ed., *Culture in Art*, pp. 130–46. Atlantic Highlands, NJ: Humanities Press, 1976.

Goldstein, Leon J. "Historical Being." *The Monist* 74, no. 2 (1991): 206–16.

Goodman, Nelson. "Comments on Wallheim's Paper." *Ratio* (1978): 49–51.

————. *Languages of Art: An Approach to a Theory of Symbols*. London: Oxford University Press, 1968.

————. and Elgin, Catherine Z. "Interpretation and Identity." In *Reconceptions in Philosophy and Other Arts and Sciences*, pp. 49–65. London: Routledge, 1988.

Gracia, Jorge J. E. *A Theory of Textuality: The Logic and Epistemology*. Albany: SUNY Press, 1995.

————. "Textual Identity," *Sorites* 2 (1995): 57–75

————. "Author and Repression." *Contemporary Philosophy* 16, no. 4 (1994): 23–29.

————. "Can There Be Texts Without Historical Authors?" *American Philosophy Quarterly* 31, no. 3 (1994): 245–53.

————. "Can There Be Texts without Audiences? The Identity and Function of Audiences." *Review of Metaphysics* 47 (1994): 711–34.

————. "Cutting the Gordian Knot of Ontology: Aquinas on Universals." In D. Gallagher, ed., *Thomas Aquinas' Legacy*, pp. 16–36. Washington, D.C.: Catholic University of America Press, 1994.

———. *Philosophy and Its History*. Albany: State University of New York Press, 1992.

———. "Texts and Their Interpretation." *Review of Metaphysics* 43 (1990): 495–542.

———. *Individuality: An Essay on the Foundations of Metaphysics*. Albany: State University of New York Press, 1988.

———. *Introduction to the Problem of Individuation in the Early Middle Ages*, 2nd rev. ed. Munich and Vienna: Philosophia Verlag, 1988.

———. "Numerical Continuity in Material Substances: The Principle of Identity in Thomistic Metaphysics." *Southwestern Journal of Philosophy* 10 (1979): 72–93.

———. " 'A Supremely Great Being.' " *The New Scholasticism* 48 (1974): 371–77.

———. "Falsificación y valor artístico." *Revista de Ideas Estéticas* 116 (1971): 327–33.

Greetham, D. C. *Theories of the Text*. Oxford: Oxford University Press, 1995.

———. "The Manifestation and Accommodation of Theory in Textual Editing." In Philip Cohen, ed., *Devils and Angels: Textual Editing and Literary Criticism*, pp. 78–102. Charlottesville and London: University Press of Virginia, 1991.

———. "[Textual] Criticism and Deconstruction." *Studies in Bibliography* 44 (1991): 1–30.

———. "Textual and Literary Theory: Redrawing the Matrix." *Studies in Bibliography* 42 (1989): 1–24.

Greg, W. W. "The Rationale of Copy-Text," *Studies in Bibliography* 3 (1950–51): 19–36. Rep. in J. C. Maxwell, ed., *The Collected Papers of Sir Walter Greg*, pp. 374–91, Oxford, 1966.

Grigely, Joseph. *Textualterities*. Ann Arbor: University of Michigan Press, forthcoming.

———. "The Textual Event." In Philip Cohen, ed., *Devils and Angels: Textual Editing and Literary Criticism*, pp. 167–94. Charlottesville and London: University Press of Virginia, 1991.

Hancher, Michael. "Three Kinds of Intentions." *Modern Language Notes* 87 (1972): 827–51.

Harari, Josué. *Textual Strategies: Perspectives in Post-Structuralist Criticism*. Ithaca, NY: Cornell University Press, 1979.

Harris, Wendell. *Interpretive Acts: In Search of Meaning*. Oxford: Clarendon Press, 1988.

Hay, Louis. "Does Text Exist?" *Studies in Bibliography* 41(1988): 64–76.

Hernadi, Paul. "Literary Theory." In *Introduction to Scholarship in Modern Languages and Literatures*, ed. J. Gibaldi, pp. 98–115. New York: Modern Language Association of America, 1981.

Hill, Archibald. "Some Postulates for Distributional Study of Texts." *Studies in Bibliography* 3 (1950–51): 63–95.

Hirsch, E. D., Jr. "Three Dimensions of Hermeneutics." *New Literary History* 3 (1972): 245–61.

Hobbes, Thomas. *Leviathan. On the Matter, Forme and Power of a Commonwealth Ecclesiastical and Civil,* ed. Michael Oakshott. New York: Collier Books, 1962.

Howard-Hill, T. H. "Variety in Editing and Reading: A Response to McGann and Shillingsburg." In Philip Cohen, ed., *Devils and Angels: Textual Editing and Literary Criticism,* pp. 44–56. Charlottesville and London: University Press of Virginia, 1991.

———. "Playwrights' Intentions and the Editing of Plays." *Text* 4 (1988): 269–78.

Ingarden, R. *The Literary Work of Art: An Investigation on the Borderlines of Ontology, Logic, and Theory of Literature,* trans. with an Introduction by George G. Grabonicz. Evanston, IL: Northwestern University Press, 1973.

Iser, Wolfgang. *Prospecting: From Reader-Response to Literary Anthropology.* Baltimore: Johns Hopkins University Press, 1989.

———. "The Reading Process: A Phenomenological Approach." In Jane P. Tompkins, ed., *Reader Response Criticism,* pp. 50–69. Baltimore: Johns Hopkins University Press, 1980.

———. *The Implied Reader: Patterns of Communication in Prose Fiction from Bunyan to Beckett.* Baltimore: Johns Hopkins University Press, 1974.

Jameson, Fredric. "The Ideology of the Text." In *The Ideologies of Theory,* vol. 1, pp. 17–71. Minneapolis: University of Minnesota Press, 1988.

Jones, Peter. *Philosophy and the Novel: Philosophical Aspects of "Middlemarch," "Anna Karenina," "The Brothers Karamazov," "A la recherche du temps perdu," and of the Methods of Criticism.* Oxford: Clarendon Press, 1975.

Juhl, P. D. "The Appeal to the Text: What Are We Appealing To?" *The Journal of Aesthetics and Art Criticism* 36, no. 3 (1978): 277–87.

Katz, Jerrold J. *Propositional Structure and Illocutionary Force: A Study of the Contribution of Sentence Meaning to Speech Acts.* New York: Thomas Y. Crowell, 1977.

Kearns, John T. "Sameness or Similarity?" *Philosophy and Phenomenological Research* 29 (1969): 105–15.

Kenney, E. J. *The Classical Text: Aspects of Editing in the Age of the Printed Book.* Berkeley: University of California Press, 1974.

Kermode, Frank. "Institutional Control of Interpretations." *Salmagundi* 43 (1979): 72–86.

Knapp, S., and Michaels, W.B. "Against Theory 2." *Critical Inquiry* 14 (1988): 49–68.

———. "Against Theory." *Critical Inquiry* 8 (1982): 723–42.

Koestler, Arthur. "The Aesthetics of Snobbery." *Horizon* 7 (1965): 80–83.

Krausz, Michael. "History and Its Objects." *The Monist* 74, no. 2 (1991): 217–29.

Kripke, Saul A. *Naming and Necessity*. Cambridge, MA: Harvard University Press, 1987; reprint of 1980 edition.

Kristeva, Julia. "Theory of the Text," trans. Ian McLeod. In Robert Young, ed., *Untying the Text*, pp. 31–47. London: Routledge, Kegan Paul, 1981.

Lessing, Alfred. "What Is Wrong with a Forgery?" *Journal of Aesthetics and Art Criticism* 23 (1964): 461–71.

Levine, Michael P. "Historical Anti-Realism: Boethian Historians Tell Their Story." *The Monist* 74, no. 2 (1991): 230–39.

Lewis, Charlton T., and Short, Charles. *A Latin Dictionary*. Oxford: Clarendon Press, 1966.

Long, Douglas C. "Particulars and Their Qualities." *Philosophical Quarterly* 18 (1968): 193–206.

Mailloux, Stephen. *Interpretive Conventions: The Reader in the Study of American Fiction*. Ithaca, NY: Cornell University Press, 1982.

Makkreel, Rudolph A. "Reinterpreting the Historical World." *The Monist* 74, no. 2 (1991): 149–64.

Margolis, Joseph. "The Ontological Peculiarity of Works of Arts." *Journal of Aesthetics and Art Criticism* 36, no. 1 (1977): 45–50.

McGann, Jerome J. *The Textual Condition*. Princeton, NJ: Princeton University Press, 1991.

———. "Theory of Texts." *London Review of Books*, 16 Feb. 1988, pp. 20–21.

———. *A Critique of Modern Textual Criticism*. Chicago: University of Chicago Press, 1983.

———. *Historical Studies and Literary Criticism*. Madison, WI: University of Wisconsin Press, 1985.

———. ed., *Textual Criticism and Literary Interpretation*. Chicago: University of Chicago Press, 1985.

McKenzie, D. F. *Bibliography and the Sociology of Texts*, Panizzi Lectures. London: British Library, 1986.

McLaverty, James. "Issues of Identity and Utterance: An Intentionalist Response to 'Textual Instability.'" In Philip Cohen, ed., *Devils and Angels: Textual Criticism and Literary Theory*, pp. 134–51. Charlottesville and London: University Press of Virginia, 1991.

———. "The Mode of Existence of Literary Works of Art: The Case of the *Dunciad Variorum*." *Studies in Bibliography* 37 (1984): 82–105.

———. "The Concept of Authorial Intention in Textual Criticism." *The Library* 6, n. 2 (1984): 121–38.

Meiland, J. W. "Interpretation as a Cognitive Discipline." *Philosophy and Literature* 2 (1978): 23–45.

———. *The Nature of Intention*. London: Methuen, 1970.

Mill, John Stuart. *A System of Logic, Ratiocinative and Inductive; Being a Connected View of the Principles of Evidence and the Methods of Scientific Investigation*. New York: Harper and Brothers, 1850.

Miller, J. Hillis. "Ariachne's Broken Woof." *Georgia Review* 31 (1977): 44–60.

Miller, Nancy K., ed. *Arachnologies: The Woman, the Text, and the Critic*. New York: Columbia University Press, 1986.

Mowitt, John. *Text: The Genealogy of Anti-Disciplinary Objects*. Durham, NC: Duke University Press, 1992.

Morgan, Michael L. "Authorship and the History of Philosophy." *The Review of Metaphysics* 42, no. 2 (1988): 327–55.

Nehamas, Alexander. "Writer, Text, Work, Author." In Anthony J. Cascardi, ed., *Literature and the Question of Philosophy*, pp. 267–91. Baltimore: Johns Hopkins University Press, 1987.

———. "What an Author Is. "*The Journal of Philosophy* 83 (1986): 685–91.

———. "The Postulated Author: Critical Monism as a Regulative Ideal." *Critical Inquiry* 8 (1981–82): 133–49.

O'Doherty, Brian. *Inside the White Cube: The Ideology of Gallery Space*. Santa Monica and San Francisco: Lapis Press, 1986.

Ohmann, Richard. "Speech, Literature, and the Space Between." *New Literary History* 4 (1972–73): 47–63.

———. "Speech Acts and the Definition of Literature." *Philosophy and Rhetoric* 4 (1971): 1–19.

Panofsky, Erwin. "The History of Art as a Humanistic Discipline." In *Meaning in the Visual Arts: Papers in and on Art History*, pp. 1–25. Garden City, NJ: Doubleday, 1955.

Parker, Hershel. *Flawed Texts and Verbal Icons*. Evanston, IL: Northwestern University Press, 1984.

Pebworth, Ted-Larry, and Sullivan, Ernest W., II., "Rational Presentation of Multiple Textual Traditions." *Papers of the Bibliographical Society of America* 83 (March 1989): 43–60.

Peckham, Morse. "Reflections on the Foundations of Textual Criticism." *Proof* 1 (1971): 122–55.

Peirce, Charles Sanders. *Collected Papers*, ed. Charles Hartshorne and Paul Weiss, 6 vols. Cambridge, MA: Harvard University Press, 1931.

Petöfi, J. S. "A Frame for Frames." *Proceedings of the Second Annual Meeting of the Berkeley Linguistics Society* 2 (1976): 319–29.

Phelan, James. "Validity Redux: The Relation of Author, Reader, and Text in the Act of Interpretation." *Papers in Comparative Studies* 1 (1981): 80–111.

Plato. *Phaedrus*. In Edith Hamilton and Huntington Cairns, eds., *The Collected Dialogues of Plato, Including the Letters*, pp. 475–525. New York: Pantheon Books, 1961.

Porphyry. *Isagoge*, trans. Edward W. Warren. Toronto: Pontifical Institute of Mediaeval Studies, 1975.

Proctor, William, and Abbott, Craig S. *Introduction to Bibliographical and Textual Studies*. New York: Modern Language Association of America, 1985.

Putnam, Hilary. *Reason, Truth and History*. Cambridge: Cambridge University Press, 1981.

Quine, W. V. "Indeterminacy of Translation Again." *The Journal of Philosophy* 84 (1987): 5–10.

Ricoeur, Paul. *Hermeneutics and the Human Sciences*, ed. J. Thompson. Cambridge: Cambridge University Press, 1987.

———. Creativity in Language: Word, Polysemy, Metaphor." In Charles E. Reagan and David Stuart, eds., *The Philosophy of Paul Ricoeur: An Anthology of His Work*, pp. 109–33. Boston: Beacon Press, 1978.

———. *Interpretation Theory: Discourse and the Surplus of Meaning*. Austin: University of Texas Press, 1976.

———. "Metaphor and the Main Problems of Hermeneutics," *New Literary History* 6 (1974): 95–110.

———. "The Model of the Text: Meaningful Action Considered as a Text." *Social Research* 38 (1971): 529–62.

Rorty, Amélie Oksenberg, ed. *The Identities of Persons*. Berkeley: University of California Press, 1976.

Rorty, Richard. *Philosophy and the Mirror of Nature*. Princeton, NJ: Princeton University Press, 1979.

Rosenblatt, Louise M. *The Reader, the Text, the Poem: The Transactional Theory of the Literary Work*. Carbondale and Edwardville: Southern Illinois University Press, 1978.

Russell, Bertrand. *Logic and Knowledge, Essays 1901–1950.*, ed. R. C. Marsh. London: Allen and Unwin, 1956.

———. *Human Knowledge: Its Scope and Limits*. New York: Simon and Schuster, 1948.

———. *An Inquiry into Meaning and Truth*. London: Allen and Unwin, 1940.

Said, Edward. *The World, the Text and the Critic*. Cambridge, MA: Harvard University Press, 1983.

Saunders, John Turk, and Henze, Donald F. *The Private Language Problem*. New York: Random House, 1967.

Scaltas, Theodore. "The Ship of Theseus." *Analysis* 40 (1980): 152–57.

Schank, Robert C. *Conceptual Information Processing*. Amsterdam and New York. North Holland and Elsevier, 1975.

Schmitz, Kenneth. "The Actual Nature of Philosophy Disclosed in Its History: Comments on Jorge J. E. Gracia's *Philosophy and Its History*." Unpublished commentary delivered at the 1994 Eastern Division meetings of the American Philosophical Association. Spanish translation forthcoming in *Revista Latinoamericana de Filosofia*.

Searle, John R. *Intentionality: An Essay in the Philosophy of Mind*. Cambridge: Cambridge University Press, 1984.

———. "Reiterating the Differences: A Reply to Derrida." *Glyph* 1 (1977): 198–208.

———. "The Logical Status of Fictional Discourse." *New Literary History* 5 (1975): 319–32.

———. *Speech Acts: An Essay in the Philosophy of Language*. Cambridge: Cambridge University Press, 1969.

Shillingsburg, Peter L. "Text as Matter, Concept, and Action." *Studies in Bibliography* 44 (1991): 31–82.

———. "The Autonomous Author, the Sociology of Texts, and Polemics of Textual Criticism." In Philip Cohen, ed., *Devils and Angels: Textual Editing and Literary Criticism*, pp. 22–43. Charlottesville and London: University Press of Virginia, 1991.

———. "An Inquiry into the Social Status of Texts and Modes of Textual Criticism." *Studies in Bibliography* 42 (1989): 55–79.

————. *Scholarly Editing in the Computer Age: Theory and Practice*. Athens: University of Georgia Press, 1986.

Shusterman, Richard. "The Anomalous Nature of Literature." *British Journal of Aesthetics* 18 (1978): 317–29.

Skinner, Quentin. "Conventions and the Understanding of Speech Acts." *Philosophical Quarterly* 20 (1970): 118–38.

Smith, Barbara Herrnstein. "Literature as Performance, Fiction, and Art." *Journal of Philosophy* 67 (1970): 553–62.

Smith, Edward L., Jr. "Text Type and Discourse Framework." *Text* 5, no. 3 (1985): 229–47.

Stern, Laurent. "Factual Constraints on Interpreting." *Monist* 73 (1990): 205–21.

Stout, G. F. "The Nature of Universals and Propositions." *Proceedings of the British Academy* 10 (1921). Reprinted in *Studies in Philosophy and Psychology*, pp. 384–403. London: Macmillan, 1930.

Suárez, Francisco. *Metaphysical Disputation V*. In Jorge J. E. Gracia, *Suárez on Individuation*. Milwaukee, WI: Marquette University Press, 1982.

————. *Disputationes metaphysicae*. In Carolo Berton, ed., *Opera omnia*, vols. 25 and 26. Paris: Vivès, 1981.

Tanselle, G. Thomas. *A Rationale of Textual Criticism*. Philadelphia: University of Pennsylvania Press, 1989.

————. *Textual Criticism since Greg: A Chronicle, 1950–1985*. Charlottesville: University Press of Virginia, 1987.

————. "Historicism and Critical Editing." *Studies in Bibliography* 39 (1986): 1–46.

————. "Recent Editorial Discussion and the Central Questions of Editing." *Studies in Bibliography* 34 (1981): 23–65.

————. "The Editing of Historical Documents." *Studies in Bibliography* 31 (1978): 1–56.

————. "The Editorial Problem of Final Authorial Intention." *Studies in Bibliography* 29 (1976): 167–211.

————. "Greg's Theory of Copy-Text and Editing of American Literature." *Studies in Bibliography* 28 (1975): 167–229.

————. "Textual Study and Literary Judgment." *Publications of the Bibliographical Society of America* 65 (1971): 109–22.

Thorpe, James. *Principles of Textual Criticism*. San Marino, CA: Huntington Library, 1972.

Tolhurst, W. E. "On What a Text Is and How It Means." *British Journal of Aesthetics* 19 (1979): 3–14.

————. and Wheeler, S. C. "On Textual Individuation." *Philosophical Studies* 35 (1979): 187–97.

Tomas, Vincent, ed. *Creativity in the Arts*. Englewood Cliffs, NJ: Prentice-Hall, 1964.

Unamuno, Miguel de. "On the Reading and Interpretation of *Don Quixote*." In J. R. Jones and K. Douglas, eds., *Miguel de Cervantes, Don Quixote*, pp. 974–79. New York: W. W. Norton, 1981.

Urmson, J. O. "Literature." In *Aesthetics: A Critical Anthology*, ed. G. Dickie and R. J. Sclafani, pp. 334–41. New York: Martin's Press, 1977.

————. "The Performing Arts." In *Contemporary British Philosophy*, 4th series, ed. H. D. Lewis, pp. 239–52. London: George Allen and Unwin Ltd., 1976.

Wachterhauser, Brice. "Interpreting Texts: Objectivity or Participation?" *Man and World* 19 (1986): 439–57.

Walton, Kendall L. "Style and the Products and Processes of Art." In Berel Lang, ed., *The Concept of Style*, pp. 72–103. Ithaca, NY: Cornell University Press, 1987.

Weber, Samuel. *Institutions and Interpretation*. Minneapolis: University of Minnesota Press, 1987.

Wellek, René, and Warren, Austin. *Theory of Literature*, 3rd. ed. New York: Harcourt, 1956.

Whitehead, Alfred North. *Process and Reality*, corrected ed. by D. R. Griffin and D. W. Sherburne. New York: The Free Press, 1978.

Wicker, Brian. *The Story-Shaped World. Fiction and Metaphysics: Some Variations on a Theme*. Notre Dame, IN: University of Notre Dame Press, 1975.

Wilsmore, Susan. "The Literary Work Is Not Its Text." *Philosophy and Literature* 11 (1987): 307–16.

Winston, P. H. *Artificial Intelligence*. Reading, MA: Addison-Wesley, 1977.

Wittgenstein, Ludwig. *Tractatus Logico-Philosophicus*, trans. C. K. Ogden. London: Routledge & Kegan Paul Ltd., 1981.

Wollheim, Richard. *Art and Its Objects: An Introduction to Aesthetics*, 2nd ed., 1968. Rpt. Cambridge and New York: Cambridge University Press, 1980.

————. "On an Alleged Inconsistency in Collingwood's Aesthetic." In *On Art and the Mind*, pp. 250–60. London: Allen Lane, 1973.

Wolterstorff, Nicholas. "Toward an Ontology of Art Works." *Nous* 9, no. 2 (1975): 115–42.

Zemach, E. M. "Nesting: The Ontology of Interpretation." *The Monist* 73 (1990): 296–311.

INDEX OF AUTHORS

This Index was prepared by Yishaiya Abosch.

INDEX OF SUBJECTS

This index is intended as a guide to readers who wish to find the main places where key topics and terms are discussed. No attempt has been made to record all the places where those topics and terms are discussed.

act(s): illocutionary, 33, 46, 57–58, 160, 180; locutionary, 33, 46, 57–58, 160; perlocutionary, 33, 46, 57–58; speech, 57–58, 180; universal vs. individual, 57–58

actual author, 182

actual text(s), 7

aesthetic experience, 6

aesthetic object, 121

aggregate(s), 34, 41

artifact(s), 5–6; vs. art object(s), 6; historical, 12; vs. text(s), 5, 9, 41

artistic experience, 6

art object(s), 5, 6, 121, 177, 186, 188; artifactuality of, 6; vs. audience(s), 6; vs. author(s), 6; vs. creation, 106; ontological status, 173–174; vs. sign(s), 6; vs. text(s), 5, 6, 12

audience(s), 2, 8, 141–169, 187, 188, 189, 190; vs. art object(s), 6; vs. author(s), 59, 91, 92, 99–100, 141–142, 155, 157–158, 160, 188; composition of, 148–153; contemporaneous, 116, 146, 153, 160, 165, 169, 171; contemporary, 116, 147–148, 153, 165, 169; determined by text(s), 188; freedom of, 130, 140, 188; function of, 141, 154–158, 168, 171, 185; historical, 148; identity of, 141–153, 169; individual vs. type of, 59; intended, 144–145, 153, 160, 166, 169; intermediary, 146–147, 153, 165, 169; and interpretative author(s), 102, 116, 128;

as interpreter(s), 144; knowledge of, 144, 145, 146, 147; and meaning(s), 118; need for, 141, 158–161, 189; vs. oral text(s), 155; paradigmatic, 153, 171; repressive character of, 142, 165–166, 168, 171, 189–190; sameness of, 58–60, 86; and signs, 143; subjectivity of, 142, 166–168; subversive character of, 142, 161–165, 168, 171, 189–190

author(s), 1, 2, 8, 91–140, 182, 183, 184, 185, 186, 187; actual, 182; vs. art object(s), 6; as audience(s), 97, 142–144, 153, 160, 164, 165; vs. audience(s), 59, 91, 92, 99–100, 155, 157–158, 160, 188; vs. composer(s), 95; composite, 94, 101–102; contemporary, 56; function of, 91, 95, 104–117, 139, 154, 157–158, 171, 185; historical, 53, 57, 93–97, 104, 138, 171, 182; human and nonhuman, 92; identity of, 93–104, 138–139, 180; individual, 11, 59; intention of, 4, 27–29, 91–92, 121–126, 161, 169, 174, 178, 179, 186; interpretative, 102–103, 104, 126, 139, 153; and meaning(s), 118, 189; and multiple interpretations, 118; need for, 117–129, 139; *of* a text vs. *in* the text, 99; vs. oral text(s), 182; original historical, 93; originality of, 45, 88, 126; vs. person(s), 94–97, 188, 190; pseudo-historical, 94, 96, 97–101, 138, 171, 182; and repression, 92, 129–134,